It's A Match!
The Guide
to Finding Lasting Love

Natalie Moore. MsEd.MFT.ChT

Natalie Moore
Natalie@NatalieMoore.net
www.NatalieMoore.net

It's a Match! The Guide to Finding Lasting Love/Natalie Moore. —1st ed.
ISBN: 978-0-9965320-0-6

Contents

CHAPTER ONE

Why Another Book on Dating?

Man meets woman and woman meets man. Love, life, family, generations, and dynasties follow.

This has been the story of humankind throughout history. In the past, though, romances developed offline. Technologically speaking, dating and mating remained pretty much the same—until now.

Online dating has changed everything. We're in a whole new world. We need whole new skills.

Digital dating enlarges the pool of possible mates, giving you millions of choices. Increasing the numbers improves the odds; but this only improves the odds that you'll find *some* one, not necessarily "*The* One."

Meeting your ideal match, a person who shares your interests and values, "The One" you can stay with forever and be happy with... isn't just a numbers game; it's also a skills game. Finding "him" or "her" still depends on the "finding." And now we can search online.

The game-changing nature of the digital dating scene has put a focus on skills and talents that are remarkably different from before. You need to know what you want and how to get it.

Your success depends on you.

To attract the best person for you, you have to be the best "you" that you can be. To stop going from failed relationship to failed relationship, you have to understand what caused your previous romances to fail. To stop bringing the wrong men or women into your life, you have to understand why you've been drawn to them, and how you have drawn them to you. To find the "right" match for yourself, you have to know what "right" is.

Over 50% of marriages end in divorce because we, unknowingly, choose relationships that are doomed to fail. Since I'm a professional Relationship Coach, with several academic degrees and many years of experience, I became curious about the relationships that lasted, those that seemed to thrive despite hardship and survived the test of time. You know the ones... the couples married thirty or forty years, who still look longingly into each other's eyes.

Why are their relationships different? Over the years, I studied many successful couples in hopes of learning their secret.

I took my information and developed a system that would help my clients avoid becoming yet another divorce statistic. My extraordinary psycho-spiritual approach for lasting romantic happiness is called "The 4 Levels of Love." My system will teach you how to identify the qualities that successful, happy, and long-lasting relationships share, and you will learn how to find out if the potential partners you meet are people you could really be happy with—for a lifetime. There's no longer any reason to waste your time with someone who weeks, months, or even years down the road will turn out to be another mistake.

After years of informal research, interviewing, and analysis, I understood what made great relationships great—and, most importantly, I figured out how every one of us could get this kind of relationship.

I found a way to recognize "The One," someone who could join you in a truly great, fulfilling, happy, and lasting relationship—right from the start.

The 4 Levels of Love System allows you to quantify, through a scoring system, each of your relationships, so you can figure out which of them has the potential to bring you lasting love. You will also find out why you should try to find a Level III or Level IV match. Historically, the world has been plagued with subpar, or doomed, Level II relationships. I will explain all of this to you, later.

The good news is that there's really someone out there just for you. And your Mr. Right is looking for you—right now!

With the right skills, you can find him, get him, and keep him. I will tell you how. You just have to be willing to do the work: to learn the lessons and practice the exercises in this book. I recommend that you get a notebook of some kind so you can keep track of the results of your exercises, because this info will be very helpful to you as you search for your own high-level romantic match.

To find lasting love you have to, first, be sure you are emotionally ready for a committed relationship. I will guide you toward becoming ready, and in the process I will help you become the best version of YOU that you can be.

This means you have to break free of the limiting beliefs and fears that have held you back in the past. You need to do this so you can stop repeating the same old failed love story over and over again. Then, you have to be prepared to declare your magnificence to the universe.

I'll show you how.

My Five-Step Process to Find Your Perfect Match

I have defined a five-step process for finding *your* perfect match. This book will guide you through the process.

Step I: Embark on an accurate self-assessment in which you take an inventory of your best qualities, characteristics, and beliefs about yourself and relationships. This includes making a list of the areas in which there is room for you to improve.

Step II: After undergoing this process of self-assessment, you will be ready to look at the things that you can realistically change, and you will decide which of your characteristics or habits you are willing to change. For example, you might identify that you want to lose twenty pounds and stop smoking. Or you might chose to take some classes in order to attract a more educated man.

You might realize that you have certain beliefs about yourself such as "I could never get any man I would want." What you believe becomes your reality. So these limiting beliefs have to be addressed. Your single best investment in life, and in achieving happiness, is in becoming the best you that you can be, period. This will not only increase your self-confidence and help you grow as a person, but will also help you find a better match.

The law of attraction says that like frequencies attract each other. So wouldn't it make sense to become the best version of yourself, in order to attract exactly what you want in someone else?

Step III: At this point you will be ready to focus on your search process. This begins with creating an inventory of qualities that are important to you in a mate (versus a date). After all, if you don't know what you're looking for, how will you know when you've found it?

I am also going to help you understand the incredible new world of digital dating, and how to navigate successfully through the ocean of romantic possibilities. If you have the right skills, you can expand your list of potential love matches exponentially because you are no longer limited by geography and time.

Step IV: After you've gotten several potential candidates, you can begin the culling process. At this point, you should be dating several people at the same time. I call this step the "interviewing process."

As you get to know your dates, you will see them under different circumstances. You will meet their friends and get to see who they really are. This process should take about two months with each person.

The point of this process is to take things slowly and to first get to know them as a friend. After all, you are not desperate and, before you invest too much time with someone, it is best to see if they are worth your investing your time. We will talk about the rules of dating during this stage.

This is where my 4 Levels of Love System is especially useful, as the system will help you assess whether you have discovered a potential Level III or Level IV match.

Step V: Now that you've chosen to date your potential "One" exclusively, it's time to evolve your relationship while continuing to evaluate it.

Once you've decided that this is *The One*, I will give you some proven guidance on keeping this person. I'll show you how to get exactly the person you want, and how to hold on to them happily, in a long-term relationship.

In other words, I'm going to give you the knowledge that will give you the power to joyously change your life. I will help you become a better version of you, and, because you are a better person, you will attract a better person into your life.

A Numbers Game

In olden times (I mean, of course, in the dark ages before the Internet), our options were limited. We generally relied on proximity and connections.

Sometimes people met their significant others through friends or matchmakers (such as a *yenta* or a *shidduch*, if she was really a professional). Maybe you relied on your well-meaning Aunt Sadie who worried at every family gathering about why you didn't "settle down—before it's too late!" Aunt Sadie would mention "this nice boy" she met through a friend at the Garden Club. Maybe you gave "this nice boy" a chance... Sparks flew or they didn't.

Or perhaps a man or woman caught your eye across the aisle at church, or while buying flour at the General Store. He or she smiled. You smiled back. And ...

Perhaps this person was not exactly what you dreamed about when you closed your eyes at night, but this person was there. They were eligible. They seemed interested.

Good enough. He or she might not have been perfect, but perhaps this was the best you could find. Before, the pool of possibilities depended on the number of available men or women in your village. This was, for all intents and purposes, a numbers game, and there were only X number of possibilities. Even if you traveled outside your village, the pool remained limited to people you'd bump into on your own, or be introduced to.

So, sadly, people took what they could get. Too often, they settled for less than they wanted, because their options were limited. They took a Level I or II match because they didn't have many choices.

Going to bars and nightclubs with your friends is just a variation on the theme, with the added element of chance. Meeting "The One" depends not only on proximity, but also on timing. You both had to be at the same bar, at the same time. If one person left at 8 to have dinner with friends, and you got there at 8:15, you wouldn't meet.

That's still a numbers game—your choices are limited to the people you meet in the places you go.

Not anymore.

Online Dating—The Game Changer

With the advent of online dating, these physical boundaries vanish. There are endless possibilities for finding a perfect match if you are skillful, honest, determined, and focused.

With online services like Match.com, eHarmony, Hinge, OkCupid, JDate, and an ever-expanding list of others, the possibilities are limited only by the characteristics and qualities that you decide are important to you. You no longer have to wait for a chance meeting or introduction. You're in control. And there is absolutely no need to settle for anything less than exactly what you want.

This explains why more and more people are going online to find a relationship.

In fact, a recent survey by the Pew Research Center's Internet Project found that 11 % of all American adults have used online dating services. Among those who are currently "single and looking" for a partner the statistic is more than three times higher—38 %.

And, Pew found, the percentages go up among those with higher incomes and higher education:

"57% of all college graduates know someone who uses online dating, and 41% know someone who has met a spouse or other long-term partner through online dating."

Among Americans with an annual household income of $75,000 or more, 57 % know someone who uses online dating, and 40 % know someone who met their spouse or partner that way.

Enough numbers. You get it. Online dating works... if you know what to do.

But...

Yes, there's a "but." And it's a big one.

Let's face it, you're reading this book because you're looking for *lasting* love. You've had relationships that, for one reason or another, didn't work out. More often than not, you've faced the same problems over and over again.

The romance started great. He seemed perfect. And then...

I know. I've been there.

This Works! I'm Teaching You What I've Done Myself

Everything that I suggest you do, I've done myself, so I know you can benefit from this process. I'm constantly trying to improve myself in order to be a happier person, and to work with the universe so I can attract and hold onto my own best match. I've learned how to make the 4 Levels of Love System work.

When I got divorced, I decided I was going to go to therapy in order to learn how to choose a partner who was better suited to me. Obviously, given my divorced status, I hadn't done a good job before in finding an enduring relationship.

My therapist took me through an in-depth process, over many sessions, costing thousands of dollars. The experience helped me get a lot of insight into all of my patterns of behavior: my relationship patterns and the patterns of the men I was attracted to.

I realized that I was repeating the past. I was having a problem choosing the right man and there was something that I wasn't doing well. I wasn't unique in that.

As I'll explain later, we are always inclined to choose the same guy, though each new prospect may seem totally different. His name or background might be different. He might be an entirely different physical type from whoever you were with before. But, invariably, the new person mirrors the very qualities that we need to improve within ourselves, or he triggers all of our emotional wounds. These wounds point to what we need to heal within ourselves.

I am going to guide you through the very process that I went through. You will learn, through a series of exercises, to recognize the things that are driving you, and how those things impact your choices and relationships. Most importantly, I will give you tools to heal your hurts at your own pace, so you can stop attracting same "wrong" partner.

I felt empowered when I was able to identify the things in myself that kept me making the same poor choices. I knew what I had to change in order to get a different result. When I took responsibility for my part in making the wrong choices, I was able to make better choices.

I had to excavate my authentic self, to find the real me, by clearing limiting beliefs and defense mechanisms that were interfering with my relationships. I had to learn how to make choices from an inspired and empowered place inside myself, instead of reacting from a place filled with fear.

Once I knew what was motivating me, what was triggering my reactions, I stopped letting the wrong impulses control me. Instead of being driven by childhood triggers, by fears and limiting beliefs, I started doing the driving. I could act, instead of react. I was in charge of my life, and of my love life.

I thought to myself: *Wouldn't it be great if there were a book that could teach everybody what I've learned? I know most people don't have the time or thousands of dollars to spend in therapy... but think how much happier people would be if they could find the right person? And what if I could actually provide a basis for people to find lasting love and bypass potential failures?*

These thoughts stayed with me as I continued working and growing my own business. At the time, I ran a financial services company, advising and guiding people on the best places and ways to invest their money to secure their financial future.

As time went by, I found that I could share what I'd learned with girlfriends who were going through relationship troubles. They were calling me because I'd gained a great education through my own therapeutic process. Their issues were different, but they were all repeating past experiences and patterns of behavior.

I loved helping others find happiness so much that I decided to go back to school to earn a Masters Degree in Marriage and Family Therapy; and I also trained to become a Clinical Hypnotherapist.

I was also dating. My children were grown. I had done a lot of self-work. I had a lot of interests and hobbies and friends, but I was missing a romantic companion.

My friends helped me find potential partners, but the men they fixed me up with just weren't for me. There was a very limited pool of candidates. Once you pass your twenties, the number of men who are single, and whom you can randomly meet through friends, decreases.

I decided to try online dating. I knew several couples that had met through one service or another, and I'd heard from my therapist friends that many of their clients had found romantic partners that way. They said, "Just put up your profile and see what kind of people get in touch with you."

So I did.

Now I look back and think my actions were funny, because I'm now very academically oriented—but back then I didn't do any research first. I had friends help me with my profile—and I wound up having to rework it over and over because I realized it wasn't showing the authentic me. I also wasted my time by going out with men I would have instantly passed up once I got better at reading a man's profile.

I thought online dating meant that you would have to kiss a lot of frogs before you found your best match. Well, maybe not literally kiss them, but I thought I'd certainly have to go on a lot of dates with them.

I went through periods of going on three to five dates a week. I developed rules, and eventually knew after only one date whether I was dealing with a man who had romantic potential, a man who might become a friend (because I did make some friends in the process), or a dud.

I learned to refine my culling process so that I wouldn't waste my time going on a date with someone who was not a potential match. Sometimes I felt like I was panning for gold... sifting through the online river for worthwhile nuggets, with about as much luck.

One of the first guys I went out with traveled with an entourage. He needed to be constantly surrounded by people who liked him, laughed at his jokes, and basically made him look—and feel—like the life of the party. He was nice. He was smart. But going out with him was like becoming a part of a three-ring circus. I got tired of the jugglers and the clowns. Soon, his entourage drove me crazy. I wanted to be "just us"...

at least some of the time. Not him. I'd suggest a quiet dinner or a movie at home; he'd bring a half-dozen friends.

Unfortunately, he needed external feedback. He needed to be validated by others.

That's a technical way of saying he didn't know who he was, and he didn't feel good about himself unless he heard complimentary feedback from someone else.

And I just wanted to cuddle.

Oh well…

Basically, I learned as I went—by doing, reading, and helping others. I also learned by listening to what my girlfriends and my male friends told me about their experiences. I was additionally able to apply the knowledge I'd gained through my own academic learning.

I was smart enough to know that finding my perfect match was making an investment in myself. The process would take time, but I'd get more efficient and skilled. And I did.

I realized that I had to write this book, and that the book would make a big difference in other women's and men's lives. I was now academically trained with a post-graduate degree in Marriage and Family Therapy, and I had valuable personal experience. I knew I could put together a system for those who could not afford to pay for the many sessions that it would take to learn all of this.

The guidance *It's a Match* provides will help the average person have a much happier romantic outcome. Even if you can only make a few changes in yourself, your life will be forever changed for the better, because your interactions with others will be forever improved.

Why Is This Book Different?

There are other books out there, of course. But, the ones I found only cover certain parts of dating. They might talk about using the "Law of Attraction" to summon someone into our lives, and then they leave out the part about how our self-limiting beliefs undermine our power. Or they might talk about how to have a relationship, without telling us how to avoid repeating the same failed love story over and over again. Or they might explain the technical aspects of online dating, without explaining how to write a profile that attracts exactly what you want, or how to really read a man's profile in order to tell if he's just a serial dater looking for sex.

And the other books left out the most important part: none of the other books showed the 4 Levels of Love, so a reader could know when he or she had found "The One" instead of just another one.

What I wanted to do was write what no one else had written: a comprehensive guide to finding lasting love in today's modern world.

That's why this book is different. Yes, you'll find out how to find him, get him, and keep him—in the digital age. But you'll also learn how to understand why your previous romantic relationships failed, so you can so you can stop making the same mistakes. You'll learn how to look deep inside yourself, and at the kind of thoughts you might not even realize you have.

My goal is to empower you so that you can find your own real and lasting love. You no longer have to remain a prisoner of your past. You can take charge of your life. *It's a Match* shows you how to understand when you're falling into the victim mentality, so you can choose a different path; and if you're willing to do the work, this book will give you the keys to having a lasting relationship, and to become happier with yourself than you've ever been.

You'll start by taking a good look at yourself, and at your personal love story. In other words, what has your history been? And what has your role in that history been?

Our relationships don't just happen *to* us. We are part of them. So we have to take ownership for how we have behaved in past relationships. All of us are driven by the ideas that were put in our brain from the time we were little.

Some of us develop inflated views of ourselves. Others— too many of us—think just the opposite. Subconsciously, we think we are unworthy. We think that we do not deserve love or happiness, that we're not good enough. Those are the things that drive us to make decisions and act in ways that can undermine our relationships.

This book shows you how to improve yourself so that you are the best version of yourself that you can possibly be. If you love yourself, you can truly love another. By improving yourself, learning how to love and accept yourself, and becoming the best version of you that you can be, you can become genuinely ready for a relationship. At that point you'll be ready to find "The One."

I'll show you how to do that: how to cast the net, as it were, to bring in the type of person you're really looking for, and not just another *Wrong One* or another, *I Should Have Known Better*.

I'm assuming that you're reading this book because you want a long term committed relationship, whether that is a marriage or lifetime partner. I'm assuming that you don't just want a date. A date is easy to get—just skip to the chapters on writing your profile. I'm assuming you want something more. I'm writing from the perspective that you've gone through the candy store phase after your last big breakup, you've sampled what's out there and sought validation by seeing how many men or women want to go out with you. Now you're tired of looking for Mr. Right and finding only Mr. I Should Have Known Better, Mr. I Should Have Seen That Coming, and their not-so-distant cousin, Mr. What Was I Thinking?

If that's the case, I'm going to be your guide.

First we're going to examine, and you're going to figure out, what you really want in a partner. What your deal breakers are. We're going to go through the process of self-discovery so you can find the partner you want.

In this process of self-discovery you'll probably be surprised by what you learn about yourself. For example, some women think they like bad boys. But you can never have a real relationship with a bad boy—because, by definition, he's not available. He's too busy thinking only about himself, and sabotaging his own life, to be available for a relationship between equals.

Or your self-examination might lead you to realize that you're attracted to emotionally unavailable men because part of you is afraid of being in a relationship.

Or perhaps you like the adrenaline rush of new relationships, so you pick romantic partners who excite you—you like falling madly and head over heels in love with them, only to have your romance end within months, weeks, or even days when you get bored because "you've lost that loving feeling" (the adrenaline rush!)

That's not uncommon.

We'll talk about the stages of romance and how the first stage of romance is actually driven by our hormones, which is really just chemistry, after all. The thrill of the new encounter releases hormones that make you feel like you're experiencing an adrenaline rush. This falling in love stage might last six months, a year, whatever. Yes, this honeymoon state feels good.

Eventually, though, the excitement wears off. What this means is that the relationship has moved to the next level. But there are people who become so addicted to the adrenaline rush of the honeymoon stage that they need to keep re-creating it.

These people are what I call "adrenaline junkies," and they're usually identified by their love of very dangerous sports, which trigger that same rush of adrenaline. Stay away from these people because they move on when the thrills run out. As soon as the honeymoon stage is done, they say, "This one is not the one for me."

And then they go out to find the next adrenaline rush.

So, I will teach you about the stages of romance. That way, you'll understand and recognize each stage, and you'll realize when your relationship is evolving in a healthy way or not. This will keep you from making false assumptions.

To have love, you have to be willing to be open and vulnerable. But that doesn't mean you have to let yourself become a victim. I'll show you what the red flags are, how you can identify the ones you should stay away from and how to avoid them.

When you understand all of this, you'll be ready to write your online profile to attract the right person for you. You'll learn how to use words that will reveal exactly who you are, and which will send out the vibrations to connect you with the best pool of potential matches.

You'll learn to choose your best screen name, and how to take—or, better yet, to have taken—and to select the photographs that project the best and most accurate "you." That's what you want your mate to be attracted to…

Basically, you need to represent yourself, as you are, in the best possible light so that you'll attract somebody who really is interested in you as a person.

Yes, exactly as you are.

There are men who are into heavy women, or men who like curvaceous women with a few extra pounds. There are women who like a man with a few extra pounds too, someone they can comfortably cuddle with. If you put up pictures of the way you looked ten years and twenty pounds ago, what you're doing is calling in the wrong potential mate and bypassing the people who could be attracted to the real you.

Truth in advertising is a good plan in your profile and in your pictures. I'll show you how to show yourself as an attractive person who respects herself.

You'll want to differentiate yourself from others. You're entering a search process so you want somebody to find your unique traits, and you want to find somebody who is interested in the real you.

This is, after all, a two-way street.

So I'll also teach you how to read another person's profile—and to read between the lines. You'll learn how to find the otherwise hidden clues in what he says, and what he doesn't.

We will do the same with their pictures. You'll discover how photographs reveal a person's personality, character, and intentions.

In short, the skills you'll learn here will show you how to look for—and find—Mr. Right For You, instead of yet another Mr. Wrong.

Let's begin.

CHAPTER TWO

The Four Levels of Love

What's the most serious disease in America? Divorce.

Close to half of all marriages end in divorce. And the more marriages you've had, the more likely you are to be divorced.

And it's not just in America.

Studies show that couples everywhere are uncoupling at alarming and increasing rates. A British couple divorced every five minutes in 2012, up slightly from the year before, which was up from the year before that. France, Germany and Canada aren't far behind.

There are many explanations for this. Some people blame the high divorce rate on living in a "disposable society." Others blame our desire for instant gratification, or on decreases in church attendance, or on Internet porn.

They're wrong. All these things may be factors, but they don't cause couples to divorce. The same goes for infidelity or the loss of sexual attraction.

Factors. Not causes.

There's really only one cause of divorce. We chose the wrong person.

We don't choose wrong on purpose—at least not consciously. It's just that most of us don't know that there are 4 Levels of Love, and that Level I and II matches are likely to end in divorce.

Most people think you have to be lucky to find your "soul mate," your one, true love. And, the rest of us, well... "He seemed so perfect when we met. We worked in the same department. We had so much to talk about. But then, after we got married..."

We don't know how to tell the difference between the different levels of love matches, so that we can avoid the ones that are doomed to fail even before they start.

I didn't know how to avoid this either. But after my divorce, I started wondering what caused some marriages to fail, while others continued to work. As I observed, questioned, and correlated I discovered what made some relationships great and enduring.

That's how I developed the Four Levels of Love. This system provides a way for you to define, analyze, and evaluate your relationships—and the men you meet—so that you can look for and find the committed, long-term connection you really want and deserve.

Lasting Love

I've been lucky to meet many couples who've been married for a long, long time and still have great relationships. You've probably seen them. They're holding hands and looking lovingly into each other's eyes because they are still deeply and intensely in love.

Over the years I started asking these couples for their secret to success. I just knew there had to be a secret, a magic formula.

They all came up with different ideas. One couple said, "We obviously agree to disagree sometimes."

I understood that. There are going to be differences of opinions by the mere fact that there are two different people in a couple. They'd better know how to disagree and find some sort of compromise!

The difference is, the successful couple knew how to argue. They accepted that they wouldn't always agree on everything, and they knew how to argue without attacking or being hurtful. (Don't worry: I'll talk about how to do this, in detail, later.)

I knew that "arguing well" couldn't be the whole answer, though, so I kept asking. And I started making a list.

Obviously, respect for each other came up frequently. So did the idea of having some level of admiration for each other.

Then I heard about the importance of having shared values and shared interests. The more shared values and interests, the better. This doesn't mean you have to be interested in the all the same things. You don't even have to participate in your shared interests together. Let's say you and I like to read. If we like the same kind of books, that's great! We could have our very own intimate book club in which we read the same book and then discuss it.

But we don't have to read the same books. We might like different kinds of books. If I like science fiction and you like biographies, that's okay. Sharing a love of reading, sitting down to read together, is enough. Or maybe you like cooking together, or swimming, or taking a walk in the evening.

Some successful couples are intrigued by different activities, but they still manage to find a way to share.

Let's say I was really excited about art and you weren't, but you were really ready to share my excitement and wanted me to talk with you about it. You might have something you love to do that I don't like doing. I'd still want to share in your enjoyment, even if I didn't want to share in the activity—like the golfer who loves to golf while the wife paints. That's okay. As long as each person comes back and tells each other their stories, and they encourage each other's areas of growth, this counts as sharing their interests.

These "successful" couples were committed to making their relationship work, no matter what. As they each evolved as individuals within the relationship, there were inevitable growing pains. But their commitment to working through the bumps in the relationship was paramount.

These couples also never took each other for granted. They often behaved with each other as though they were still dating.

One great example of this is my colleague, Larry and his wife. They were college sweethearts. Decades later, he still opens his briefcase in the morning to find little love note Post-its his wife has written and stuck inside. The only phone calls he will always answer— he doesn't care what meeting he is in—are from his wife. This is true, even after 40 years of marriage.

Larry and his wife understand that maintaining the romance in their relationship is very important. They always had a weekly "date" night with each other, and their only rule is that they cannot discuss their children. This keeps them connected to the person that they fell in love with, and at the same time they've got room to continue to grow.

Also, unfailingly, every successful couple said that they were sexually compatible. Sexually compatibility involves frequency, desire, and what you like in sex. If you have somebody who is really into S&M and somebody who's not... that's a problem. Someone who likes sex once a month is not sexually compatible with someone who wants it once a day. There is always going to be some difference in the sex drives of partners, but there needs to be a compromise that leaves both people satisfied.

As I started tallying my findings, I started connecting the dots—or, more accurately, connecting the circles. I started seeing that *all* the successful couples had many things in common.

As I talked to more couples, I began to notice more. I could identify what their level of connection was – what their level of love was – by examining some basic, but key, elements. Once I had that, I could tell if they would fail or succeed as a couple.

I discovered that I had only been in Level II relationships. I never went into my relationships thinking, "*This is only a Level II relationship, and it's never going to fulfill me." I'm never going to be truly happy.* I didn't know what made a good relationship versus a so-so relationship.

Now I do.

The Four Levels of Love

As you can see from the following graphic, there are four types of matches.

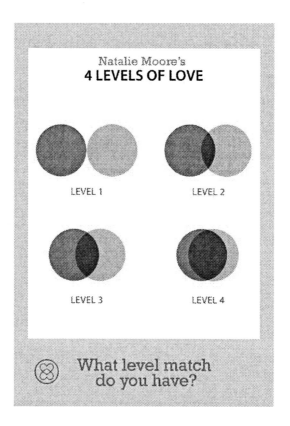

You might think of them as Bad, Blah, Blissful, and Breath-taking. I call them the 4 Levels of Love. Most of us are unaware that these four levels exist, which is why most of us choose the wrong man.

The key components of a great match are the aggregate of the number of shared intimacies and core values. This sum of the shared values and the number of shared intimacies creates the area of intersection in each of the 4 Levels of Love.

A Realistic Vision of Love

As I said before, there is no such thing as a perfect match. Each person you meet is going to have both positive and negative characteristics. You have to be realistic about that. If you're not, you're setting yourself up for perpetual disappointment: constantly looking for that elusive "perfect" man. Instead, look for the best match you can find, check that his negative qualities are not on your list of deal breakers, and that his baggage fits your baggage. (More about this later...)

What is Intimacy in a Relationship?

Intimacy is a journey of mutual discovery between partners. It is a process of moving past discussing just the facts of one's life to being open enough to discuss deep feelings, dreams, faults, failures, and needs.

The ability to be intimate in a love relationship takes self-awareness, time, trust, commitment to the relationship, honesty in communications, and authenticity in behavior (no manipulation or game playing).

Healthy intimacy requires the willingness to be vulnerable, which should increase over time in a healthy relationship, as you build your trust that you are safe emotionally and physically with this person. Both partners have to be able to stand the tension of someone really seeing them for who they are. Both partners must feel safe.

For a relationship to last, there must be a high level of intimacy and commitment to the relationship. All good relationships require a lot of work. They don't just happen!

The number of shared intimacies is probably the most important determinant of your relationship level, or of what level you can achieve with your beloved. In short, the intimacies are broad categories that are important to evaluate in your relationship. Do you trust your partner enough to discuss deep feelings, dreams, faults, failures, and needs in every area?

These shared intimacies will show you how well you and your potential mate align in terms of your physical, emotional, social, psychological, and other needs. My college professor, Marilyn Volker, PhD, identified eight types of intimacies.

I add two more to her list of intimacies: financial and work, for a total of ten. Our beliefs and expectations about our finances and how we handle them have become increasingly important in light of the changes in women's participation in the work force. Women have become an active and successful part of the work force in the past three generations, and as a result their role in relationships has changed drastically. Our financial independence has earned us a voice in the family finances.

Of course we all carry a lot of emotional baggage around money and finances. So it shouldn't be a surprise that financial issues can become a source of marital strife.

Many therapists don't include work and finances under the list of intimacies because they don't fall neatly under what they consider to be emotional or physical needs. But the ability to address financial goals, strategies, and issues as a couple is often emotional and stressful because many of our conflicting values and philosophies are involved.

Many of us define ourselves through our work because we spend so much time doing it. Our work is one of the first things we disclose when we meet someone. In Western culture, our work is so central to our core that it impacts most aspects of our lives. Thus, our ability to discuss work issues and fears without feeling judged or belittled is crucial to the success of a long-term relationship.

Refer to the following list of ten intimacies as you are evaluating your budding relationship. Use it as a way of measuring your relationship and its potential. You can use this list as a tool in growing your relationship by expanding your shared areas of intimacy.

1. Affection

How does each one of you express and interpret affection or love? Some people need to hear endearments in order to feel loved, while others prefer to be showered with little gifts or receive a lot physical touch.

Do you feel comfortable talking with each other about your different ways of receiving affection? Can you express affection to your mate in a way that he can receive it? It's important to assess how well you meet each other's needs to give and receive affection.

We each have different levels of needs and desire to be held, to be caressed, and to be reassured. Again—different people, different needs.

I have seen couples in which one person loves to touch and be touched, while the other person does not. She associates love with physical attention. He doesn't like to touch or be touched. She subconsciously interprets his inability to touch her as his not loving her. You can see how this is a problem! This relationship is probably not a good match.

2. Social Intimacy

How well do you share friendships and social interactions with each other? Are you both comfortable with a girls' or a guys' night out? Do you consider it important that you like his friends? And that he like yours? Do you interact well as a couple when you are with other people?

Does one of you have a vastly different need for social interactions with other people? Can you discuss these differences and be satisfied with the compromise?

I once dated a man who had a high need for social interaction. He liked for us to go out with different friends and business people every night, while I enjoyed going out with others only two or three nights a week. It became a juggling act to find the right balance between his and my needs. For me, this became too exhausting to continue.

3. Emotional Intimacy

How easily do you share our feelings with each other? Do you feel safe in sharing your feelings and needs with your partner without fear of being belittled, ridiculed, or disregarded? When you speak about your feelings, is he interested? Is he empathetic and compassionate? Are you?

When you speak about how his actions make you feel, how does he respond? Does he take responsibility for his actions, or does he blame you for them?

Are you able to discuss your hopes, dreams, and goals?

The willingness to be vulnerable, and to be seen for who you are, should increase over time in a healthy relationship as you build trust that you are safe and accepted.

If you can't feel safe to express your history, feelings, and needs, then you really have very little basis for a relationship. In essence you're saying that you do not trust him to respond appropriately or respectfully, or to accept you as you are.

4. Intellectual Intimacy

This area of intimacy measures how comfortable you are in discussing politics, books, or any intellectual subject. Can you listen to each other with respect and curiosity for the other's opinion without making the other person wrong?

Do you share a similar intellectual curiosity or range of knowledge? If one of you is more educated than the other, is this a problem?

When you travel, do you both enjoy going to museums together and learning about the culture of different countries? Or does one of you just want to go shopping while the other one is interested in going to museums?

Can you share knowledge without lecturing each other? (Lecturing as a form of communication is actually a barrier to intimacy.)

5. Companionship Intimacy

Companionship isn't about sex. It's about the ease between the two of you when you're spending time together doing everyday things such as errands, chores, or just sitting together reading a book or watching TV. Much of life is spent doing everyday things. Are you comfortable with the silent moments between you? Do you play well together?

Some people have a higher need for companionship than others. How well do you match in this area? Some people have a higher need for "alone time" or "space" than others. A person who has a high need for space would not be a good match for someone who requires constant companionship.

Do like doing recreational things together such as sports? Do you both play fairly?

6. Aesthetic Intimacy

How important is it for you to share your interests with your partner in music, art, and performance art?

How important is it for you to be surrounded by a beautiful environment? Do you have similar tastes? One couple I know had a problem with this. She liked antiques and he liked very modern furniture and art.

She would not compromise, and they lived in a house full of antiques (which he called brown furniture). She belittled his preference by saying that this showed his lack of class. He, obviously, did not feel safe voicing any further opinions because he did not want to be ridiculed.

I know another couple that spent a lot of their time and resources beautifying their home and collecting art that they can afford. They built a strong bond through their aesthetic intimacy.

7. Sexual Intimacy

How sexually compatible are you? Do you have similar sexual drives? Do you feel safe sharing your sexual fantasies and needs with your partner?

Do you have similar needs for sexual exploration and adventure? Can you share these without feeling judged? Are you equally generous in your sexual giving, as well as receiving? How satisfying is your sexual experience together? How safe do you feel expressing your needs, preferences, and setting limits in the sexual arena?

This aspect is very important to the success of any romantic relationship. Sexual needs, drives, and preferences may change over time. Your ability to be open about this and to feel safe discussing all aspects of sex is very important. Large discrepancies in sexual drive and desire for sexual exploration can limit a relationship's chances of long-term success.

8. Spiritual Intimacy

Do you share similar views regarding God, religion, and in your philosophies towards life? If your beliefs are not similar, are you each able to respect the other's beliefs? Can you discuss your beliefs without making the other person wrong? How safe do you feel when discussing your true feelings, beliefs, and experiences in these areas? Are you both able to accept your differences with respect?

How important are religious ceremonies in each of your lives? Are you able to freely discuss these topics and reach some compromise or acceptance?

9. Financial Intimacy

This is a prime cause of marital discord. Finances should probably not be discussed until you are in a committed relationship, but you can assess your views on spending, saving, and the incurrence of debt as your relationship develops. You should definitely not get married without thoroughly discussing these issues.

Do you share similar values about saving and spending? Are you able to freely discuss these topics? Are you both trustworthy with each other's money? Are you able to be completely honest with each other about your financial situation?

Can you agree about how money should be held: jointly, separately, or in some mix of the two? Can you agree on how spending decisions will be made as well, as well as how debt should be handled? If you have children from other marriages, are you able to discuss how their expenses are going to be handled? What if one child has a special need or wants a more expensive education than the others?

10. Work/Career Intimacy

Do you each value your own occupation, and each other's? Can you share work problems and situations with respect and empathy? Can you help each other formulate solutions to work problems?

If you work together in your own business, can you work as partners rather than as boss/employee?

Are you supportive of each other's growth by encouraging more education, or by encouraging the other to go for that big promotion or big job?

Does one partner's career take precedence over the other person's? Always?

Core Values

Core values are the things that define what is important to us in our lives and how we make decisions. Unfortunately, many of us have never examined and identified our own core values.

For example, ask yourself: What beliefs, principles, or convictions do you hold dear? What is the importance of religion, family, or community? Do you have a need for achievement or adventure? You might believe that honesty or trustworthiness is paramount, and that lying, cheating, or deceitfulness are things you just can't put up with.

Do you have strong opinions about politics or race?

You may have spent your childhood in poverty and consider being frugal an inviolable standard.

Core values include anything you feel so strongly about that they are an integral part of your being.

Firm environmentalists or devout vegans might feel so strongly about their beliefs that they should list them as core values. A person who goes to church every Sunday would include shared religious practices in his list.

Couples who have shared values have a higher chance of long-term success. You can find a list of core values at the end of this chapter. Please use this list to identify your own top five core values, and use this list as you do the exercises you will find at the end of the chapter as well.

Putting it All Together—
The Four Levels of Love

Level I

When you meet somebody and you don't have much in common, you have a Level I match. I call this match the null set. You might share a bus bench with this person, and maybe an ice cream or a one-night stand, but you should not share a lifetime.

Other examples of this match may include situations in which the institution of marriage is the sole purpose of the union. This could be a mail-order bride, a marriage made in order to get legal documentation, or an arranged marriage.

Most of the time this match cannot last.

Level II

A Level II match has a small number of shared intimacies and core values. Most of us enter a Level II match with great hope, though we've explored few key intimacies and core values. The amount of unexplored intimacies and values becomes apparent after the marriage, when the couple experiences conflict and alienation. Regretfully, many of these matches have a painful end. Most of the failed relationships in our society are Level II matches.

You might go to the same church and like the same TV shows. You might share political views or you might work for the same accounting firm. You might be in the same bowling league, have the same friends, or your kids might go to school together. Couples like this join together and hope for the best. They "settle" on each other, thinking that having something in common is good enough.

This couple ultimately realizes that they have very few core values or shared intimacies. They are afraid to voice their real feelings, fears, and desires with each other, so they arrive at a point at which they feel like don't even know their partner. They become resentful.

At the onset of the relationship, this lack of intimacy and common ground was not apparent or even examined. They may have shared a number of interests, which created the illusion of a viable match. But when viewed from the perspective of what makes relationships endure, you can see that there's not enough to keep this couple together long-term.

These partners usually have a nebulous vision of their future together, or they may not have discussed their future in detail. They usually try to force a fit, in order to come together as a couple.

In earlier times, when most people lived in small towns, this sort of relationship was common. People's shared proximity and social circle was all they shared. Given that there might only be two twenty-something's within a hundred miles, it made sense to settle. Some women were thrilled that at least they'd avoided becoming a spinster.

This was often a fear-based decision, based on the belief that, *I am never going to find somebody who's better, so I might as well take this match. It's better to have someone than no one.*

Sadly, too many people still engage in this kind of thinking. Sometimes family, cultural, or religious pressures come into play. But even people with lots of options often fail to make the best match.

Princess Diana and Prince Charles were in that situation. They came from the same social group. Their families were similar. They were more or less age-appropriate and he needed to have an heir.

There were several commonalities, and they figured they could make the rest work. They had the similar lifestyles, some of the same friends, and presumably found each other attractive.

Sound familiar?

It's kind of like when you meet somebody at work or through work.

Let's say you're a stockbroker. You meet another stockbroker. You really think you have a lot of interests in common. There's the people you know, the work you do, the sports you like. (Sound familiar?)

That couple would probably get married. But guess what? When they start living together, they're going to discover that they're just a Level II match: their relationship revolves around superficial things. They've confused interests with shared values and true intimacy.

This sort of situation happens all the time. Because so much of your dating life is concentrated around the interests that you have in common, you tend to avoid dwelling on your differences. Many couples are so busy talking about work and socializing with their same group of friends, they just don't realize that there are other aspects of their lives that will become important to the long-term success of their relationship.

Another reason people settle for a Level II relationship instead of moving on is due to what I call "perceived investment." Maybe that comes from my background in finance, but the idea of "perceived investment" is a lot like that old saying: "throwing good money after bad."

Except that instead of throwing away money, you're throwing away time.

You meet somebody—at work, through a friend, whatever—and, again, because of your work or your friends or your bowling league or whatever, you have enough in common to have a good time together.

You start dating. And even though there are times when you feel a little twinge of doubt, when your inner voice is telling you that something might be lacking in your relationship, a year goes by, or two, or three.

Both of you may realize that you don't have a lot of things in common, but you think, *I've already invested two years of my life.*

You rationalize.

I've spent so much time with him already, and it works well enough.

And you end up settling. You end up marrying your Level II match.

That's when you throw good time after bad.

Two or three years of so-so dating and engagement leads to two, three, or four years of so-so marriage. Then, you guessed it! You join the divorce statistics. And, by the time you divorce five years later, you've got seven or eight years invested and you have to start over.

Been there, done that? Me too.

That's why I know we both would have been a lot better off *knowing*, and facing facts at the beginning. That way we could have ended our Level II relationship and spent our time looking for, and probably finding, a Level III or Level IV match.

Level II matches are often started offline, and when one or both people feels like the pool of potential mates is limited.

Others accept Level II matches because they're driven by fear: of abandonment, loneliness, or that they're not worthy of something better. Whatever. These limiting beliefs or fears push people to seize any relationship they can get, like a drowning person latches onto a life preserver.

People think, "*What are my chances of ever finding somebody who will want to marry me?*" They settle. They think, "*Any relationship is better than no relationship.*" What they get is a relationship, but not a union. They settle for a Level II relationship because they think that's better than being alone.

With a lot of work by both partners, a Level II relationship may be transformed into a Level III relationship, but this is rare. So why not focus on finding a Level III relationship or a Level IV relationship? These two share many of the same qualities.

Level III

This is a very good match and makes for a very strong marriage because the couple share many core values and intimacies, and they also have a shared vision of the direction of their life together. Depending on their stage in life, this could mean a shared vision of having children together and how to raise them, or it could be an agreement regarding what age to retire and what to do after retirement.

Having a shared vision of your life together is important. I know a couple whose marriage failed after thirty years because they had very different ideas about how they wanted to spend their retirement. She wanted her entrepreneur husband to quit working and have a traditional retirement, because that's what "old" people did. He wanted to continue making "deals" because he felt alive and vibrant as he did this, and he didn't consider his chronological age to be a true reflection of who he really was.

Now these two older people live separate lives. Not surprisingly, many "empty- nester" couples divorce after years of marriage because they no longer have a shared vision of their remaining time, together.

The Level III match is sexually compatible and each one feels comfortable and emotionally safe with the other.

A couple who has many shared intimacies is usually emotionally very healthy, so it is the coming together of two independent people who can be interdependent with each other – not co-dependent, but interdependent. This means that each person is "there" for the other, but each can maintain a sense of self within the relationship. Each has gotten past expecting someone else to fulfill all their needs, and when emotional wounds are triggered, each is experienced at self-soothing. They are able to maintain healthy boundaries because there is mutual respect and self-respect. Each partner demonstrates a healthy level of self-love and emotional security. From this place of wholeness, each can truly complement each other.

No long-term commitment or marriage should ever occur unless it's at least a Level III. This alone would reduce the divorce rate and increase the success rate for relationships.

Level III matches generally make for lasting, loving, and fulfilling relationships and a lifetime of happiness. This is a very life enhancing and supportive relationship in which 1+1=3.

These relationships are easier to find online, versus the offline-dating world in which getting to know someone from A-Z relatively quickly is hard. There is also a dating efficiency due to the vast pool of potential dates and the plethora of information about each person that is available from sites that require profiles.

The online dating protocol of asking any type of question, makes it socially acceptable for you to screen for deal breakers, values, and other pertinent information within the first few dates in order to evaluate your match potential. With the advent of online dating, no marriage should ever occur unless it is at least a Level III match. You do not need to settle for anything less. Think of the impact on our society and children if we only entered into Level III relationships.

Level IV—The Divine Partnership (DP)

The Level IV relationship provides for an even higher level of connection between partners. There is no secret formula that will tell you where to find your DP. You can't look for him. But, if you're ready for him, he might just happen to come into your life.

Your divine partner may be out there. But he won't come looking for you until you are ready to be part of that match. As you come closer to being your most authentic self, by clearing defense mechanisms and limiting beliefs, and following the calling of your soul and your Higher Self, you may attract your Level IV partner. (I will give you some tools on how to do this later.)

Part of preparing for your divine partner includes working on finding your inner balance by integrating the male and female "aspects" within yourself. That means releasing gender-specific roles such as the Tyrant Male role or the helpless Princess role. We each have a part within us that can be strong and be called to action when necessary. We also have a part that can be soft and knows when to be still and receive. When you can balance these two parts within yourself, you eschew unilateral gender roles. When you have created this divine marriage within yourself, you are ready to mirror it outside of yourself with your Divine Partner.

The hallmark of the Divine Partnership is that both parties feel like there is an element of a fated union, of divine intervention bringing you together in order to complement each other's lives. This Level IV match has the largest intersections between the circles of confluence because it's really a soul level or higher union.

Your relationship may start your feeling *I've known this person before.* And then you discover that you're just so connected that, basically, your inner being tells you that there's something big going on.

This is very different than a "soul mate" relationship. "Soul mate" is a term that has been adulterated into meaning "your other half," when it really means a member of your soul group with whom you've shared many life times.

Soul mates are often couples that come together to resolve past life imbalances or issues. These relationships usually involve a lot of strife, along with an immense sexual attraction that keeps you together until these issues are resolved. They tend to be more tumultuous relationships, often filled with a lot of sexual tension and a lot of drama.

After the couple works through their "issue," they usually part. Often one person works through the issue before the other, so the breakup can be painful—one person is still very much enthralled, while the other may have already left the relationship.

The DP relationship is not about working out past karma or imbalances from other lifetimes, or about working out major relationship issues. This relationship is about something bigger. Another hallmark of the DP relationship is that both people are looking outward together in the same direction. There is often a shared goal of philanthropy or community or world service.

The DP match is much more than a chemical attraction. You might feel a strong initial attraction, but as you get to know the other person, your mutual attraction gets reinforced. Your desire to be together grows deeper and you discover that you even more points of connection. There is a sense of harmony, of "rightness," not drama. The partners are so in tune with one another that sometimes when they're apart, they can still feel each other's joy, fear, and anxiety,

When you meet your divine partner, things seem to sort of fall into place. From the first moment you feel, *I've known this person. This is amazing!* This sense of recognition and instant familiarity continues. Your soul longs to be with this person.

And everything flows into place. Level IV relationships are easier than other relationships. Divine forces seem to be orchestrating everything so you can come together. I'm not saying that the circumstances of your meeting will be perfect. Most likely there will be an initial challenge. She might be twenty years younger than her DP, or he might be of a different race. Perhaps one of these people is dating someone else.

The natural order of life is for these two to come together, despite the obstacles. If both parties are following the call of their souls and Higher Selves, they surmount the obstacles and they come together.

Perhaps their initial challenge is meant to clean up some remaining area of growth that each needed. Perhaps one needed to learn to eschew social conventions, etc.

There will always be some areas of growth that the Divine Partners must address, but the people in these relationships work through their issues in a mature way. The deciding factor of every action is whether it is good for the relationship, as opposed to what might be good for just one individual.

This relationship is not perfect. There is no such thing as a perfect match. You both are still two different people, with different experiences. But you and your DP will share large areas of commonality, as you can see from the Venn diagram. Even in areas in which you're not as compatible, you'll be willing to sublimate or bend because the relationship is so much more important than whatever it is you don't agree about.

The Divine Partnership (DP) is made of two complementary forces working together, standing in divine flow. Divine Partners do not take anything away from each other, but by being together they become much more than they are as two individuals. The sum of their union is far greater than if they were standing alone. In this case 1+1=4. This is an alchemical union in which the sum is far greater than each of its parts. Each person inspires the other to become the best they can be.

This magic plays out in almost every area of their lives. Often, each partners' spiritual gifts are amplified when they are together. If one is psychic, she becomes a clearer channel of information when she is with her DP. If another is a healer, he becomes a more powerful healer.

Finding your DP offline is a miracle. The chances of finding your Level IV match vastly improve online because you have access to a greater number of people.

For Divine Partners to meet offline, both parties have to be listening to their inner guidance and acting upon it at the same time. Online, you get repeated exposures to the same person over a long period of time. In the offline world, if you arrive at a park one hour late, you may miss your chance to meet for the rest of time.

The only way to find a Level IV relationship is to aim for a Level III match. The only one who'll know the difference between these levels is you. The difference between Level III and Level IV is the sense that you've been together before and that your souls yearn for one another.

If meet your DP, you'll know that you've found "The One." You'll feel like you're reuniting instead of just starting.

CHAPTER 2: EXERCISES

Exercise: Identify Your Core Values and Shared Intimacies

Analyzing your Core Values and Shared Intimacies will help you determine the "Love Level" of your romantic relationships whether past, present, or future.

1. In order for you to determine your most important values, begin to think about the qualities in yourself which make you the proudest. Was it that moment when you helped a stranger who was in need? Was it when you got that big promotion?

Next, think of some of the happiest times in your life. These will also show you some of your values. Do those evenings spent with your family come up as your happiest memories? If so, you know you are family oriented. Were you happiest when you were climbing Mount Kilimanjaro or spelunking? If so, you know that adventure is one of your values.

Make a list of your top five core values.

2. Now let's do the same thing one more time. This time, make a list of your intimacies. Look at all of the intimacies listed in this chapter. Have your list of core values handy.

Now think about your past and current relationships. Put the initials of each of your exes next to the values you shared and next to the intimacies you shared. Now do this with your current relationship.

When you're done, count the sum of the values and intimacies for each one:

> 2 or less = Level I
> 3 to 7 = Level II
> 8 or 12 = Level III
> 10 to 15 = Level IV

It's pretty easy to see why they're your exes isn't it?

Hold on to this list. Use it when you start going out with different men. You're looking for an 8 or higher. When you find a 10 to 15, you're in Divine Partner territory.

Let's look at the example of Peter and Mary:

Her Core Values
Family
Service to others
Spirituality
Connection
Art

His Core Values
Family
Financial independence
Knowledge
Art
Service to others

Core Values: 3

Shared intimacies: 5 | Total 8 = Level III |

In order to grow this relationship, this couple could work on increasing their shared areas of intimacies.

List of Possible Core Values

Abundance

Acceptance

Accomplishment

Accountability

Achievement

Acknowledgement

Activeness

Adaptability

Adaptability

Adoration

Advancement

Adventure

Affection

Affluence

Aggressiveness

Altruism

Ambition

Appreciation

Approachability

Art

Articulacy

Artistry

Assertiveness

Assurance

Attractiveness

Availability

Awareness

Balance

Beauty

Belonging

Bravery

Brilliance

Calmness

Camaraderie	Delight
Care	Dependability
Celebrity	Desire
Challenge	Determination
Change	Devotion
Charm	Dignity
Cheerfulness	Directness
Cleverness	Discipline
Commitment	Discretion
Community	Diversity
Compassion	Dominance
Competition	Drive
Confidence	Duty
Conformity	Ecstasy
Connection	Education
Consistency	Elegance
Contentment	Empathy
Control	Encouragement
Conviction	Energy
Coolness	Environmentalism
Cooperation	Ethics
Courage	Excellence
Courtesy	Experience
Creativity	Expertise
Credibility	Exploration
Cunning	Expressiveness
Curiosity	Extravagance
Daring	Extroversion
Decisiveness	Fairness
Decorum	Faith
Deference	Fame

Family	Ingenuity
Fashion	Inquisitiveness
Fearlessness	Insightfulness
Fidelity	Integrity
Financial independence	Intellect
Fitness	Intimacy
Flexibility	Introspection
Freedom	Introversion
Friendliness	Intuitiveness
Friendship	Joy
Frugality	Justice
Fun	Kindness
Gallantry	Knowledge
Generosity	Leadership
Grace	Liveliness
Gratitude	Logic
Growth	Love
Happiness	Loyalty
Harmony	Making a difference
Health	Marriage
Helpfulness	Maturity
Heroism	Meaning
Honesty	Meekness
Hospitality	Mindfulness
Humility	Modesty
Humor	Motivation
Hygiene	Nature
Imagination	Non-conformity
Independence	Obedience
Individuality	Open-mindedness
Influence	Optimism

Organization

Partnership

Patience

Passion

Peace

Perfection

Perseverance

Philanthropy

Playfulness

Pleasure

Poise

Polish

Popularity

Power

Practicality

Presence

Pride

Privacy

Proactivity

Professionalism

Prosperity

Punctuality

Purity

Recognition

Recreation

Refinement

Relaxation

Reliability

Religion

Reputation

Resilience

Resourcefulness

Respect

Responsibility

Sacrifice

Security

Self-control

Selflessness

Self-reliance

Self-respect

Sensitivity

Sensuality

Serenity

Service

Sexiness

Sexuality

Sharing

Silliness

Simplicity

Sincerity

Solitude

Sophistication

Soundness

Spirituality

Spontaneity

Stability

Status

Strength

Structure

Success

Support

Synergy

Teaching

Teamwork

Thoughtfulness

Trustworthiness

Understanding

Uniqueness

Variety

Virtue

Vision

Vitality

Volunteering

Warmth

Traditionalism

Transcendence

CHAPTER THREE

You Are Who You Date

Remember that old saying, "You are what you eat?" I don't know if that's true. I'm not a nutritionist.

But I know what *is* true: You are *who* you date.

We all want a relationship in order to find true love and companionship. Humans are social beings who need relationships in order to thrive.

Relationships are not only about love, but they also serve a higher purpose. They can help us to achieve personal growth and spiritual development. Each relationship is our mirror. It shows us where we need to keep working and where we are succeeding. We can discern our own limiting beliefs and unresolved personal issues by observing what triggers us in our relationships.

In short, being close to another person shows us where we stand with ourselves.

As I said earlier, before you can find the best *one* for you, you must become the best *you* that you can be. (Unless, of course, you want to keep attracting the same kind of relationships that you have attracted before.)

That's the Law of Attraction. You get what you are.

The Law of Attraction

The Law of Attraction is one of the many spiritual laws that govern our universe. In summary, our beliefs draw us toward circumstances that mirror our expectations and frequency vibration.

Our thoughts, beliefs, emotions, and actions are what create our frequency vibration. There's actually a lot of science behind all of this. In his book, *Power vs. Force*, David R. Hawkins, MD, PhD explains how he actually measured the frequency of different emotions. These emotions are a result of our thoughts, which affect our actions.

People who vibrate at the same frequency are drawn together. So, it makes sense that in order for you to manifest your perfect relationship, all you have to do is to change your vibration by changing your mind.

The Secret by Rhonda Byrne gave us tools to help us use the Law of Attraction to bring whatever we wanted into our lives. These same tools have been taught by spiritual teachers through the ages. In short, to attract our desired relationship, we can make a list of the qualities of our perfect mate, create a vision board of his qualities and the desired qualities of the relationship, and then, affirm gratitude for our already having this relationship in our life. This is a quick summary of the technique, but you get the point.

What no one mentions is that your subconscious beliefs about yourself and your relationships largely over-ride any amount of affirmations and visualizations. For example, assume that you're trying to attract a certain type of man, but deep down you feel that you are not lovable and that you are not worthy of him. As a result, no matter how many times you visualize, and how many times you imagine having him, the other 90 % of the day your limiting beliefs are creating your frequency vibration. Thus, you will attract someone who closely matches your limiting beliefs.

Why? Because, you are sending the universe mixed messages. Your overriding frequency is really that of being unlovable and undeserving. You are sustaining a higher frequency for the short time that you are visualizing and feeling this new relationship. But, most of the day, you are really projecting your belief that you are unlovable and undeserving of this great guy. In essence, one message is interfering with the other. As a result, you are likely to end up attracting a man who is similar to your exes.

Our brain works like a computer. As we experience things (data), we make conclusions and store them in our hard drive (brain). We store these conclusions as programs in our subconscious. Much of what we believe about relationships and ourselves was programmed into our brains by the time we were ten. It's scary to think that a child has programmed our computer, but that's the reality.

Young children are concrete thinkers. Everything is black or white. We made inferences about ourselves, others, and relationships based upon the experiences and the concrete thinking of our younger self. Unfortunately, we continue to make decisions about life, relationships, and ourselves from the perspective of our younger self. Hence, much of what we do and think (i.e. attract) is based upon subconscious beliefs created by these faulty early assumptions.

In order to get different results in our lives, we need to identify and clear up any incorrect conclusions and assumptions that created our limiting beliefs. We need to understand the reality, which is that we are magnificent beings who are completely deserving of love. (I will give you tools to identify and clear these limiting beliefs in the following chapter.)

This idea is simple, and it makes sense. Our thoughts and emotions create a vibrational frequency within us. That creates a corresponding frequency that we send out into the universe. Think of this as a song we compose with our hearts and minds. Happy, positive, optimistic thoughts and feelings play one tune; angry, negative, pessimistic thoughts and feelings play another.

In accordance with the Law of Attraction, you can only attract a person who matches your frequency. This is why you've been attracting the same type of man over and over into your life. Thus, doesn't it make sense that you would want to become the One that you are looking for?

If your ideal man has wonderful qualities that you do not possess, meeting Mr. Fabulous won't do you any good. You wouldn't be a frequency match, so the bond wouldn't work. You wouldn't be able to sustain this relationship.

That's why I stress that it's important to improve yourself, to be the best you can be *before* you try to attract someone. After all, as Einstein supposedly said, the definition of insanity is doing the same thing over and over again and expecting different results.

In fact, I think we should always be working on ourselves if we want to improve the kind of man we're getting, and also, in the process, improve our lives.

Frequency Matches

The good news is that you're not stuck with the same frequency for life. And, you're not stuck with the kind of men you've been with in the past.

You have the power to change and improve.

If you want to attract a different match, you have to clean out your emotional closet. That means looking at the problematic things that have existed within you, but you have not been willing to fix. Yes, it's time to get your big girl pants on because this is not for the faint of heart.

Your internal changes will boost your self-confidence, too. How you feel about yourself can change your frequency because our internal emotions often drive our actions.

I've always been a firm believer in working on myself – either through therapy, reading self-help books, or practicing other techniques. The more I work on myself, the happier I become because I'm less reactive. I can *act* instead of *react.* I am more in charge of my life and my choices.

You can always judge your progress by the differences in the people that you attract, ranging from potential romantic partners to potential new friends.

Our internal work should be coupled with becoming the best you externally, too. How you look and present yourself is an expression of how you feel about yourself. It's time to evaluate how you look and what you wear, to find out what you're saying to others about how you feel about yourself.

Consider how these external things can reflect the new "you" that you're trying to project: your look, the way you dress, your hairstyle. We often get stuck in a certain dress style or haircut. I find that when I go shopping, I often gravitate to the same clothing style or that I keep getting the same haircut. We are creatures of habit.

Why should we bother evaluating our external selves? Because men are visual. That's one reason. But further, what we see in the mirror also affects how we see ourselves. Checking the mirror on our way out the door and seeing an attractive, poised, well-dressed woman looking back will boost your self-confidence.

You don't have to be expensively dressed to look attractive. You can look stunning in jeans and a T-shirt. Wear clothing and accessories that make you feel pretty, and good about yourself.

I suggest that you enlist the help of friends who have a good sense of style. Have them go through your wardrobe and make suggestions about what works for you and what doesn't. When I see that my closet is full of the same clothes, I invite a friend whose style I admire to go shopping with me, and to pick out new clothes she thinks would look great on me (and that I like). Over the years, I've found great new looks this way.

Many stores have free personal shopper services. Another great option is to find a personal shopper whose style you like. Try several until you find the one for you. Have them notify you when the store has sales. I work with a great personal shopper, Lisa, who finds amazing things for me that I would never have considered or even found on my own.

Every once in a while, I ask my hairstylist, whom I've had for years, to change my look because I'm bored. This forces her to evaluate me as though I were a new client.

It's also important to take a good look at your physical health, your level of fitness, and how you feel you can improve in these areas. After all, you want to be the best you can be—in all areas. Plus, doing all this is likely to make you feel better.

Are You a Full Vessel?

Full vessels make full, healthy relationships.

Relationships fall on a continuum, starting with what, for simplicity's sake, we can call the immature relationship. At the other end of the spectrum we have the mature relationship.

An immature relationship involves two people who have a lot of emotional needs and who are looking for another person to fill those needs. I call these the "never enough" relationships. Each one is always demanding that the other partner fill his own unmet needs. Unfortunately, no matter how much you do for the other person, it's never enough because they are an empty vessel.

Each person in an immature relationship has an external focus. Each focuses on how the other person does not met their needs.

Sometimes the vessels are really empty. Other times they are half-full.

The reality is that two empty vessels coming together remain just as empty, and just as needy. They can't get what they want because they don't know how to meet their own emotional needs. These are important life skills that need to be learned as we grow up.

At the other end of the spectrum is the mature relationship. In reality, there are several other types of relationships in the spectrum before you get to the mature level. But, they are like shades of color in a range.

The people in a mature relationship are full vessels. Each partner is self-sustaining. Each can self-soothe his internal wounds and has an internal feedback loop. This means that she doesn't value herself based upon external feedback from other people.

Each partner in a mature relationship has an internal focus: on healing her own emotional wounds that interfere with the relationship. Someone in a mature relationship will be a neutral observer of her own actions, thoughts, and feelings. She will be the detective of her own psyche. She will take responsibility for herself.

It takes a lot of work to achieve the insight, wisdom, and self-containment necessary to be a full vessel. We all have things that trigger us, but a full vessel knows how to deal with them.

Many people have huge walls around themselves to protect themselves from being hurt. Others have smaller walls. These walls are a defense mechanism created by the ego; the walls are there to protect us. They are usually formed from our own earlier beliefs about relationships and how lovable or deserving we are.

When you create a wall around yourself and don't let somebody get close, you are never going to get hurt. But guess what? You are never going to love or get love, either.

Unfortunately, this defense mechanism perpetuates your belief that you are not lovable, because it does not allow love in. Does that really make sense? It's obviously not a good defense mechanism when it creates the very problem you're trying to avoid.

The full vessel does not create walls in order to avoid "bad" feelings. She has broken down these walls and has found better coping skills.

Others keep themselves "safe" from the perceived pain of love by finding fault with every partner they have. They convince themselves that they cannot find a worthy partner, so they are alone. They use this coping mechanism in order to avoid being hurt. They succeed at remaining unhurt. They also end up alone.

It's good to keep a list of your own coping or defense mechanisms as you notice them. We will use this list to help you identify your fears and limiting beliefs, so we can clear them and get into healthier relationships in the future.

I will give you the tools to clear these fears and limiting beliefs, but in some cases you might find it beneficial to additionally enlist the help of a therapist. A therapist would be especially helpful if your defense mechanisms are interfering in all your relationships or if you have suffered childhood abuse.

Some women can let their girlfriends become close, but won't let men into their lives. Or they allow men in as friends, but no more. Some women simply refuse to be vulnerable. They don't want to risk getting hurt.

If you find that you want to be perfect all the time, you have a limiting belief that you are only lovable if you are perfect. You need to create a wall to hide your imperfections. Don't. To be human is to be perfectly imperfect.

If you find that you cannot be yourself with a man, that you're hiding half of your feelings and faults, you've erected a wall. It's okay and appropriate to create a wall or a boundary with a complete stranger, but it is counterproductive when you're trying to build intimacy with someone close. As you get to know someone and you learn to trust them, you need to lower your walls in a healthy manner. These are called having flexible boundaries. The aim is to become a full vessel and to break through unhelpful defense mechanisms.

The full vessel uses healthy coping mechanisms such as humor. When she does something, instead of calling herself stupid and closing off, she pokes fun at herself. She thinks, *"There I go again, doing that same thing again." How silly of me! I will do better next time.* She realizes that she is a work in progress and views her mistakes with compassion for herself. Having compassion for yourself is a form of healthy self-love.

You can practice this by examining your self-talk every time you make a mistake. Pretend that your best friend was telling you about this "mistake." What would you tell her? Tell yourself these same things! You have to be able to love yourself before you can truly love another.

If you're reading this book, it's because what you have been doing has not been working for you. I want to guide you on your own personal journey of self-discovery.

Your work towards becoming a full vessel begins when you start excavating your authentic self, clearing away fears, limiting beliefs, and defense mechanisms. You can recognize the people who have achieved this, because you feel their openness and you get the feeling that "what you see is what you get." You want to be around this person.

One advantage of working towards becoming a full vessel is that you will become happier. You'll be happy being by yourself. You'll be happy to be yourself. You'll feel complete. And, as a complete person, you can be a complement to another complete person. You're both already complete, and don't need to settle for anything other than the right match. A full vessel is not afraid to be alone.

That leads to higher-level matches. Two full vessels are able to have an interdependent relationship. They can have a mature relationship, in which one plus one is more than two.

When two full or almost full vessels share values, when they look outward in the same direction and have shared intimacies, they're ready to arrive at a Level III or Level IV relationship.

But when two fairly empty vessels or semi-full vessels get together, they often end up in codependent relationships. Their relationships are based on fear: the fear of not getting needs met, or the feeling that *I've got to meet his needs so that he'll meet mine.*" This is giving to get.

If you find that you always need to have a guy, that you cannot stand to be alone, that's a sign that you're not a full vessel. You are operating out of fear of being alone, and you're making fear-based decisions. This is the situation in which people generally settle for less.

Incidentally, the process of self-improvement doesn't stop just because we might have found our match. Our new relationship will most likely bring up issues, which are clues about what else we need to address. There will always be work to be done. We're all works in progress. The good news is this: as you continue working on yourself—using some of the techniques I'll show you here, or going to therapy, or getting personal coaching—you will continue to become happier and more complete.

The point of this is to keep working on these exercises as you date. Dating lets you practice your new skills, and helps you see where your weaknesses are and what is triggering you.

Dating helps you close in on the things you need to work on so that you can grow.

You might as well start by looking at everything. Reading this book and doing the exercises gives you a chance to reinvent yourself. Just be sure you are coming from a place of self-love and self-compassion. Love yourself unconditionally, with all of your human faults. Have compassion for yourself and the experiences that have brought you to this place in your life.

This was a big lesson for me. I used to demand the highest levels of achievement from myself and would berate myself if I fell short of that. I had unrealistic expectations due to my own limiting belief that I was only worthy if I achieved something—because that is how I was recognized in my family. I had to work at learning self-compassion and self-love, so I could understand that I was worthy just by existing, that I was lovable with all of my shortcomings. By clearing away my own limiting beliefs, I was able to become my authentic self.

Certainly we have made mistakes in the past. But we don't have to be a victim of our past. We have a say in how we react to this. We can make new choices. We can turn our mistakes into lessons. We can say, "Ok, that was a mistake. This is what I could do better."

Sometimes you might repeat a mistake. Then you examine it: "OK, what made me repeat that mistake? What could I have learned from this experience?" As we move through our process, I will teach you how to become the neutral observer of your life and the events in your life. From this point of view, you will be able to clearly see what you are doing and why.

Many of us have experienced tragic events and trauma. We may not have been able to prevent this difficulty when it presented itself, but we can choose how we react to the difficulties now. We can choose to remain a victim to these events and be a prisoner of our past, or we can invoke our self-sovereignty and seek to find the power to change our reaction and our story.

That's where empowerment comes in. When you feel the power to change your life, you feel hope. You become optimistic. If you have hope and optimism, the sun is always shining and your frequency is high.

Empowerment is really about how you look at your life. It's being psychologically minded, able to be aware of your reactions and what causes them, and able to make new choices.

As you change, you'll notice a change in the type of man you attract. That's one of your barometers of progress and success. You will attract better and better matches, as you become a better and better version of you.

Begin with identifying the emotional debris that's cluttering your psyche. Start consciously clearing it out. This begins with cleaning out your closet.

CHAPTER 3: EXERCISES

Exercise: Assess Yourself and Figure Out What to Change

1. The first step is to embark on an accurate self-assessment: take an inventory of your best qualities, as well as those aspects of yourself that could use improvement. Ask your friends and family what they think your best qualities are, and what are the ways in which you could improve. Examples of great qualities are having a great sense of humor, beautiful smile, intelligence, kindness, and a love of reading. Your list of negative qualities could include things like being slightly overweight and not physically fit, having an outdated wardrobe, low self-esteem, or few interests outside of work.

   - Make a list of your top five best qualities.
   - Make a list of five aspects of yourself or your life that could use improvement.

2. After undergoing this process of self-assessment, look at the things you can realistically change. Of these things, look at the things you are *willing* to change.

For example, you might decide that you need to lose twenty pounds and stop smoking. Or you might decide that you'd like to have more of an education in order to attract a more educated man. Your best investment is in becoming the best you that you can be—period. This will increase your self-confidence and help you grow as a person.

3. Make a list of three aspects of yourself or your life that you can realistically change. Write a plan of action describing what you are going to do to address these issues.

CHAPTER FOUR

Cleaning Out Your Closet

We all carry a lifetime of experiences with us. These experiences shape us, mold us, and make us who we are. For good and bad.

They are the baggage we all carry: the emotions, beliefs, and experiences that color our outlook. Just like baggage holds our clothing and keeps it hidden when we travel, we keep many of our past experiences hidden away, out of view most of the time. We stuff it all in a closet.

Our internal closet is just like a closet in our home—you know, that one stuffed with our winter coats, the tennis racket we no longer use, a paddle for the kayak we used to have, shoeboxes full of photos we printed out and keep meaning to put in an album—along with that hideous sweater Aunt Sara gave us that we just don't have the heart to throw out.

You know what I mean. We all have our clutter closet that is full of things from the past. They were once so useful, or we thought they were, when we first acquired them. We keep stuffing things in there to drag out when we need them. The reality is that much of what's in there is not very useful. This stuff can just get in your way, even if you think it's hidden, crammed in there and unexamined.

Our internal closet is jammed full of things we picked up over the years. I'm talking about feelings, emotions, and our reactions to people, experiences, and the world around us. Some of this is useful. Some is not.

Whether we realize it or not (and I assure you, mostly it's *not*), we have a certain set of tools in our internal closet that we pull out when we face certain situations. They are our go-to reactions.

If someone sees you running up and holds the elevator for you just before the door closes, it's natural to feel pleased and to smile and say thank you. If they see you, but just let the door close anyway, it's natural to be upset and maybe frown. It's wrong, though, to let that moment ruin your day, or to think the experience is proof that you're worthless and don't even merit having someone hold a door open for you.

Another person's rudeness is not a reflection of you. For too many of us, though, we think it is. We can't help it. Instead of seeing things for what they are, clutter from our past gets in the way. This blocks our view and our way. When we trip over this clutter, we can get hurt.

Our unresolved painful memories can manifest as instinctual drives, limiting beliefs, and emotional walls that our ego has created to "protect" us from getting hurt. Unfortunately, all this can separate us from our soul or our authentic self.

That's why you have to clean out your closet. You need to address the past in order to clearly identify and eliminate the very things that are holding you back from your future path.

Cleaning out your closet is really about excavating your authentic self. It's about having the courage to let go of what is no longer working, in order to reach for a new way of being, and of having a higher perspective.

The process of cleaning out your closet starts with identifying your underlying beliefs and behavior patterns when you are in a romantic relationship, and discovering yourself as the source of how your relationship will work out. You have to begin by examining your beliefs about being in a relationship.

I had a client, Mary, who found that she was ambivalent about being in a relationship. After examination, she found that she had a fear of being in a love relationship because she thought she would lose herself and be consumed by it. Thus, she would not be able to accomplish her goals. Her underlying belief was sabotaging her efforts to find her true love.

She had a pattern of over-giving to her love interest at the expense of meeting her own needs, so naturally she had little time to pursue her own goals. When we delved into her underlying beliefs, we discovered her limiting belief about herself, definitely contributed to her experiences in relationships. She thought that no one would love her unless she provided value (over-giving) and she was indispensable.

After working through this limiting belief about herself, she had to learn to express her needs and draw clear boundaries about what she was willing and able to give. She had to learn to "not self-abandon," taking care of her partner's needs at the expense of her own, which she had been doing in her relationships in order to feel safe.

As you can see, it was very important for her to be conscious of her own limiting beliefs about being in a relationship. Then she could take responsibility for changing them. She had to look at herself as the source of her experience. This was very empowering.

When you take responsibility for your part in any experience, you stay out of the victim mentality. When you take responsibility for yourself and your actions, you can make changes. You become empowered.

The Power of Limiting Beliefs

Many of us do not even recognize that we have limiting beliefs that sabotage our success in life and in our relationships. These limiting beliefs cause incongruence within us and interfere with our achieving our desired experience.

Our subconscious mind is very clever at creating self-sabotaging behaviors, which it does so covertly that we're not even aware we're doing it. Thus, it's to our benefit to identify our own limiting beliefs and transform them into empowering beliefs.

In addition, identifying and eliminating your limiting beliefs will allow you to raise your energetic vibration because you will be more positive. This will, of course, help you to bring in that new man.

Common Limiting Beliefs

Below is a list of some of the more common limiting beliefs. Ask yourself if you ever hear your inner voice saying any of these things, or if you ever catch yourself thinking any of them. Make your own list of your own personal limiting beliefs.

I'm not good enough   I am not worthy

I am bad	I don't deserve
I am not important	It is not possible for me to
I am invisible	I will lose my identity if...
I am not lovable	I cannot trust my judgment
I am powerless	I am not strong enough
I am not safe	I am alone
I am not chosen	I am afraid of losing control
I am not wanted	I am afraid of losing myself
I am too different	I am not supported by life

Triggers and Instinctual Drives

A *trigger* is something that sets off a memory of a traumatic event or series of events. It may be activated through one or more of the five senses: sight, sound, touch, smell, and taste.

A drive, such as hunger, motivates a person to act in ways that will reduce their tension or pain. In this case, a person will be motivated to eat.

A lot of our unresolved painful memories manifest as drives, triggers, and behaviors that are actually just an attempt to ease pain. Unfortunately, these bandages only ease the pain momentarily, because we are not healing the underlying event. They result in further damage by causing separation between the ego self (personality) and the soul or our authentic self.

When we are triggered by something, we may revert to "acting out" the part of us that remains emotionally stuck at the age of our initial trauma. This part is called the inner child. We often have many inner children. Imagine that when you are triggered you may be a five year old running around in a thirty year old body. There are many wonderful books on healing your inner child, which is beyond the scope of this book.

The point is, you do not want your five-year-old self in charge of your adult love life. In order to heal the stunted development of this inner part, we have to acknowledge it, hear the message, and heal it.

One way to do that is to imagine the adult part of you, and then imagine this adult part holding the five-year-old part in her lap. Have the inner child tell you what she's feeling, thinking, and what she would like to do. Listen carefully because she has been acting out because she feels unheard.

Have the adult part of you acknowledge the feelings, hurts, and misguided assumptions of the five-year-old. Speak to her as though you were speaking to a younger version of yourself.

Then let the five-year-old inner child know that the adult you can take care of her, you now have more wisdom and resources. Write down her assumptions about herself in your Limiting Beliefs List.

In the future, when you are in a relationship, and you start feeling any of these old feelings again, you will know that this is your five-year-old inner child trying to drive the train. You can take a deep breath, acknowledge the five-year-old, and once again remind the five-year-old that you're in control. This is part of self-soothing.

If you have the need to be perfect or super good, you need to address your inner child. As a child, we may make the erroneous conclusions that if we are perfect, smart, quiet, or funny enough, etc., we can win over mom or dad and they will finally love us as we need them to—loving us unconditionally.

The child often mistakenly assumes that she's caused her own problems with her parent(s), because she is not good enough. This creates a drive to be perfect; which, since we are human beings, is impossible.

Of course, all this is subconscious. Even so, the inner child's Limiting Belief that she is not good enough will color most of her love relationships and her life. She will always strive to be "super good," or she'll give up completely and "prove" that she's really not "good enough" by engaging in self-sabotaging behaviors.

Whenever someone or something triggers her feelings of not being good enough, she will react instinctively to prove or disprove them. Or she will react with anger, which sublimates her fear of not being good enough. This unexamined fear or Limiting Belief drives her behavior. You can see that this takes a lot of energy!

But once we become aware of our drives and triggers, we can address them at the source, instead of letting them control us. Once we know how to spot the things that trigger our reactions, we can consciously choose to avoid them or heal them.

Past Relationships

The next step is to look at our relationship history.

Many of us have a chronic pattern of dysfunctional relationships. Our previous relationships share consistent similarities, both good and bad, including such features as physical and/or emotional abuse, emotional unavailability, substance abuse, instability, workaholism, etc. Each previous relationship ended because of these repetitive dynamics.

You're probably thinking something like this: *There's nothing wrong with me and my choices. Every man I date is different.*

No. I can promise you that if you chose to marry the wrong man once, you'll probably keep choosing the same man, but with a different name and body, again and again.

I know I did. The problem is that we are subconsciously attracted to certain characteristics in a man, which replay earlier unresolved dramas or meet other subconscious needs.

This is what therapists call a "repetition compulsion." We attempt to rewrite history. We're trying to fix a past relationship by re-creating it with somebody else.

Thus, it's important to make your unconscious choices, conscious.

Many of us have had one parental relationship that caused us to experience great frustration, disappointment, rejection, abandonment, neglect, or abuse. If we don't address these earlier traumas, or at least recognize them, we often try to replicate that relationship, subconsciously, with our partner.

When I examined my personal love story I found that I always chose emotionally unavailable men. These emotionally unavailable men would evoke in me the tendency to overgive. I thought if I gave enough or was wonderful enough I would earn their love.

Of course, this was impossible. So, in frustration, I would withdraw my energy from the relationship. That would cause the other person to really withdraw from me, and I would feel abandoned.

This was a classic example of how my own limiting belief that I was not worthy to be loved as I was caused me to re-create a very dysfunctional relationship pattern. I realized that

I was reliving the relationship dynamics I had experienced early in my life, with my father.

My father was a narcissist who was emotionally unavailable. My father gave me a lot of attention, but only for my academic knowledge and achievement. He rewarded me when I did things well. If I didn't succeed or achieve, he was displeased, and he would withdraw emotionally. As a result, in my relationships and in my life, I have felt driven to be a super achiever.

And as an adult, I *chose* to be in intimate relationships with narcissists who were emotionally unavailable. I was attracted to aloof, self-involved, charismatic, *bon vivants* who lit up a room when they entered, and expected to take the light with them when they left.

Initially these men would seem to be everything I ever wanted. They seemed to be very giving in the beginning and very open, but in reality they were not. They were narcissists.

Their pattern worked as follows, they would find out from me what I was looking for through my own words or other clues. Then they would become what I wanted. Often, they seemed almost too good to be real. Once they had me, they stopped giving emotionally and began only to take. (This is the short version.)

Still, I swore up and down that the men I had dated since I was seventeen had nothing in common. That is, until I was asked to make a list of each important love interest in my life from the time I started dating, and to give a one word adjective for each of their characteristics. I was shocked to see the similarities, even though they all presented differently.

Exercise: Uncovering Your Past Patterns

Let us find your pattern in choosing your partners.

- Paste pieces of papers together so that all of the names are side by side, horizontally.
- Then, under each name, write what first attracted you to each one, followed by a list of their characteristics. Use one word.
- Next, do a list of your father's and mother's characteristics.

Example:

Johnny	Harry	Mark	John
Alpha male	Alpha male	Alpha male	Alpha male
Charismatic	Charismatic	Charismatic	Charismatic
Narcissistic	Narcissistic	Narcissistic	Narcissistic
Sweet	Sweet	Arrogant	Sweet

Now I want you to look for the commonalities. You'll probably be surprised by how clearly they stand out.

You're likely to see some of the characteristics of whichever parent you had a difficult or unfulfilled relationship with showing up in your adult relationships.

I recently had a case of a young man who kept choosing very volatile partners. When we examined his relationship with his parents, it was obvious that he was re-creating his relationship with his father. His mother was a very calm and stable influence in his life. His father was a very angry and volatile person who was constantly criticizing him.

He kept choosing women that were just like his father in order to recreate that initial, unresolved relationship in order to try to have a different ending. We call this repetition compulsion in psychology. This is why we keep dating the same man (but with a different name) over and over again.

Once my patient gained this insight, he was able to identify the traits that reminded him of his father in the women he met. When he realized what his subconscious was doing, he was able to consciously choose *not* to re-create this pattern, by avoiding the women who were like his father.

If you have parents who were very self-absorbed, or were ill, you probably have abandonment issues because your parents did not meet your needs emotionally, or maybe physically, at pivotal times in your life. They were too absorbed in their life's work or their own activities, so you often felt abandoned, or that you were not good enough, or maybe you thought you were unworthy of their attention.

Now, as an adult, if you're in a romantic relationship with a man who is very withdrawn emotionally—absorbed by his work, his studies, sports, or whatever it might be—he's going to trigger your abandonment issues. Dating or marrying a workaholic would probably not be a good fit for you, because his focus on his work will constantly trigger your feelings of abandonment—unless you were willing to resolve your underlying limiting beliefs.

Your relationship with this man would probably be managed by your inner five year old every time your fear of abandonment was triggered. Imagine how well this would work out!

I had another client, Mary, who constantly chose men who had great potential. She thought that if she came in to the relationship and helped them enough, they would reach their great potential. At that point, of course, they'd be overcome with gratitude. They would realize how wonderful she was and give her the love she wanted.

The first thing we know about relationships is that you cannot go into a relationship hoping to change someone. You can only change yourself. In essence, Mary was taking on a project.

Initially, these men would be grateful for her help. But as these relationships progressed these men began to resent Mary's nagging, and they started to feel unloved for who they were. Eventually, these men would withdraw and end the relationship.

Mary would be left feeling abandoned. She'd think she was a failure. Instead of recognizing how her actions had hurt the relationship, she'd think the opposite. She'd conclude that she hadn't tried hard enough. If she'd tried harder, or been good enough, they would've loved her.

Mary's pattern of self-talk set her on a downward spiral, making her feel even worse. This is what I call the negative spiral self-talk, which is very disempowering. I showed Mary how to take her power back by observing how she was contributing to this pattern, so that she could start to make life-affirming changes.

We examined her relationship story, the plot line of most of her relationships, in order to help her identify how she was the author of her own story. Mary was able to understand her contribution to her romantic failures. She was able to write a new story by changing her plot. She changed her behavior.

Listen to Your Gut

Another important source of helpful information about your limiting beliefs and other clutter in your unconscious mind can come from what I call your gut reactions. These are usually reactions that are out of proportion to the incident at hand. They come very, very fast. And they can very quickly spin out of control. That's one way you can tell that you're responding to past hurts.

An example of a gut reaction would be if your boyfriend doesn't answer your text right away, and you immediately start thinking, *He doesn't love me anymore* or *He's cheating on me.* If your relationship has been fine until then, yet you're worried about infidelity, that's usually a reaction that's out of proportion to the circumstances. Your reaction stems from something else. You're re-enacting and you're over-reacting, based on the facts.

Gut reactions usually come from Limiting Beliefs that grew out of our childhood traumas. They are the result of a trigger.

Being Psychologically Minded- Becoming the Neutral Observer

The first part of healing is to be willing to pay attention to our drives, triggers, and behaviors through dedicated self-awareness. We need to be psychologically minded. We need to be our own inner detective. A detective gathers facts without judgment and is a neutral observer.

The proper way to handle an emotion is to respond with something like this, *Okay, this is what I'm feeling in this moment.* You have to be very present with yourself in order to do this. It takes a lot of practice, because most of us are very out of touch with our body and our emotions. When something is happening to you that has triggered a reaction, you should try to take a deep breath and just ask yourself, *What am I feeling?*

Once you identify the feeling, ask yourself, *Okay, what is my feeling telling about my assumptions and about the situation?*

Your goal is for you to observe yourself, from the neutral observer point of view. Notice every feeling and reaction that isn't coming from your authentic self. That is, step back and watch your own actions without judging. Just watch the facts and your response as though you were watching a movie.

Be curious, not critical. If you start berating yourself, you disempower yourself. Look for facts not judgments. Don't conclude, *I've been a failure,* or *You're so stupid. You're doing that again.* Stop shaming yourself!

I call shame and guilt the "Mafia of the Mind." Shame and guilt drag you down and disempower you.

If you only look at the facts, you can deal with the facts in a rational way.

Ask and Receive

Now that you've learned about identifying your limiting beliefs, it's time to learn how to clear them.

You can use the "Ask & Receive Protocol" for clearing limiting beliefs about anything. "Ask & Receive" is an energy psychology approach pioneered by Sandy Radomski, LCSW and Tom Altaffer, LCSW (www.askandreceive.org). Their approach is very effective at resolving emotional and physical symptoms and in helping to clear limiting beliefs.

The process they use bypasses the ego or conscious mind by using various methods to find and access higher parts of our *self*, which are beyond the bounds of our awareness. This helps us find answers, and facilitate the healing of physical or emotional symptoms. You can learn more about this protocol on the website askandreceive.org or on my website natalie-moore.net.

I love to teach this approach because it's easy, and anyone can use it to make a difference in her life. There are other energy psychology techniques that work, such as EMDR and Body Talk, but they require a lot more knowledge.

Exercise: Clearing Limiting Beliefs Using the Ask & Receive Technique

I'm going to walk you through a simple clearing of a limiting belief: *I am not lovable.*

Start by turning your limiting belief into an *empowering* belief: *I am lovable.*

Use the following sentences and breathe deeply after saying each one aloud. Remember that limiting beliefs and emotions are stored in our bodies in our cellular memory. Emotions are energy. Breathing is a way of moving energy.

The Six Statements:

A. There is a part of my being that already knows *I am lovable.* (Breathe)

B. That part of my being is willing to inform the rest of me now. (Breathe)

C. It is doing so now with grace and ease (Breathe)

D. My mind, body, spirit, and soul are receiving this information now (Breathe)

E. Information transfer is now complete (Breathe)

F. Full integration is now complete (Breathe)

If there's a feeling of tightness as you say your empowering belief, then keep trying to clear the tightness, which is just another way that your body stores your belief that you are unlovable. Identify where the tightness is in your body.

A. Insert the following statement for the first statement above. Say this aloud: There is a part of my being that already knows how to heal and release this tightness around my chest, and already knows what this tightness means, and already knows how to release this from its source of origin. Now continue with the following five statements.

B. That part of my being is willing to inform the rest of me now.

C. It is doing so now with grace and ease.

D. My mind, body, spirit, and soul are receiving this information now

E. Information transfer is now complete

F. Full integration is now complete

Now repeat, *I am lovable.* If the tightness is gone, you're done. If some other sensation shows up, keep repeating the process.

At this point you are ready to look at your own list of limiting beliefs, and ready to turn each disempowering belief into an empowering one. Start by clearing two or three a day. Finish each set by repeating the empowering statement with each of the six statements after clearing any body sensations.

Continue adding to your list of limiting beliefs as you notice them.

Our Self-Assessment

The journey of life is about excavating your authentic self and discovering your unique gifts. Many people will never do that because they just settle into what society tells them they should do or be or whatever. But everybody has a unique gift. I'm a firm believer in that.

By doing a realistic self-assessment, you can discover your unique gifts and get a realistic view of the people you're going to attract. This is a way for you to see who you really are, and to see what you might need to work on, so that you can be the best "you" that you can be.

Our inventory of our own personal characteristics should include complimentary statements. Here're some examples: *I have an easy-going personality. I can be a great friend. I'm very supportive.*

These are all very good qualities. Our list should include some not-so-good qualities, as well. Here's an example of that: *I like having my own way, and get upset when I don't. I tell it like it is, and if that hurts another person's feelings, that's their problem.*

Be honest with yourself. This self-assessment is for you. You don't have to be overly critical. You don't have to go looking to make a list of negatives. But you are human, so a list with absolutely no negatives would be pretty odd. A realistic self-assessment should include both positives and negatives.

Your friends can help you do a reality check.

After you make your list, ask a couple of friends, "What do you think of this?" And, "Can you add anything?" They might tell you you're being too hard on yourself. Also they may come up with characteristics of your personality that you don't see, good and not-so.

That's okay. We're all perfectly imperfect. Some people's baggage fills trunks and some people have little carry-on bags. The amount of baggage you have just depends on how much work you've done on yourself.

It doesn't matter when you start working on yourself. You're never too late. Even if you're seventy years old, it's a good time to start minimizing the size of your baggage.

If you start with a trunk and you get your baggage down to the size of a carry-on bag, that's a successful life. Further, you'll be more likely to have a successful match and a healthy relationship with another person.

Then you can focus on finding Mr. Right for You.

CHAPTER 4: EXERCISES

Exercise: Discover Your Limiting Beliefs and Repetition Patterns

1. Everyone has a relationship history (story). Look back at each of your major relationships.

2. Write down the plot line of each, from falling in love to breaking apart. Ask your friends to help you identify your patterns.

3. Note your limiting beliefs about yourself and relationships. Start clearing!

4. Make a chart of all of the characteristics that describe your father.

5. Make a chart of all the characteristics that describe your mother.

6. Then make a chart to describe all the characteristics of every important romantic relationship that you've had.

7. Next, look at the list of every characteristic that all of your dates/mates have shared. This is your pattern of the dates that attract you. What do they have in common?

8. Compare the shared characteristics of your dates/mates with each one of your parents. Are there any similarities? If so, was your relationship with that parent tumultuous? What do you wish had been different with your parental relationship? Recognize the repetition compulsion.

CHAPTER FIVE

Mr. Right For You

Bottom line: you want Mr. Right, not the same Mr. Wrong over and over again. To get Mr. Right, you have to know what you're looking for. Most of us start dating with the thought that we'll know that *he's the one* when we find him. But how do we know if we've found him, if we don't even know what he looks like?

When we go to buy a house, we usually know what we want before we look for the house. We have an idea of the neighborhood we want, how many bedrooms we need and how many bathrooms, of how much the home should cost, and whether we prefer a one story or a two-story structure, etc. You get the idea.

These same principles work when you're looking for a romantic partner. You need to thoroughly evaluate your situation so that you know what you want. Figure out what you're looking for; then make a specific list of the qualities that you want to have in your mate. This way you won't end up compromising and excusing away characteristics that are problematic and unacceptable. You don't want to end up living in a one-story house, when what you really wanted was a two story one.

This is your list. Only you know what's important for you to have in your ideal mate. You decide. Some people like the color blue; some like red. Some like tall, blonde, blue-eyed, professional men who wear dark suits and silk ties and know exactly which wine goes best with Chilean sea bass. Others like dark-haired, dark-eyed men in jeans who know when the BBQ is exactly the right temperature. Start thinking about what you really like and what is important to you.

Of course you have to have realistic expectations. You're looking for Mr. Right For You, not Mr. Perfect. There are no Mr. Perfects out there. Not for anyone.

That doesn't mean you're going to settle for less. You're not. You want your Level III or Level IV match. And you'll get him. Superman doesn't exist in real life, but according to the Law of Attraction, you get what you ask for. So if you don't want cold fish, don't ask for sushi.

Making the List

I believe that online dating gives us the ability to be more selective. But you can only be selective when you know what you want. Otherwise, you only get what you stumble across. Once you figure out what you're selecting for, you can see who meets those qualities.

Of course I'm assuming you want a committed relationship leading to marriage or a life partner. I'm assuming that your goal is not a hook up, and it's not just to have dates to keep you entertained while you fulfill your other priorities in life.

Start by defining your goal: a lasting relationship. This becomes your intent that you project to the Universe. This becomes your focus. If you're going to ask the universe, through the Law of Attraction, to deliver the one you want to spend the rest of your life with, you don't want to aim your energy at his next-door neighbor.

Be specific.

Make a list: What does he look like? Yes, you might think that seems superficial, but it does matter. We all have some image that pops into our head when we think of our ideal partner, the person we really want to be with. If tall turns you on, be honest about it. If you melt for blue eyes, say so. You're not going out looking for second-best or a nice runner-up. You're making a list of your ideals.

Think about his personal qualities. If you're into fitness, a man who is twenty pounds overweight won't do it for you. Maybe you want somebody who is kind and funny.

What does he like to do? This is just as important. Does he like movies or sports bars? Does he fish or cook? Does he dance? If you love salsa or ballroom, and moving to the music with a sure-footed partner is your idea of heaven, then you won't want to spend your life with someone with two left feet.

If financial security and sagacity are important, list these characteristics. What kind of work does he do? Maybe you don't like accountants? Does he have a college degree, a graduate degree, or a high school degree? What education level would best compliment yours?

Continue by adding to your list the qualities that your ideal Level III or Level IV partner would have. Examples could be: responsible, physically loving, affectionate, having a great sexual appetite. Or you might prefer someone less sexual. Think about what *you* want. Perhaps you want someone who is mature, kind, honest, or trustworthy.

You might say you want "somebody who matches well with my personality." But, it's better to follow up with some words that describe what that means: Outgoing? Funny? Quiet?

If being physically fit or health-conscious is important to you, then you probably want someone who's the same. If you like to run, you might put in, "He enjoys running with me."

Think about the intimacies and values you'd like to share with that special person. If you're philanthropically minded you might want to say, "Somebody who can be involved in my philanthropic activities."

The more specific you are, the better you'll be at focusing your energy on attracting exactly what you want. And the sooner you'll know that you found "Him." You'll immediately know that you've found someone with the qualities that are important to you. Your heart will also know.

This is a very personalized list. You can use this list and the exercise at the end of the chapter to begin harnessing the power of the law of attraction.

Realistic Expectations

Most of us have a fantasy ideal of the man we would like. Usually he looks like Prince Charming or Brad Pitt or whomever. Our ideal usually looks like Mr. Perfect. But remember, Mr. Perfect does not exist in real life. You want Mr. Perfect for *You*—your Level III or Level IV match.

What I'm suggesting is for you to have a realistic view of the person you want to attract. And whose frequency will match with yours. If, for example, you're a couch potato who doesn't like working out, you don't want to attract a guy who likes to work out five times a week. Your lifestyle and values aren't compatible.

We have to look at our lifestyle, our interests, our values, and ourselves.

If you're an introvert and you don't like to entertain, you don't want to date a master of the universe. His social life will be way more active than what you're interested in doing. This would be a mismatch and you would both end up feeling resentful.

If you like spending your time watching daytime TV, you probably won't want to look for a Mensa member or scientist. The physical chemistry may be great, but he's not likely to share your love for "The Price is Right." And you're bound to get tired of going to physics lectures.

If rock-climbing is really important to you, your list should include the qualities of "adventurous" and "risk-taking."

I'm just the opposite. I don't like physical risk-taking. A guy who likes to ride motorcycles is not going to make my list. Neither is a racecar driver.

Go back to that honest self-assessment you did in the last chapter. Take a good look at your habits. Do you like to wake up at noon versus waking up at five in the morning? How often do you exercise? How important are healthy eating habits?

If you're not into health and you're a drive-through at McDonald's kind of girl, you're not a match with a guy who's into health and is a vegan.

If you never go to the gym and you're overweight, you shouldn't expect to be compatible with a muscle-bound gym junkie who has a different lifestyle and outlook about his body. Having this kind of difference is like asking for conflict.

You get it. You need to be honest with yourself. That's what matters.

Being realistic doesn't mean lowering your standards. It means being truthful about what you really like—to do and to be. No matter what your fantasy match is like, you're going to be much happier with someone who's compatible with you.

I had a client who was very athletic and health conscious. After the marriage and over time, his wife gained 100 pounds. He felt resentful and lost his sexual interest in her. They had a difference in values—being healthy and physically fit were important to him. She pretended that she shared the same values while they were dating. She got him. But then she lost him, and many years, because she'd pretended to be what she was not. He also felt betrayed by her. You know how the story ended—another divorce statistic.

The Two of Us

Your ideal relationship is not just about him. Or you. It's about *both* of you. How do you envision your ideal relationship?

Think about the following: *What does my ideal relationship look like for me?* Look at your past relationships. What worked? What didn't work? You know what your old love story looked like. You know what didn't work.

Now, I would like you to think about how you would like this new relationship to be. Write a list of the qualities that you think are important in a relationship. This list will eventually be written out into a paragraph or two that will become your relationship vision statement. This will be your personal vision of what you are looking for in a healthy relationship with the qualities that are important to you.

If you're finding that you're putting down things like, "He meets all my needs," that's a sign that you're looking for a parent, not a mate. No one can meet all of your needs except yourself.

Write your list in the present tense, and speak only in positive terms. For example:

"I am involved in this wonderful relationship with this incredible man who respects me, loves me, and trusts me as much as I respect, trust, and love him. We have mutual goals, a shared vision of our future together..."

You get it. It's your vision, so start thinking. You can include physical attributes and qualities like, "He's physically fit and healthy. He's emotionally and physically available."

You can put down things like, "We each value each other's family and have a shared vision for raising our family together."

Anything you want. It's your ideal relationship, so put in the things that are important to you.

Many of us do not know what makes for a healthy relationship. So, I'm going to give you some guidelines of these qualities so that you can think about including them in your statement.

Two independent people coming together to become interdependent with each other form a healthy relationship. Each person can change and grow in separate ways without having the other person feel threatened. In fact, they expect that there will be differences between themselves because they are each individuals. The partners encourage each other to grow and pursue their separate interests. Luckily, both have good conflict resolution skills and know when to compromise.

One partner is not expected to fix or fill all of the unmet childhood needs of the other. Each is expected to meet their own emotional needs so that they can come together as two full vessels. If issues or childhood triggers come up, each partner looks inside their own self for healing. Neither expects the other to heal or fix the past. When one of the partners cannot fix their own pain they get professional help.

A healthy person in a healthy relationship is honest and takes care of their own emotional wounds.

They share mutual respect, trust, commitment, gratitude, generosity in giving and sharing, love and patience. Healthy partners feel safe to ask for what they need and want. At the same time they can say "no," and accept "no" for an answer when appropriate.

There is reciprocity in giving and receiving. They each receive pleasure in both the giving and in the receiving. One gives to please; one does not give to receive.

A healthy partner does not attempt to change or control the other. They see each other realistically and accept each other's shortcomings because humans are perfectly imperfect.

When we meet somebody, we have to accept him as he his. Don't start a relationship thinking that he would be perfect, if only... Don't come up with an agenda to change him. He's not a project. If the things that you don't like are deal breakers, move on. If they are not, learn to live with the situation, and don't expect him to change.

You can only change yourself, so change your reaction to the thing that annoys you.

Partners in healthy relationships do not attempt to control each other. Control is about fear. When you seek to control someone you are operating under the premise that if you control all of the elements, you will ensure a desired result. Control is actually an illusion, because we can never control all of the variables, and the other person always has free will.

The issue of control is so pervasive in relationships that I want to give you an example of a case that illustrates how often this backfires.

When Mark and Anna married, they were full of illusions, and each had his or her own emotional baggage resulting from two failed marriages.

Anna's ex-husband had cheated on her with many women. He got away with it for so long because he paid cash for his trysts. Anna made it a condition of her marriage to Mark that she'd control all the money in the relationship.

He would receive an allowance of $300 a month in cash, and he could use his credit cards for whatever he needed because she could track those. If he needed a check, he would have to explain his need and, if she approved, she would write it out and sign it. (Relationships should be based on trust, so right away it's clear that their relationship did not have a strong foundation.)

Mark was very successful and came to resent Anna's need for control. He didn't like having to ask Anna for money once a month, as though she were his mother. Over time, he became more and more resentful and he actually began to look at her as his mother, not as his wife.

Anna ended up losing Mark, not because he had an affair, but because he could no longer tolerate her irrational need for control and her inability to take responsibility for her own insecurity and lack of emotional healing. She created the very problem she wanted to avoid. By controlling the money, she lost her husband.

(I had to ask Mark what was it about himself that made him think he deserved this type of control and treatment when he agreed to the original request. He had to address that.)

Deal Breakers

Ok. So now you know what you're looking for. But, you also have to know who to stay away from.

You are probably thinking to yourself, *I will know a "bad" guy when I see him.* Unfortunately, people do *not* openly present their negative qualities when you first meet them. And the *really* toxic people are highly skilled at fooling others.

So you need to identify what your personal deal breakers are before you start dating. Only then can you know how look for "deal breaker" traits, and figure out how to ask the right questions in order to ferret them out.

If you don't identify what your personal deal breakers are, you will probably be on your way to falling in love by the time he lets down his guard and reveals his real self. This leads to people accepting the unacceptable. You'll find excuses such as, *this time will be different,* even when you see that he has the very same qualities that have not worked out for you in the past.

There are certain characteristics and behaviors that should *never* be accepted in a romantic partner, such as being physically or emotionally abusive. These are the real deal breakers. When you see these qualities in your date, you must run, no matter how great everything else seems to be or how sorry he seems to be after doing it.

Everybody has certain personal deal breakers—things you just won't, or shouldn't, accept in a partner.

If you come from an alcoholic family and have not done your emotional healing, dating a recovering alcoholic might be a deal breaker for you because you would be constantly triggered and watching for a potential relapse. You might also refuse to date anyone who uses drugs or abuses alcohol.

There are some qualities that should probably be on everyone's list of deal-breakers: he has a bad temper which he can't control; he's verbally abusive; or he attempts to control what you wear, whom you see, and what you do.

Discovering that someone is lying about his past or his present—his marital status or criminal history, for example—should be a deal breaker.

One of my earlier dates, before I had my "rules," was with a local professional I met online. After a delightful chat on the phone, during which we seemed to have much in common, I accepted a date to meet for coffee.

When I first saw him, he looked older and a little heavier than his photos, but he was charming. On our way out, I asked him, "By the way, what is your last name?" He turned to me and sarcastically asked me if was going to Google him. This was a big red flag! At that point I had not even thought about doing a Google search on a potential mate.

I was only being polite when I asked for his last name. Of course, I went home and promptly Googled him, only to find out that he was fourteen years older than what his profile stated.

The man had run for public office, so there was plenty on the Internet about him. When he called to ask me on a second date, I asked him about this. He actually denied the info. And asked me, "What, do I look like I'm that old? Maybe I should call a plastic surgeon?" Obviously, I declined his invitation. Why start a relationship with someone you already know to be a liar? (Another lesson here: get his last name and do a Google search before you meet him.)

Other deal breakers might be more individual. If you're six feet tall, dating a five-foot-three guy might be a deal breaker for you. Someone else might not mind.

Your core values play an important part in your list of deal breakers. If you're deeply religious, that might rule out atheists. If you're highly political—say strongly conservative or staunchly liberal—someone firmly wedded to the opposing view probably belongs on the deal breaker list.

Men with the characteristics you identified in your failed past relationships, *definitely* belong on the deal breaker list. You already know how those relationships turn out.

In the end, your list of deal breakers is very personalized. And it's very important. If you start dating without a clear idea of what your deal breakers are, you'll make concessions and end up in yet another doomed Level I or II relationship. Or, worse, you could end up in danger.

It doesn't matter if everything else is good, or even great about him, if you see one of your deal breakers as you get to know him, move on! You have fantastic sex together? Good for you. But sex is only one part of a relationship. If you can't stand what comes out when he opens his mouth, run! If he's a brilliant conversationalist, successful, handsome and romantic but he calls you "stupid" and treats you like an inferior, throw him out and lock the door.

True deal breakers are non-negotiable. That's why they go in the deal breaker category in the first place. There are no concessions. I had a girlfriend whose previous husband of many years suffered from addiction problems, which ultimately led to their divorce.

When she started dating again, she knew that drug use would be a deal breaker. Later, she started dating someone who liked to smoke marijuana everyday. When I asked her why she was willing to override this deal breaker that she had previously identified as crucial, she said, "Well, he's not an addict." I explained to her that someone who needed to smoke marijuana every day clearly had a substance abuse problem. And that she was just simply repeating her past pattern, which she already knew would not work.

Then I asked her why she was making excuses for compromising on her deal breaker. We discovered her underlying limiting belief that she could not find someone better.

If you do find yourself yielding on one of your deal breakers, rationalizing... *Well, the only reason he won't let me see my girlfriends is because he wants to be with me so much, and it's not really so bad. I do like being with him*, you need to stop and do a self-check.

Be psychologically minded. Ask yourself: *Why am I making this concession? I already identified this as a deal breaker.* One of your limiting beliefs might be the culprit. Dig deeper: *What am I feeling? Am I afraid I won't get anyone better? What is it about me that makes me feel like I deserve this behavior?* Clear anything that you identify.

Remember that part of being empowered is that you never act out of fear. You never make fear-based decisions. You *will* find someone better. Move on.

Revising Your List

As a good rule of thumb, a deal breaker should never be eliminated. In fact, as you go along in your dating process, you might find that you discover new deal breakers to add to your list. For example, let's say that you're in your 50's and have grown children. After you date a couple of guys who have young children you may wonder, *Do I really want to be raising a child again? Even part-time?*

Even something that you might not have previously thought about can go on your list of deal breakers.

Sometimes, though, something you thought was a deal breaker really isn't. I'm not talking about the big things, like physical or verbal abuse. If he hits you once, he will do it again. No matter how sorry he says he is, or how sweet he acts for the next two weeks. It's amazing how many men and women will continue with someone who hit them. *Well, he said he was sorry. He just lost his temper or I made him angry...*

It doesn't matter what you did or what excuse he gave you. Physical abuse is *never* okay. He *will* do it again. Continue to check your deal-breaker list as you get to know each new potential partner. If he's doing any of the deal breakers, then you know what to do. And don't look back. These big ones never come off the list.

Something that is *not* critical, though, may possibly come off the deal breaker list. For example, I had a girlfriend who was gorgeous. She was well over 5' 11" and a striking blonde. All the men loved her.

She liked men who looked a certain way, who were taller than she was, and who had a certain bank balance. She had many dates and some short-term relationships, but these men left her after a time.

Finally she met a guy who was taller than she was, which was great. But one of her deal breakers had to do with "appearance," how a guy dressed and the way his house was decorated. This guy was a terrible dresser. His teeth needed some whitening. His house looked like a college fraternity.

Everything else about him was great—exactly what she wanted and, I thought, needed.

So I said to her, "Let's talk about his qualities. What do you like about him?"

Well, he had great moral qualities and almost all of his personal characteristics were exactly what she was looking for.

So I told her, "Frankly, you can teach him how to dress. You can encourage him to get his teeth whitened. You can redecorate his place.

Those are superficial things that can be changed. He probably doesn't even notice them. They're not deal breakers." My point was that superficial aspects of a person's appearance are not a true deal breaker. She had found an attractive guy; he just needed some polishing up.

His being unpolished was not actually a deal breaker in the sense that character faults are deal breakers or active addiction. With some teeth whitening, a new haircut, and an updated wardrobe this guy was just as attractive as she liked, he looked great. Getting him to whiten his teeth was possible without any real work on her part; it would have been much harder, maybe impossible, to get him to change his character traits.

My point is that you have to look at the things you put on a deal breaker list. She had previously failed because she had some superficial things on her list. Some traits are more important than others, and you may have to compromise on superficial things.

Another example is that character traits trump eye color. I personally compromised on a potential mate's age if they had great character and other important qualities.

My client ended up marrying the man she had been dating, and he has been a wonderful partner. They've agreed that she can be in charge of decorating their home and buying his clothes.

Exercise: Make Your "Mate" and "Date" and "Deal Breaker" List

There are certain types of guys that you just date. They will never make it to your "I would marry this person" or "That person could be my life partner" list.

They're fun. But perhaps they're irresponsible. Or they're great conversationalists but there's no chemistry. They're great dancers, but that's *all* they ever want to do.

Fun. Maybe friends. Not mates. There's only *one* you spend the rest of your life with.

It's easy to get confused, though. You've seen it happen to friends. Maybe even to yourself.

Don't.

Here's how to make sure you don't.

1. Make a list with three columns.
    a. The first one is "Mate." That means someone you could marry. This is a life partner list.
    b. The second column is going to be "Date."
    c. The third is "No Way"—the deal breaker list.
2. Look at the first column as the list of: *I am looking for my life partner or my husband. What qualities must he have?* Must. These are not negotiable. These are the qualities that he must have if I am going to spend a

lifetime with him. You already made that list earlier in the chapter. List these qualities under this column.

3. Label the second column "Date." These the qualities you would accept in a man you would just go on a date with. You can be flexible about these because he's only a date or Mr. Right Now. You would not be flexible about these if he were your mate.

For example I'm anti-drugs and don't enjoy being with anyone who drinks too much when they're with me. I find this disrespectful. But I might go on a date with a guy who parties because he's a great dancer or really funny. I might meet him for dinner or at a dance venue. But I know that's as far as it goes. And I don't let him drive me home if he's been drinking. He's fun for a night.

Another friend was a great dinner date, but he's Jewish and he knew that he would only marry a woman who shared his faith. I'm not Jewish. And I didn't plan on converting. We had fun dinners together and shared many values, but we had mutually exclusive criteria for our life partners. So he was always ONLY a date.

You want to be very careful that someone on the "date" list never becomes a "mate." It's easy for this to happen. You enjoy each other and keep going out. Before long you're in love with Mr. Wrong for *You.* They soon become the man you never should've married.

The purpose of this list is to keep you safe from doing that, because we tend to have a lot more flexibility about accepting qualities in guys we would date that we would never accept in a mate. Dates can be Level II matches. Mates should never be.

You have to keep your eye on your goal, a lifetime partner or marriage. Go out with a "date" no more than once or twice a month, if you must. You should be focusing on going out with potential mates, Level III or Level IV matches. This is dating efficiency. Why waste your energy and time on what you know you don't want?

4. The third column, the "No Way" list, is for the deal breakers. This list is inviolable. You don't ignore them or modify them. Even if a man fits every other part of your qualifications and exhibits just one deal-breaker, you walk away.

   If you don't, your relationship will end anyway. Just like all of the relationships before it.

Keep these three lists handy as you date. Be sure to continuously check them. A date should never become a mate. Keep these three lists where you can easily find them thereafter, as a helpful reminder. Refer to them often.

Exercise: Make a Vision Board

In this exercise, you will make a vision board filled with images of what makes your perfect "Him." You won't have pictures of the actual "Him" yet, of course, but you can make a collage using pictures of the activities you want the person in your life to like doing, and that you want to do with that person. Maybe you'll have a picture of a couple playing tennis, relaxing on a beach, hiking, painting, reading, or cooking—whatever you want.

You can also include pictures of couples doing things that are important to you, or that you find romantic. You might want to include a picture of the type of house you envision sharing. This is your vision board. Have fun with it.

Once a day, look at your completed board and imagine doing and having all the moments that are pictured. Then thank God, the universe, or Spirit for bringing all of this to you—instantly, with Grace, and in perfect ways.

Exercise: Use the Law of Intention

You are a self-sovereign being with the universal right to determine your life and direction. When you state your intent, you are telling the universe exactly what you want. If you intend red, the universe does not deliver pink. That is the Law of Intention. It serves to strengthen the Law of Attraction.

Now let's put it to use.

I want you to read aloud and to yourself all the qualities of that ideal relationship, using the Relationship Vision Statement that you wrote earlier in the chapter.

State before reading it, "It is my intent to..." Picture yourself with our special someone as you read it.

At the end, finish with: "Thank you for bringing this to me instantly, under grace, and in perfect ways."

Add this vision statement to your vision board.

Exercise: Find the Relationship Road

Find a quiet place to sit. Close your eyes and take some long deep breaths. Continue breathing and relaxing, letting go of all your stress and worries.

Imagine you're walking along on a beautiful tree-lined road which represents your current life and that includes all of your past dating experiences, marriages, successes, and failures. The road of your life as it has been up to now.

As you continue walking, you see a fork in the road. Do I stay on my current path because I'm afraid to make changes both within and without? Or do I take a chance because what I've done has not worked? You decide to leave your past and that old story behind. You're done with that.

You boldly step onto the new path. You're not a victim. You are the creator of your life. You are empowered!

Imagine yourself walking down this new road upon which *all is possible.* The past is behind you, and gone—because you're now on a new road with new possibilities.

As you walk down the new road, there's a grassy area. You sit down in the grassy area and imagine yourself with your mate, in this new wonderful relationship.

Imagine that he is sitting with you. Imagine how happy you feel, how contented and safe you feel. Actually *feel* the feelings.

Imagine your children with you, and recognize how happy they are. Imagine everybody interacting harmoniously and how wonderful this experience is.

Spend a few minutes on this visualization and then close the meditation by saying, "Thank you for bringing this to me instantly, under Grace, and in perfect ways."

The Law of Attraction works best when you combine your list, thoughts, and feelings to create the new higher frequency of your desired match. Your new frequency vibration will draw to you your new higher frequency match.

As you're working on this vision, you're working on clearing the limiting beliefs that interfere with your happiness and your romantic future. And you are maintaining a higher and higher frequency for longer periods of time. This allows you to attract the right person into your life.

When you're doing this, I also want you to notice any feelings that come up. For example if you hear your inner voice saying something like this: *That's impossible, I'll never get someone like that*—write that down.

To believe, *I'm never going to get someone like that,* equals *I am unworthy.* Continue finding and identifying any limiting beliefs that would interfere with your getting what you want. Each time you do this visualization notice all your feelings around it.

Remember that you are forever that neutral observer of yourself in every action. You are a detective of your own psyche. As that neutral observer, write down anything that comes up. Something different might come up each time. As you resolve some issues, secondary issues might appear.

You can return to the Ask & Receive clearing exercise in the previous chapter and clear any limiting belief.

CHAPTER SIX

Dating in the Digital World

Welcome to the "new" world of online digital dating. Well, not really so "new" any more. The idea of computer-assisted dating first appeared in class projects like the "Happy Families Planning Service" experiment at Stanford University as early as 1959. That one involved 49 men and 49 women, introduced to each other based on their answers to twenty questions. None of these matches lasted.

In 1965, a pair of Harvard undergrads launched Operation Match by inviting participants to a "social experiment." Within six months, some 90,000 people had returned the 75-question survey, along with $3, in hopes of finding a mate. Six weeks later, they got letters listing their matches and their phone numbers.

They paved the way.

But the real impact didn't come until thirty years later when Match.com went live in 1995. In the twenty years since, hundreds more sites have followed, and digital dating has profoundly impacted our ability to search and find true love. In essence, the world is now your oyster.

Even more wonderful, online dating is not a dirty little secret anymore. Once upon a time, people might have looked at digital dating as somewhat disreputable, or even slightly sleazy—a dark cyber-alley meeting place for losers or lusters.

Not anymore. A Pew Research Center report released in 2014 said, "59% of all Internet users agree with the statement that 'online dating is a good way to meet people, a 15-point increase from the 44% who said so in 2005."

More and more people are using online dating services; and more and more are finding meaningful long-term relationships this way.

About 40 million Americans use online dating services. Match.com alone boasts of having 17 million users, who visit the site a total of 93 million times a month.

It's easy to see why. There are obvious advantages—you're fishing in an ocean instead of a pond, or a puddle if you live in a small town. And, used properly, online services can increase your dating efficiency. You can sort through the possibilities much more easily and zero in on the dating prospects whose qualities come closest to those on your "mate" or "Mr. Right For You" list.

As we've mentioned before, online dating is powerful and it works with outstanding results if you have the skills to use the sites correctly.

However, with great power comes…

Yes, you know.

The truth is this new change brings tremendous opportunities, and a whole new set of problems. It's like being tossed the keys to a race car and told you can hit the road – you can cover a whole lot of ground fast, but you better take some time to learn how the racecar works before you hit the accelerator.

It's pretty easy to get hurt if you don't know what you're doing. Or you could wind up going in circles as everyone else whizzes past you to the finish line.

So fasten your seat belt. Here we go.

Dating Efficiency

Not long ago, the search process was the most difficult part. We had to look for potential suitors in church, through friends, at work, through activities we enjoyed, or in bars. Finding our true love among limited possibilities required a lot of luck.

With the advent of digital dating, there are no physical boundaries. Off-line dating is like going to a brick-and-mortar store where your choices are limited by what you find in the one store; online you can get, pretty much, anything you want, almost instantly.

Now we have no problem searching, because digital sites like OKCupid and EHarmony allow us to see thousands of prospective suitors instantly. We now have a huge available pool of potential mates.

Today's problem is that we have *too many* choices.

Having thousands—actually, millions—of options can be a nightmare of excess. Trying to read every profile for every man using dating sites today would be impossible, even if you made this your full-time job.

I'm not exaggerating.

If you dedicated forty hours a week, and spent just three seconds looking at every one of those profiles, it could take you eight years to look at them all. Give them each the amount of time a TV commercial takes—a short one—and you'll be at it for the next eighty years.

When I first started looking for a potential date online, I was overwhelmed. I decided to apply some of my financial training in using search algorithms to develop my own process, so I could efficiently cull through the pool of potential mates and find the one who was just right for me. (I will share this process with you later in the book.)

Luckily, these sites have tools that, when used properly, will help you weed out the men with deal breakers and other undesirable qualities. The point of online dating is not to deluge you with possibilities, but to help you winnow down the many potential candidates so that you can find Mr. Right for You.

Truth in Advertising

The best way to get to your best match is to practice truth in advertising.

You want to attract a man who wants *you*—just as you really are. If you create an online persona, some made up version of who you wish you were, or someone you think is most likely to catch a man's attention, the man you attract won't be your true match. He'll be that make-believe person's match.

Still, people lie.

A University of Wisconsin-Madison study found that about 81 % of people fibbed about their height, weight, or age in their profiles. Another study, in which academics checked the true weight, height, and age of eighty online daters, found that the women in the group claimed to be, on average, 8.5 pounds thinner in their profiles than they really were. Men fudged by two pounds. But the men tended to lie about their height more—stretching the truth by a half-inch.

Women, though, were inclined to distort reality in a different way. They posted photographs that were, on average, a year and a half old. The men generally used pics only six months old.

My own experience was worse. Many men posted photos that were at least ten years old and fifteen pounds ago. Men have told me that women do the same.

Don't.

One man I met told me his worst online dating experience was with a beautiful woman in her forties. She looked really great in all of her pictures and everything else in her online profile seemed great. They went out a couple of times and she looked as good as she did in her pictures. She wore wonderful flowing clothes and when they went out dancing, he held her and she felt marvelously firm in his arms.

Well, things went really well, until the night they were going to get intimate. As he took her clothes off, he discovered that she was almost completely encased in something like heavy-duty Spanx everywhere. Her arms and legs—everything. As she started pulling her garments off, he said, she literally had huge rolls of fat coming out.

He told me that he couldn't go on. He was in shock. He told her he had to leave.

That may be an extreme case, but here's my point: there's nothing wrong with being heavy; and there's nothing wrong with wanting to look less heavy. But not telling him? Even after they'd gone out a few times? That's pretty much the ultimate in lying.

I've heard countless men tell stories about going on dates where they agreed to meet at a bar. They're sitting there waiting, and they don't see the person anywhere. Suddenly the woman comes up to them looking totally different from her pictures online. Usually the pictures were ten years and twenty pounds ago.

Naturally, the guys feel awkward that they didn't recognize their date. They also feel like they've been deceived.

I know how they feel. I've been sitting at a bar or coffee shop waiting for my date to show up, and some stranger says hello. That's the way it feels.

Of course, you want to be polite, so you stick it out and have the drink or whatever. But the whole time, you may be counting the seconds until you can make your escape because you feel like you've been deceived. And who knows what else they could be hiding.

Starting with deception ends up in disappointment and wasted time for you both. The sad fact is, there are people who would've been perfect for those guys or for those women if they had been truthful.

So be honest. You don't want the initial impression made on your potential mate to be something like this: *That person is a cheat!* or *That person lies!* You want to begin a relationship with a strong foundation of trust.

There is someone for everyone, and someone who really wants you just the way you are. With online dating, the odds of meeting that someone are exponentially in your favor. If your goal is to find a committed relationship, it's important to go out there looking your best and being your best. But it's most important that you be *you*.

So Many Sites to See

There are hundreds of digital dating sites. Hundreds. And new ones spring up all the time.

Every site, of course, tries to be different from the others. Generally, they each succeed.

There are sites for Christian singles and Jewish singles, single parents and "marriage minded people." There are sites for "big bodied" people, middle-agers, and seniors. There are sites for vegetarians, "geeks," farmers, and fans of Apple products. There are even sites for married people looking for affairs, and for people just looking for adventurous sex.

The sites share some similarities, but each has its own rules of the road, and each has its own slightly different goal.

It's impossible to list them all, but here's how some compare.

Match.com

Match.com claims "more relationships & more marriages than any other site." It's certainly one of the largest, with nearly as many active users as there are people living in the entire state of Florida. You can search for people, send "winks" and get matches, but you have to buy a monthly subscription if you want to get in touch with any of them.

This was my own personal favorite because I liked the amount of information available about my prospective match.

I also liked receiving the 24 Daily Matches based upon my own criteria where I could say "yes" or "no" or "maybe" about each one. The same 24 men would also receive my profile as a potential match. If they said, "yes" to my profile, I would receive an email telling me that he was interested. I could then proceed, or not, accordingly. The same for them.

eHarmony

eHarmony is one of the oldest and most respectable names in the business, claiming even more subscribers than Match.com—20 million. It also contends that 565,000 of its members have married, and that "on average, 438 people get married every day in the United States because of eHarmony; that accounts for nearly 4% of new U.S. marriages."

The special sauce: Signing up involves answering hundreds of questions designed to analyze compatibility and connect you with your perfect match. Unlike the other sites, you don't even get a peek at the possibilities until you're done.

Beware because your matches can look at every one of your answers to these questions. On the plus side, you can also look at theirs. This site tends to self-select people who are willing to answer these questions. Some men do not have the patience for lengthy questionnaires. But if they are seriously looking for someone, they might be.

OKCupid

Owned by the same folks who own Match.com, OKCupid is completely free. You answer a number of multiple-choice questions and you are constantly urged to answer even more to help refine your matches. The site also asks you to say how you'd like your ideal match to answer, and how much their answer matters to you. It then calculates a comparison based on a "patent pending" process. In short, as its website puts it, "We use math to get you dates."

This site's accuracy depends on your being honest and your knowing what you want.

JDate

JDate is almost as old as Match.com, JDate is a religious affinity site with a clearly stated mission: "JDate's mission is to strengthen the Jewish community and ensure that Jewish traditions are sustained for generations to come. To accomplish this mission, we provide a global network where Jewish singles can meet to find friendship, romance and life-long partners within the Jewish faith."

ChristianMingle

ChristianMingle is one of the Christian versions of JDate (in fact, they're both owned by the same company), this site bills itself as "an ideal destination for Christian men and women to find friends, dates, and even soul mates, all within the faith."

Tinder

One of the most recent dating services arrived on the scene as a mobile app and rapidly transformed the way singles connect, making it worth mentioning separately—and with a note of caution.

Tinder was launched in 2012, is quick, minimalist, and designed for participants to make dating decisions unabashedly based on looks, roughly the equivalent of a glance across a crowded bar, with decisions to wink or move on made in seconds. Users often see nothing more than a few photos before deciding to swipe left for "no" or right for "yes." If both users swipe right on each other's pictures for "yes," they can text each other and start a conversation right away.

I mention Tinder only because you will hear about it. But I don't think this is the most efficient way to meet The One. It is more focused on finding dates, or casual sexual "hook-ups," than on long-term relationships.

Tinder says it makes 13 million matches a day—which often last less than that. Sheer odds indicate that some of these matches become longer lasting, and the app claims it has resulted in at least 2,000 engagements and weddings. But that should tell you something; this is an almost infinitesimal amount compared to the number of daily connections.

Other narrowly focused niche services target smaller demographics.

VeggieDate: The name says it all. VeggieDate is aimed at "vegans, lacto vegetarians, ovo vegetarians, pescatarians (fish and vegetable eaters), semi-vegetarians, those who are becoming vegetarian, and macrobiotic eaters."

FarmersOnly: Its tagline is "City Folks Just Don't Get It!" The point, according to founder Jerry Miller, is that farmers tend to be tied to their work, connected to the land and their livelihood, in ways others might not relate to. Miller's concept makes sense. He's recognized a shared interest that's also a core value, which already puts like minded couples in a better place to succeed.

OurTime: For 50+ men and women looking for someone within their own age group.

Tastebuds: Matches people based on their musical interests.

LinkedUp: A mobile app that syncs matches potential partners using their LinkedIn account information. If professional resumes matter to you, here's a place to look for a mate.

The list goes on and on.

Exercise: Picking the Site for You

You can use as many sites or services as you like and can afford. But zeroing in on the ones most suited to you is the most efficient way to get the results you want.

How do you pick?

First, think about your core values. Write down your top one or two.

Is religion important? Then consider using one of the affinity sites focused on religion.

If you're a staunch vegetarian, or have firm political views, one of the affinity sites dedicated to those interests might be a good place to start.

Do you still have kids at home? Caring for them is bound to be one of your core values, and an important consideration when you're bringing someone else into your life. Sites like SingleParent.com might be a good fit for you.

Also consider demographics, health, and lifestyle issues. List one or two that are important for you.

If you're an empty nester nearing or already retired, one of the sites for people over fifty, or for seniors, is most likely to connect you with people in your own age bracket.

Is race important? There are sites for Blacks, Latinos, Asians, Native Americans and other specific groups.

There are also specific sites for hearing and visually impaired people, and sites dedicated to helping the disabled find matches.

Next consider your interests. You know that shared interests are important for higher-level matches, so targeting sites for people who have things in common with you is another way of improving the efficiency of your search. Write down your top two.

I already mentioned sites that serve special interest groups, like the site for farmers only, and those for Apple product fans or people who share musical interests. There are also sites for book lovers (including at least one just for fans of Ayn Rand), art lovers, and tattoo lovers.

Finally you should decide how much you're willing to pay.

If money is an issue, look to the free or "freemium" sites like Zoosk, OKCupid, or Plenty of Fish.

Now look at your short list of criteria and number each item, putting them in order of their importance to you.

Last, look at your list, and decide if any of the criteria are important enough to warrant your choosing a site based on that one factor.

Does one item on your list stand out? If so, choose a dating service dedicated to that.

If none are "most important," you probably want to choose one of the general-interest sites.

Remember that the top dating sites, such as Match.com and eHarmony, allow you to filter for several, if not most, of your key criteria, and they automatically tailor your search to consider those factors. OKCupid's free search algorithm allegedly does the same.

Keep all our important criteria on every site you choose, no matter what specific criteria you decide are most important.

Words of Warning

As I said before, dating services give you tremendous power over your search. But you have to be careful.

You wouldn't trust every person you meet on the street, would you? You wouldn't just give them your social security number, or the keys to your house.

Don't do those things online, either.

The vast majority of the people you meet on a dating service are just like you – they're honestly looking for true love. They want a life-mate.

But some are con artists. Or predators. Or sexual abusers. Or thieves.

Be careful.

Every one of the reputable dating sites offer safety tips. Read them. Pay attention.

We'll cover usernames, pictures, and what to say in your profile a little further ahead, but there's one hard and fast rule to note here—do NOT use your real name, or other identifying info such as your birthday, as your username or in your profile. You'll give out this private info when *you* decide it is safe. Period.

By the same token, don't use your real email, personal or work, in your communications until you get to know the person better. These sites are deliberately set up to serve as a safe space for meeting, chatting, and getting to know someone anonymously.

Also be careful about which email account you link to a site. I know of a case in which a woman had her work email connected to an online service, so the notifications of incoming mail, etc. arrived in her work inbox. While she was traveling, she left her auto-reply "out of office" message on.

Unfortunately, anyone who wrote to her on the dating service got a message giving them her real email, name, where she worked, and her office and cell phone numbers.

The same is true of connecting through Facebook. Most services have safeguards in place, but you must use them. Check the settings. Make sure that you know which information strangers can access.

Carefully read all the messages you get. Online meetings are like meeting a stranger in a coffee shop. If he starts asking deeply personal questions right away, or asking for personal information, be wary. If he wants your address, presumably because he wants to send you flowers or something else, run!

On its tips about avoiding online scammers, the Federal Trade Commission says to be wary of anyone who does any of the following:

- Wants to leave the dating site immediately and use personal email or IM
- Claims love in a heartbeat
- Claims to be from the U.S. but is traveling or working overseas
- Plans to visit, but is prevented by a traumatic event or a business deal gone sour.

Naturally, don't send online dating prospects your money. Don't offer your bank account for him to transfer money into yours. Scammers sometimes say they have to shield some cash from their ex, and you'd be doing them a huge favor if they could put the money in your account. This is just a way to get access to your account.

Also look for signs of instability or danger in the emails you get. The majority of people using a dating site are law-abiding citizens who are online for the same reasons as you. But some aren't.

Use your common sense. Look for clues. If you spot signs of anger or obsession, if he starts making demands or threats— basically, if he writes anything that makes you uncomfortable in any way, step away. Your Level III or Level IV match won't make you feel ill at ease.

CHAPTER SEVEN

You Have 30 Seconds

A blink. A wink.

Or not.

Face it—decisions can take place quickly. You see someone and, in the blink of an eye, you decide whether or not he's attractive. Malcolm Gladwell dedicated a whole book to the subject. This was, he said, "The Power of Thinking Without Thinking."

Yes. We all do it.

You glance at a guy across the room and *zing!* There's a tickle—or not.

The same thing happens online, but based on a picture. Same effect.

You may do this with the profile pictures you look at. The same thing will be done with yours. That's why, online, you have 30 seconds to "make the sale." Or less.

In the first three seconds, your picture does all the work. In the next five, it's up to your screen name. Then comes the hook: maybe it's some of your basic information and profile; but, almost definitely, his decision will take into account what he thinks of your additional photos.

It makes sense, right? We all know men are visual. (So are women, but we'll get to what his pictures tell you later.)

So the pictures you choose better be good. And, as I'll show you, there are certain rules for the most effective ones: no sunglasses, make eye contact, and smile. There are additional things you should absolutely avoid.

Every picture says something about you. Usually, a lot more is revealed than you think. We all pick up on the subliminal cues in pictures.

"There is this idea that attraction stems from a very superficial outlook on people, which is false," Tinder co-founder Sean Rad told the *New York Times*. "Everyone is able to pick up thousands of signals in these photos. A photo of a guy at a bar with friends around him sends a very different message than a photo of a guy with a dog on the beach."

Take a Good Look at Yourself

Before we get to your picture, though, let's look at you as the subject of the picture.

As we discussed in the "Cleaning Out Your Closet" chapter, this is a chance to reinvent yourself, because what you've been doing previously has not brought you lasting love. You might as well start by analyzing everything. This is a great time to decide what works and what doesn't; what stays and what goes; what's fine just the way it is, and what needs some work.

Madonna has always been a source of inspiration for me because she's always reinventing herself into a better version of herself. It takes a lot of courage and hard work, but look at her now! She's not only changed her look numerous times throughout the decades, and kept herself fit, but she's also grown personally and spiritually. This doesn't just happen. Her achievements require introspection and a willingness and need to always improve. You can adopt this outlook and strategy, too.

You already began this process of improving yourself on the inside by cleaning out your closet, identifying childhood triggers, and clearing out any limiting beliefs. We also alluded to some outward changes that you could start thinking about.

We're going to focus on all these changes here, so you can reflect the changes in the new pictures that you will use for your online dating profile.

Your picture will be the first impression that you will make online—the one that captures his attention before he realizes all your great inner qualities.

Stand in front of a mirror, a full-length mirror if you have one. (If you don't, go into the dressing room at your favorite clothing store and use their full-length mirrors. This won't take long.)

What do you see? Look at yourself as though this was your first time seeing yourself. Take critical look. That doesn't mean to be negative, although that's what most of us tend to be when we're evaluating ourselves. It means examine what you see: the good and the not so good. Be a neutral observer of your outward appearance.

Everyone has something that she likes about herself. And something that she wishes was a little or a lot different.

Exercise: The Me I See

After you've taken some time to look at yourself in the mirror, it's time to take notes.

Make two columns. Label one column "Good." Label the other, "Needs Work."

List at least three good things about yourself and one—that's right, *one*— thing that could use improvement or that you plan to change.

Why the 3 to 1 ratio? Because most of us are too hard on ourselves. If you find a second thing that needs work, then add two more good things.

See a third with room for improvement? Add another two that are positive.

The point is not to minimize the number of things that could use improvement, but to force you to see what you should already realize—the good outweighs the bad, at least 2 to 1. And, if it doesn't, look at your limiting beliefs about your appearance.

Your finished list might look like this:

Good	Needs Work
1. Nice smile	1. Lose 10 pounds
2. Great eyes	2. Outdated hairstyle
3. Pretty lips	
4. Good legs	
5. Firm arms	

Here are some things to consider:

Weighty Matters

Do you think you need to lose weight? Or gain some?
Do you really?

Be careful with this one. We're so used to obsessing about our weight that it's very hard to be realistic about this. A lot of times we think we need to lose weight when we don't.

The "blind-eye syndrome" can be a problem, too. It's easy for us to treat our bodies like our homes – we're so used to seeing them that we don't notice the paint has faded or the rug is worn. We're so used to the sagging sofa ("It's so comfortable!") that we don't realize how shabby it looks.

If you think you could lose ten pounds, maybe you're right. Maybe you need to lose even more. You can get a second opinion from your friends, your doctor, or a physical trainer. If you do need to lose some weight, get started.

But if you don't need to lose any weight, don't. If you like what you see, keep it. There are plenty of health reasons to be slim, but if you're healthy, don't change yourself just to match some Madison Avenue ideal. I'll repeat this: there are a lot of men—a lot!—who prefer full-bodied women.

The bottom line is that you have to practice self-love and accept the things in yourself that you can't change, and focus on improving what you can. You will be healthier and feel better about yourself. You will, then, project a self-confidence that is very attractive and magnetic.

Brush up, touch up

Get a consultation with the best hairstylist you can find to see if your hairstyle needs updating, or if it's the most flattering style for your face shape and age. As we age, our face changes.

Get a makeup consultation. If you can't afford a professional makeup artist, go to the mall. Go to your favorite makeup counter to make sure that your makeup and techniques are up to date and the most flattering for your age. I find that it's best to choose a makeup company that advertises a look that you like.

For example, I like the natural look that Bobby Brown markets, so whenever I want an update, I go to the manager of the Bobby Brown counter so that she can show me how to use the new season's colors in a way that flatters me. Additionally, they are usually willing to help you on "Picture Day." Just tell them you are having pictures taken, and you need help with makeup that will photograph well.

Next examine your teeth, which can be a sure sign of aging and excessive coffee and red wine consumption. Are your teeth too yellow? This might be the time to go to your dentist and get your teeth whitened. Or if you're on a budget, there are over-the-counter teeth whiteners that work very well. You can whiten up to eight shades—that will lead to a more beautiful smile. Make sure your teeth are in good condition.

Don't forget your nails and your feet. When was the last time you had a pedicure? Get them done or do them yourself. Men notice hands and feet. (So do women!) Plus, you will feel great after the treatment.

What looks good to a woman is not necessarily what attracts a man. So stick to colors that are in the normal range. Most men do not like frosted nail polish or nails that are exceedingly long. I've heard men say that super long nails look like claws. You don't want him to feel like you want to get your claws into him!

Also, no frosted lipstick because this dates most women. Unless you're twenty-something, frosted lipstick will only accentuate the lines in your lips.

You should aim for a classy, clean look. A man may want to date someone who looks like a stripper, but he won't want to introduce her to his family or kids.

Look at yourself realistically

How does your skin look? Do you have deep lines from years of sunbathing? You might want to consider a trip to a dermatologist, who might suggest that you consider getting some fillers. Or maybe now is the time to consider cosmetic surgery. Even so, remember that it's essential that you feel comfortable with yourself and how you look. Don't do anything because you feel pressured. If you're happy with the way you look, don't change a thing.

I once had a dermatologist who suggested that I needed Botox even though I was only thirty years old. I knew that I had beautifully unlined skin, and I was happy with the way I looked. I passed on his recommendation and found a new doctor.

The reason you're doing this external self-evaluation is so you can present the best you that is possible—and within your budget. Most important, though, is for you to feel good about yourself.

Dressing the Part

You also need to take a good look at your wardrobe. When was the last time you updated your wardrobe?

Most of us always shop in the same places. We buy the same styles. We tend to get stuck in the same old look. Before we know it, we've been sporting the same look for the past decade.

Your clothes are an integral part of your new image. Think about the message you want to project, and make sure that your wardrobe reflects that. Don't become someone you're not, though. Become the best you, with a wardrobe to match.

You can still be a jeans and T's girl, if that's who you are. But nice-fitting, attractive jeans and a stylish, flattering T can show off who you are in a way that baggy, tattered work jeans and a stretched-out, stained T with holes does not.

By the same token, dress age-appropriately. When women become single at certain ages they often want to go out looking really sexy. Okay. But guess what? Really short, sexy dresses are only appropriate at certain ages.

If you're over forty, you probably shouldn't be wearing mid-thigh dresses—even if you have killer legs. It just looks like you're trying to be something that you're not. (These are comments from men!)

Plus, you want to attract a man for the right reasons. You want him to see your shapely legs? You can accomplish that by wearing a skirt that's above the knee.

For the same reason, you want to be careful with showing a lot of cleavage. If you wear tops that accentuate your cleavage, you're going to attract a lot of men, yes—but not necessarily for the right reasons. If you post a picture that's all cleavage, I guarantee that you'll get a lot of online attention. But most of it won't be from potential long-term mates. You're more likely to end up with dates. Sometimes less is more. A formfitting dress that doesn't reveal cleavage, but that shows your body's shape underneath, can be sexier than something that shows more skin. And the modesty sends a better message.

Most men want their significant other and potential mate to be someone who looks attractive and well put together, someone that they can introduce to their families and colleagues.

Your Picture

After you've gotten yourself looking the way you think you want, it's time to show off.

Your pictures should be realistic representations of you. When you show up to your date, you should look like your picture.

This means your photo(s) should be recent. Most should have been taken within the past three to four months, although you could have some from the last six to nine months. There may be one photo that's almost a year old, say from last New Year's Eve, or maybe a photo taken during your daughter's wedding when you looked particularly stunning in your party dress. Maybe include a photo from before that, when you went horseback riding on the beach in Puerto Rico. But don't post photos that are more than a year-and-a-half old. None.

The pictures should reveal the way you look now. So don't Photoshop 10 pounds out of the picture, or blank the wrinkles out of your neck. If you're curvaceous or overweight you don't have to hide it. Just wear something that flatters your figure.

Your pictures are your "brand," in ad-speak. The man who responds to your picture is saying, "I like what I see. He probably doesn't want you to lose weight or doesn't care about your wrinkles.

It's false advertising to offer him someone who's not the one he's going to get, whether that's now or later.

I'll say it again: There really is a match for everybody. That means there really is someone out there who wants you just the way you are.

So show the best you—just as you are.

First Impressions

Most dating sites let you include a number of photographs with your profile. One photo, though, will be the most important. This will be the picture that people see first. You might pick it, or the site may pick it from those you submitted.

You want a profile picture that really shows who you are, and shows you in the best light. First impressions, right?

Yes, that first one should be your best headshot. Because the first thing he wants to see is your face—close enough for him to quickly decide if he likes what he sees. Hopefully, you're wearing your best smile. I say this because I had someone who lived far away—geographically undesirable – who told me that he occasionally looked at my pictures because my smile was infectious and it made him smile. How awesome is that! So make someone smile today.

Put up a picture of the seashore, your dog, or one of your favorite sayings, and he's going to move on without looking any further. He's not dating your dog. He doesn't care what Walt Whitman has to say that's particularly meaningful to you. (So many men complain about this.)

He wants you. Or not.

So make sure he can get a good look. Don't make your main picture the one of you standing in the distance looking out over the canyon at sunset – with your back to the camera. He's not there for the scenery. Yet. He's there for you.

Also, if you seem to be far away and can't be seen, the immediate natural reaction will be for him to wonder: *What is she hiding?* He may think the same thing if you're wearing sunglasses.

So have a picture that's up close and personal.

Let him see your eyes. I'll say it again and again—eye contact is very important. Covering your eyes or looking away from the camera distances you. It makes people wonder if you're hiding something. American culture associates direct eye contact with honesty.

But if you normally wear regular prescription glasses, wear them. This should be an honest picture of the best you. Remember truth in advertising? It really does matter. You want him to see the person he'll be meeting if you both hit it off.

Also don't use a group shot of you and your best friends out on the town as your main photo. Don't play a guessing game. You want him to see you, not force him to have to figure out which of the three is you.

Let him see your hairstyle. Whether you shave it all or let it down, it's you. We tend to put a lot of thought and care into our hair for a reason. It's one of the most distinctive and alluring things about us, no matter how we wear it. It frames our faces. It makes our look. It's a statement.

Go Pro

If you don't have a friend who can take a good picture of you, my advice is to invest in some professional photographs. Not the kind that you do at Sears. Those may be great for family albums or "Baby's First Year" but generally those poses are stilted. Definitely, don't do "Glamour Shots." We all know that no one looks like that in real life.

You want to find a photographer who will photograph you while you're moving so that the shots look natural. Believe it or not, this can be done with a headshot. Have him photograph you wearing three different outfits so that you can choose the pictures that look best or use them all.

You're looking for your lifetime partner; invest the money so that you stand out. Don't be like the people who post out of focus photos with terrible composition.. The cost of professional pictures in Miami is about $300.

I can't stress the importance of getting professional photos. You can also use your professional-quality photos on Facebook and other online social media sites. Many people meet their lifetime partners via social media as well.

You have thirty seconds to get his attention, make it the best thirty seconds.

Rounding It Out

Okay—you caught his attention with your main photo. If he likes what he sees there, he's going to want to see more.

"Candid" pictures—in social settings, on vacation, or just out and about—speak volumes.

What you wear sends a loud message, so does where the shots are taken, and what shows. If every picture is of you at a church function, that says something. If every photo was taken in a bar, that says something else.

Most of the pictures should be of you doing "normal" things, like cooking, going to a boat show, art gallery, farmers' market, etc.

Try to avoid beach shots in which you're wearing your bikini. The subliminal message that this picture sends is not what you want. You're "advertising" for sex with those pictures. You will attract men who are looking for a quick fling or a one-night stand. A message from a man looking for a long-term relationship may be in there among the many responses, but in terms of dating efficiency you're fishing with the wrong bait.

Remember, you are looking for a mate not a date.

Your candid shots should show you smiling, not just with your mouth, but also with your eyes. You'll seem like what you are: truly happy and genuine. He will want to join you in the fun you're having.

But please don't post dozens of pictures of yourself. You need a good assortment so he can see you in different ways, but five to ten photos are enough. You don't want to send out the message that you're so into yourself that there's no room for anyone else. I posted four of myself.

Ideally, you should include one full body shot of you in which your shape is defined in a classy way, perhaps showing you in a dress, or a nice top and slacks.

You should definitely have a picture or two of you doing something that you really love. For example, if you love to horseback ride, you should have a picture of you riding horses, wearing jeans and boots. If you love kayaking, have a picture of you kayaking.

But don't fake it.

If you don't have any interests outside of TV and your work, it might be time to develop some outside interests, and then you can photograph yourself doing those things. But if you try to pass yourself off as somebody you're not, you'll get somebody you don't want or who doesn't want you.

Think carefully about the message your activity conveys. If you post a picture of you holding a rifle at a gun range, be aware what that says to people. If guns are important to you, and you shoot regularly, then this photo is perfect. But if you've only been to a gun range once, and you aren't truly a gun-lover, lose it.

Do the same with any other pictures involving controversial or adventurous activities. If you don't long to be on the back of a Harley every weekend, think twice before you post that picture of yourself on a motorcycle. Yes, the photo shows that you like to have fun. Yes, it says you're willing to try new things. But guys who like motorcycles tend to be passionate about them. Guys who are attracted to women on motorcycles may be looking for someone to hit the road with them. Constantly.

Pay similar attention to other activities that people—especially men—can be passionate about. Golf. Tennis. Fishing. If you don't want to be on a boat smelling fish every weekend, consider what you're telling an avid fisherman when he sees that picture of you smiling next to a fish dangling off your line. If you don't want to sit through nine innings of baseball all the time, be wary about posting photographs of you at a game.

If you have too many pictures at functions and galas, they may send a message that might turn some men off—or others on. But if your life really revolves around functions, you should have a few of those because the man you want will have to be comfortable going to those events.

Uh Oh's, No No's, and So So's

Please, no selfies. They're rarely as flattering as you think they are, and they carry a subtle message that you don't have any friends. If you did, why won't they take pictures of you?

If you do decide to ignore my advice and use selfies, don't have the phone showing in the photo. And make sure that the background is clean, and that your room is tidy. If you're doing that one where you aim the camera at the bathroom mirror (Ugh!), you should definitely clean everything up. Remove all your shampoos, creams, lotions and depilatories because they will show up in the mirror.

I have seen so many selfies that show clothes piled up around the room. What does that say about a person? I am sure that the poster only noticed how good he looked and never saw his own mess on the floor.

The pictures you choose to post say a lot about you. And they should be about you. A group picture or two is fine: you do have friends and have fun with other people, after all. But the majority of your photos should be about one person—you.

He's seen a sunset. He doesn't need to see a shot of one on your profile page. He's seen the ocean. And the photo showing your brightly painted toes in front isn't saying much, except that perhaps you have nice feet.

There's one big No No: Definitely do not post pictures of your kids! Such postings aren't safe for your kids. Further, a man wants to first envision you as a woman, not as a mother—even if you are a mother.

Yes, being a mother is a very important part of your life, but the point of going to an online dating service is to attract a man. And a huge part of being a parent is protecting your kids and being concerned about their safety. You don't want to wonder if you attracted a man because he wanted to meet you or because he's a pedophile who wanted to get near your daughter or son.

Exercise: Picture Checklist

Main Photo

Close enough to see your eyes?
Making eye contact?
A nice, honest smile?
Evenly lit?
Skin looks nice?
Hairstyle visible?

Additional Photos

At least one full-body picture? Appropriately dressed?
Two additional photos in different settings: a party, by a lake, at a museum, etc.? Classy? Natural? Not revealing?

One to two more photos pursuing activities you truly enjoy: dancing, playing tennis (or, at least dressed for it, on the court, holding a racket), etc.?

If you have more photos, are they of something significant? For example, do they show a place you traveled to recently or that was significant to you for some reason (it was a place you always wanted to visit, or where your ancestors were from, etc.)?

Are numerous photos in the same type of setting? In bars, church, the gym? If yes, two questions: What does that say about you? And can you get rid of the extra photos?

Do any of the photos show you involved in an activity that men can be passionate about (golf, football, biking), but you don't really want to do that activity regularly?

What else is visible in every photograph? Study them all carefully. Is your room or bathroom a mess? Is there a man in the picture, perhaps with his arm around you?

It's better to leave out photos of other men, even if the guy is your brother; but if you do choose to use a photo of another guy, try to explain who they are in the photo's caption. Look at every photo with an extremely critical eye, then follow the old rule: When in doubt, throw it out. Do any of your photos show your children? Cut them out.

This exercise is intended as something of a guided critique. It's highly subjective. In the end, only you will know if your pictures truly represent who you are, accurately and tastefully. If you're not sure about anything, ask a friend to go through the exercise with you.

A "You" By Any Other Name

After your main photo, your screen name carries the most weight. Most likely, before he even clicks to see more pictures, he'll glance at your screen name. It will tell him something, consciously or unconsciously.

Choose wisely. A Rose1234 by any other name is easily a missed opportunity. Your screen name is your "brand." And here's the truth: You wouldn't buy a car called "Unreliable" or "Gas Hog," or a cereal named "Tastes Terrible." In the same way, he probably won't click on "TiredOfItAll," "Betrayed," or "SoSad."

There's also a big difference between "HotMama4U" and (don't, it's overused) "LovinLife." One says, "I'm easy." The other says, "I lack originality."

You want a name that follows the three rules for a good one: It's original, clever, and simple. That makes it memorable and good for attracting the man you want.

Original and clever means it's good if your screen name reveals something about your personality, your favorite hobby, or something you're passionate about. Mine, for example, was "1InYourMind." It was intended as a play on words – both, "number one in your mind" and, since I'm a therapist, as "one who works in your mind."

Clever? I hope so. But certainly original, and definitely meant to be a conversation starter.

If you love swimming, or teach it, you might use something like "Aquagirl." Tennis your thing? How about "LoveSetMatch?"

Short is good. Catchy is best.

You have to be security conscious with your user name. Never use your own name, or parts of it. Not only is it not very clever to use "SallyJones1" for your user name, it says too much about you. It makes it too easy for a predator, abuser, or thief to track you down. He can guess you live alone, that's why you're looking for a match. That makes you an easy target.

The same advice applies to revealing other personal information: your birth date or the name of the street you live on.

Use the same kind of caution with online dating as you do when you get out of your car and you walk to your front door alone. There are predators out there.

Exercise: Picking your user name

Your turn. Time to pick a user name.

Get some paper, or your computer or tablet.

Make your first column a list of some of your favorite things. This doesn't have to be in any particular order. Just let yourself brainstorm. The list might look like this:

Swimming
Music
Movies
Dancing
Sunsets
Cats
Comedy clubs

Now choose the three items you like the most. Put each one at the head of a column. Under each, be more specific. Like if swimming is your top thing, list where you like to swim or your favorite swimming stroke.

Use synonyms, play word associations…. brainstorm.

For example:

Dancing	**Bicycling**	**Art Galleries**
Ballroom	Two wheels	Picasso
Salsa	Free Wheeling	Gallery Girl
Stepping Out	Pedals	Louvre
Dancing shoes	Mountain bike	Canvas

List as many activities and favorite things as you want, the more the better.

Now choose your favorite one or two from each column, and let loose, let your creativity run free.

Each might be good enough on its own, saying everything you want. Or a variation might come to mind. You might want to mix and match, putting items from several columns together.

For example, you might call yourself "TinyDancer," "SalsaWheels," or simply "FreeWheeling." Give yourself two or three possibilities and pick your favorite.

You might want to ask a friend what she thinks before you make your final selection. Sometimes wording that seems perfect and innocent might have connotations we didn't consider. "Girl2Ride" could attract a lot of men looking for sex, instead of a cycling partner.

Think about it.

CHAPTER EIGHT

The Main Event! Creating Your Profile

Your "profile" closes the sale. He loves your pictures and is intrigued or amused by your screen name. Now, he wants to know more. You're on the final stretch!

Here is your chance to stand out from the crowd. Yes, he thinks you're attractive. That's why he clicked on your pic. But this is your chance to show him that you're more than just a pretty face—and a chance for you to find out if he's there for something more than skin-deep.

That's right, your profile works both ways. It's your bait and your hook, and a vital part of the search process. It's a way for you to narrow the field down to the ones you want to attract, and to sort through the many possibilities for the man you want to keep, the "keeper"—your potential Level III or Level IV match.

Your profile serves one purpose, to attract the right kind of man and to create a desire in him to contact you. He needs to find you so appealing that he really wants to get to know you better.

The ultimate purpose of your profile is to get you a first date with your potential Mr. Right, not Mr. Right Now. The right profile can get you there.

Power Extras

There's a lot more to a profile than just the profile.

Several sites include a tagline or catch phrase. Almost all include at least some "About You" info. Some ask you to describe "Your idea of a first date."

Every element is a part of the message you're sending out into the universe of potential mates.

The tagline

This is basically your slogan, a way to describe yourself or your philosophy in just a few, catchy words.

"Catchy" is key.

If the best tagline you can come up with is "Live, laugh, love"—really? It's so hackneyed that even if it's true and it's been your personal motto for the past twenty years, it has become dull, trite, and overused. And guess what? That's exactly what he's going to think of you: that you're dull, trite, and—well, let's hope not.

If that's really the description of you or the personal philosophy you want to be known by, try saying it in your own words. "I enjoy every moment I can, learn from the ones I can't, and laugh as often as possible."

It's more words, but it's also more genuine. It sounds like you, not something from an inspirational poster.

You don't have to be profound: "I have a bicycle built for two with one empty seat." Or "Need help breaking in my new dancing shoes."

Bottom line: Keep it simple and fun,

"About You"

When it comes to the "About You" information, what you do say and what you don't say are both relevant.

Almost every site asks you to provide some information about yourself. Some present this section as a simple survey. Others ask a series of questions and ask how "your ideal partner" would answer. Some use multiple-choice questionnaires. Some use open-ended forms. OKCupid asks you to tell, "Six things I couldn't live without" and "On a typical Friday night, I am…"

Still others use a hybrid. Zoosk has a somewhat lengthy and wide-ranging section that asks a variety of multiple-choice questions such as "How much does physical attractiveness matter to you in a match?" and "Do you believe that there exists a statistical correlation between race and intelligence?" Every question offers a limited number of answers as choices, but they also offer you a chance to "Add an explanation."

All are aimed at refining the matches the service offers. Whether the algorithms those central computers use work or not is a subject of ongoing debate. Whether they do or not, you can still use them as a way to narrow your search.

I believe you should answer every question on a dating platform because, as I said, what you don't answer says as much about you as what you do. If you are truly looking for lasting love, you will want to invest the extra time so that you can give the matching algorithms a chance to work for you. If you're unwilling to do this, you need to ask yourself if you are truly looking for love.

Some questions very are simple and obvious. Some are trickier.

My advice is always the same: be honest in all of your responses.

For example, almost all sites ask about your income level. If you don't answer, it can look like you're ashamed of how much you make or are afraid you'll attract con artists. Don't be. This is actually an important part of the culling process and, honestly, an important point of compatibility. If you make $25,000 and somebody else makes $150,000, you may have two very different lifestyles. Also, the person making $100,000 will have to assume that he or she will be paying for most of the couples' expenses.

On the flip side, if you're considering holding back because you want to be cautious, you may be doing yourself a disservice. Someone may be attracted to you because you have similar incomes.

The other questions that people often don't answer truthfully are the ones pertaining to their children such as: how many children do you have, and do they live at home. I really don't understand this thinking because the answer will soon come out when you start dating. It's very important to be truthful here.

If you have kids, they're a big part of your life, especially if they still live with you. They're a huge source of joy, pride, worry, and stress. They're a great responsibility. You'll want to be with somebody who understands this and can handle it. You don't want to attract someone who is not willing to accommodate the needs of your kids. You are a parent first. If you are not—that says something about you, too.

If you have children who live at home, whether that's full time or part of the time, you should say so, and expand on it in your profile. Mention their ages. Teenagers and pre-schoolers present different challenges and involve different lifestyles. Not every guy wants to go to kiddie birthday parties at Chuck E. Cheese or deal with the drama of a high-schooler staying out all night without permission.

In my case, I have two grown children who live on their own. We're very close and see each other a lot, but they're adults. It's different. I love kids, but I don't want to start all over again with small children. That would entail a big commitment on my part to be a part time parent. I know this about myself so it's a deal breaker for me. Someone like me would probably want another empty-nester, not someone with kids at home—even part time.

I put this in my profile so that anyone who has younger children or teenagers knows and they don't waste their time or mine. If you're up front about having children still living at home, those who do not want to date someone who has younger children or teenagers can automatically pass you by and not waste your time or theirs. This helps to create dating efficiency by ruling out your deal breakers.

Many dating site platforms have a question about religion. Religion is a very tricky thing because it means many things to different people.

Obviously, if it's important to you and you wouldn't want to date anyone outside of your own religion, you should make that clear. List your faith in the question and answer section if it calls for it, and say a bit more about it in your profile.

Be clear. If your answer is "Christian" and you're very devout say something like "My faith is an important part of my life," or "I want to meet somebody who shares my religion and wants to attend services and church-related activities with me."

Those answers don't leave room for doubt.

I chose to put "spiritual but not religious." To me that really means, "I'm open to all religions and respect everybody's beliefs." I believe it also subtly indicates that I'm not looking for someone who wants to impose their religious beliefs on me, or who expects me to convert.

Several dating platforms ask what type of relationship you're interested in. The options range from "friendship" and "casual dating" to "serious" or "committed relationship."

Again, honesty is the best policy and clarification makes everything better. Since you're reading this book, I assume you want a committed long-term relationship. Tell the world!

But in the body of your profile, let it be known that you want to take your time and get to know somebody. You're interested in a long-term relationship, yes, but that doesn't mean you're ready to fly off to Vegas with the first guy who answers.

The Main Event—Your Profile

Now, the essay question feels like some kind of difficult test, but is really just a chance for you to present yourself in the best light and, if your response is well written, to pique a man's interest.

In short, if your main photo was the digital equivalent of a meaningful glance across a crowded room, and this is the initial conversation.

It's flirting; it's *not* your life story. The goal of this essay is to intrigue your potential mate enough so that he wants to know more about you and go on a first date.

It's important that you be yourself. Above all, stick with the golden rule of attracting the right match: Truth in advertising.

This isn't the time for a "makeover." You're not presenting the person you wish you were. You're presenting who you are. If you're not who you want to be yet, then you shouldn't be trying to bring that "someone" into your life just yet.

That includes everything from what you like to do and what you're looking for, to what you really look like.

Additional Profile No-No's:

One of the things that I've heard from men is that a lot of women seem to cut-and-paste from other women's profiles. They always "want somebody with a good sense of humor who will take them traveling."

Please don't even bother reading anybody else's profile. If you're like everybody else, there's no reason for him to pick you. Mr. Right For You is looking for you; so be you. This is a search process. You want to differentiate yourself from others. Let him see what's unique about you.

Don't lie about your weight. Don't lie about your age or your goals. Your Mr. Right wants you just the way you are.

It seems like that should be obvious. But, as I've noted before, studies show that men lie about their height; women lie about their weight. And both tend to shave off a few years.

I don't necessarily encourage it, but I understand why you might want to change your age in order to outsmart the sites' search engines. Age is a search tool. Dating service servers sort by it. So do prospective matches.

Most services ask you if you're a) a man or a woman, b) looking to meet a man or woman, and c) between what ages. You both get the same questions.

If someone says that he's looking to meet someone between the ages of 45 and 55, the service computer is designed to weed out people who are younger or older. If you're 42 or 57, that someone—who might have clicked on your picture— may never see it.

I've seen women who are 51 say they're 48; and men who are 61 say they're 58. I'm OK with that, as long as they tell the truth as soon as possible. That should be in the body of the profile itself. Or at least on your first email or phone call.

I don't encourage, or advise, people to take entire decades off their age. This is particularly offensive because they often don't look anywhere near the age they're claiming.

If you want to bypass the age sorting system, create your own search in the site. Look for men who are looking for women who are five years younger or older than you are. Find the ones who meet your list of requirements and send them a wink. Let them decide if the age difference is that important. This is more honest.

Lying about your age is tantamount to putting up pictures that are from that vacation twenty years ago, when you still fit into a size two. Part of self-love is accepting yourself exactly as you are at this point in your life.

I have heard from many men that there are several things they always get very upset about: one is that they expect somebody who was much younger and it turns out they're much older. The other is that the pictures don't match the age.

Why bother? The guy who winks at you or emails you isn't looking for the real you. He wants that younger woman. (And, do you really want that man who wants to be with someone 30 years younger?)

For the same reason, if you don't really "Exercise five or more times a week," don't say that you do. The work out aficionado who answers will be a little disappointed when you don't want to join him for workouts every day.

If you're really "curvy" don't call yourself "slim" or "average."

Don't talk about your ex. Don't talk about sex. Don't talk about anything you wouldn't if you were meeting in person for the first time.

And never—never—write anything like, "Princess Seeking her Prince." This isn't a fairy tale; this is your life. The message between the lines is: *I'm needy. I need to be rescued.*

Don't write, "I'm tired of being alone," or "Lonely too long, now I'm looking to live." Who wants to go out with a desperate, depressed, needy person?

If you're advertising that you want to be rescued or you're needy, what you need to do is wait. You need to work on yourself before you're ready for a relationship.

Profile Yes's:

You want to present yourself in the best light without embellishing, without lying. So every piece of the profile should be well thought out, but keep it light. Make it conversational. Make it fun or amusing. You're flirting!

You're trying to get a first date, not tell your life story. You want to give a sketch of your life so that he knows there are enough points of interest, but you don't want to make your statement too long.

Use your own words; don't borrow quotes. He wants to have an idea of what you're like, how you speak and think. Rattling off a list of inspirational quotes makes you sound like a greeting card, not a person. If you're funny, be humorous. If you're not, don't. You want to give someone an insight into your personality, not be somebody you're not.

You want to project an air of confidence. Your profile is definitely not the place to be humble. But it is a place to talk about your great qualities without exaggeration.

So how do you do this? How do you show them what a great life you're living and how much fun they would have with you?

Imagine you're sitting at a bar and a handsome guy comes up to you and says, "Hi. Tell me about you."

You'd say something catchy, a little flirty, and tell them some facts about you that make you sound interesting and fun. Well, this is the same idea.

The only difference is that a profile is written down where it can be reread, so be careful what you write. Please have someone read your profile draft and check it for grammar, spelling, and typos.

You definitely want to include what you do for fun, hobbies, or activities that you love and that give an insight into who you are, what you do for a living, and anything that makes you unique.

You want to use descriptive language that draws them into your story instead of creating a laundry list of your attributes.

As you'll see from the example that follows, I like to put something in my profile that let's me know if he's actually read it. If he addresses that piece in his email, then I know that this man may be seriously looking for a mate. Men who are looking for dates or flings don't usually bother with profiles—reading them or writing them.

I prefer sites that require profiles, rather than sites that do not. People in their twenties seem to prefer sites that don't require the time commitment necessary to start interacting, and they're right that it takes time and introspection to write a good profile. But I would rather know as much as possible about someone before I go on a first date. This is safer and more efficient. Further, this is the kind of investment people make when they're hoping to end up in long-term romantic relationships.

Following is a copy of my online profile, followed by an explanation of why I chose to write what I did.

Section 1: Headline

Life is a wonderful adventure to be fully explored and lived ...

As I mentioned above, the headline should serve as a one-sentence catch phrase. It can be your philosophy on life. It could be something catchy like "I'm witty and quirky," or "sophisticated and refined." It can be anything that you want. But its job is to make somebody want to read the rest.

Section 2: In your own words

Friends tell me that I'm easy to talk to and have a quick wit. I often have a smile on my face and a laugh not far behind. I'm as comfortable in jeans and a t-shirt hiking down a trail as I am putting on high heels and a cocktail dress to attend a social event. My friends and family also tell me I am loyal and the person they know they can count on to give great advice and to be there for them. I value direct communication and believe that honesty is the best policy when it comes to dating and relationships. My friends also describe me as refined, well educated, and cultured.

I also look at life as an adventure to be fully explored and lived. I love traveling to exotic locations and experiencing them as though I were a local. I am comfortable in my own skin and am not into wasting your time or mine by showing you a facade or playing games. I am financially responsible and assume that you are, too!

In 2003, I decided to follow one of my passions by going back to college for my Masters in Marriage and Family Therapy, while managing my own financial services company full time. It was no small achievement re-learning high school geometry after twenty years in order to pass the G.R.E.! You can see that not much daunts me. I graduated in 2006.

I just moved back to Florida in October 2013 after living in Santa Fe, NM for 2 1/2 years. In the spirit of life is an adventure.... I wanted to experience living in a place filled with raw, natural beauty and immerse myself in following some artistic pursuits. (I designed jewelry.) I also ran my financial company from there. Miami has been my home since 1983. I have a close network of eclectic friends in both locations with whom I enjoy spending time.

Three somewhat random facts about me:
#1 I was a gymnast and a dancer until I was 18
#3 My shoe collection rivals Sarah Jessica Parker's in Sex and the City
#2 I will tell you if you tell me something interesting about yourself in your email.

My perfect match is a man who is a take-charge kind of guy. You are comfortable making decisions and taking action - and, occasionally, accepting some input. Keeping (or getting) in shape and being healthy is a priority for you. You also know that confidence is sexy. You are cultured, enjoy traveling, are generous of spirit and have a positive outlook. You are playful and adventurous. You have your feet firmly planted on the ground and your imagination is soaring like a kite! You have an even temper, are patient, honest, ethical, and affectionate. You also understand the value of getting to know someone before jumping into a relationship. (I know. You're thinking that I don't ask for much, but I am also offering a great deal!!!) If you are this man, I'd love to hear from you... and maybe, I will tell you my # 2!

Let's look at paragraph 1:

Friends tell me that I'm easy to talk to and have a quick wit. I often have a smile on my face and a laugh not far behind. I'm as comfortable in jeans and a t-shirt hiking down a trail, as I am putting on high heels and a cocktail dress to attend a social event. My friends and family also tell me I am loyal and the person they know they can count on to give great advice and to be there for them. I value direct communication and believe that honesty is the best policy when it comes to dating and relationships. My friends also describe me as refined, well educated, and cultured.

It's usually hard when people have to talk about themselves. Our culture has taught us that it's not nice to brag or to compliment ourselves. In order to overcome this and to let people know that I actually have friends, I decided to write about myself from my friends' point of view.

Now, of course, they're my friends because they love me and they think I'm great – at least most of the time! So here I get to describe myself in a way that sounds inviting and gives a lot of information in a short space. I let men know that I value humor, that I'm easy to talk to, and I'm always smiling. So I'm already inviting them in with my smile.

I also want to tell them about my character. I throw in the part about loyalty and how my friends can count on me. I'm also letting them know that these are qualities I value, and that I'm hoping they have those qualities too, because I have chosen to speak about them.

Next, and right up front, I let them know that honesty is very important to me and clear communication is key. That should tell them that if they're lying anywhere in their profile and they want to have anything to do with me, they should tell me up front.

> *My friends also describe me as refined, well educated, and cultured.*

This lets a man know that I'm looking for the same or at least someone who is comfortable with a woman with these qualities.

Paragraph 2:

> *I also look at life as an adventure to be fully explored and lived. I love traveling to exotic locations and experiencing them as though I were a local.*

Here I'm giving them a glimpse into what drives me. It also shows them my outlook on life. I want to live life fully and completely. I also talk about one of my passions, which is traveling. So what I'm saying here is that if you're a couch potato or your idea of traveling is going to Disney World, you are not the man for me.

> *I am comfortable in my own skin and am not into wasting your time or mine by showing you a facade or playing games. I am financially responsible and assume that you are, too!*

With this phrase I let you know that I've done a lot of work on myself and I'm going to let you see the real me. I want to show you. And I want you to show me who you are because I'm not into wasting my time or his.

This also lets him know that I'm serious about finding a relationship with the right person for me. I'm not saying it explicitly, but implicitly.

Paragraph 3:

In 2003, I decided to follow one of my passions by going back to college for my Masters in Marriage and Family Therapy, while managing my own financial services company full time. It was no small achievement re-learning high school geometry after twenty years in order to pass the G.R.E.! You can see that not much daunts me. I graduated in 2006.

This third paragraph serves to let a man know what my passion is, and what I'm willing to do for something I'm passionate about. It also tells him something unique about me.

Notice how I talk about what I do for a living? I mention that I have a financial services company and that I'm also a therapist. What I do for a living is three paragraphs down. That's because my work does not define me, but the therapy part of my work is one of my passions.

When talking about your work, you want to highlight the positive aspects, not the mundane or bad aspects. This is not lying, it's focusing on what you like. Most people are attracted to happy, positive people who enjoy what they do.

For example, I could talk about my therapy work by describing it as, "I spend my day helping people lead happier lives."

Doesn't that sound better than saying, "I spend my day listening to other people's problems." Both describe the work of therapists, but the first sounds so much more appealing! (By the way, the first way of saying it is how I actually do look at my work!)

Paragraph 4:

> *I just moved back to Florida in October 2013 after living in Santa Fe, NM for 2 1/2 years. In the spirit of life is an adventure.... I wanted to experience living in a place filled with raw, natural beauty and immerse myself in following some artistic pursuits. (I designed jewelry.) I also ran my financial company from there. Miami has been my home since 1983. I have a close network of eclectic friends in both locations with whom I enjoy spending time.*

I am a woman of many interests and passions, so I wanted to talk about my jewelry designing endeavors and my fabulous experiences in Santa Fe. I also wanted to tell those men who live in Miami that I have actually spent most of my adult life living in that wonderful city.

Notice how I also mentioned that I have eclectic friends. My friends are from all walks of life and have all types of interests and jobs. This is important to point out because if someone is too settled in his ways, he might not fit in with all of the different types of people that I enjoy.

Paragraph 5:

> *Three somewhat random facts about me:*

#1 I was a gymnast and a dancer until I was 18

#3 My shoe collection rivals Sarah Jessica Parker's in Sex and the City

#2 I will tell you if you tell me something interesting about yourself in your email.

Okay this is the "tell!"

It is a well-known fact that most men don't read most profiles unless they are seriously screening for a mate. Many men just look at the pictures and send you winks or quick emails saying things like, "Wow!" "You're beautiful!" Or "Great smile!" (Don't! If you're going to interact with someone, make it meaningful.)

Other men take the time to write something witty or interesting letting me know they've read my profile. Please do the same when you write to someone who captures your interest.

Whose response do you think will elicit more interest from me?

I know if a man has read my profile when he writes to me and tells me something interesting about himself and asks for my number two!

This does several things for me. First, I get to learn an interesting fact that I probably would not have learned otherwise, and I now know this guy a bit better. This will probably make him more interesting to me. Second, I can tell if he's writing because he's interested in me as a person, or just because he liked my picture.

Hopefully it's both!

Additionally, this paragraph allows me to be witty, flirty, and lets the guy know that I'm really into shoes!

The challenge for you is to come up with your number one and number three. After all, don't you want to be appreciated as a person as well as for your looks? Plus—a guy who is more serious about looking for a relationship actually reads profiles. If he's a serial dater he might not take the time.

Paragraph 6:

My perfect match is a man who is a take-charge kind of guy—from planning a date or our next get-away to fixing a lamp (or, finding someone who does!). You are comfortable making decisions and taking action - and, occasionally, accepting some input. Keeping (or getting) in shape and being healthy is a priority for you. You also know that confidence is sexy. You are cultured, enjoy traveling, are generous of spirit and have a positive outlook. You are playful and adventurous. You have your feet firmly planted on the ground and your imagination is soaring like a kite! You have an even temper, are patient, honest, ethical, and affectionate. You also understand the value of getting to know someone before jumping into a relationship. (I know. You're thinking that I don't ask for much, but I am also offering a great deal!!!) If you are this man, I'd love to hear from you ... and, maybe, I will tell you my # 2!

What are you looking for in a man? Tell him. This way you're also telling all those who aren't what you're looking for not to bother. Yes, some will still try. But generally, your wording becomes a powerful tool for culling through the sea of endless possibilities.

There you have it. That's mine.

When I first wrote it I thought perhaps it was a little long, but I garnered a lot of replies. Yours doesn't have to be this long. And it doesn't have to include everything mine does. Your words are yours—as unique as you are. Just make sure they serve three functions: to tell, lure, and cull.

CHAPTER 8: EXERCISES

Exercise: Your Tagline

This one's easier than it may seem at first.

Ask yourself what you want in life. Write your answer down.

If your answer is something like, "To be rich," get more specific.

Why do you want to be rich? What would you do with the money? Would you travel? If so, write, "I live to see the world."

Do you want "To live in a cabin on a mountaintop?" Why? What would you do there? Maybe the real answer is "I want to be close to nature and do yoga." Then your tagline might be something like, "Tranquility. Serenity. Nature."

There are no right or wrong answers. You're just trying to explain what drives you, and what you want your lifetime companion to share.

Exercise: The Profile Checklist

Ultimately, your profile needs to sound like you. But use this checklist to make sure it includes all the things you want to say.

(Character) What would your friends say (or you wish they would) about what you're like as a person. Are you loyal? Friendly? Smart? Helpful? Dedicated?

(Qualities) What is your personality like? Cheerful? Sensitive? Happy? Thoughtful? Funny? If you like to laugh and often do, that's worth noting.

(Hobbies and activities) What do you like to do? Cook? Go to movies? Paint? Ride horses?

(Interests) Do you like motorcycles or opera? NASCAR or ballet? All of them? Interests are similar to activities, except that you don't necessarily do them all the time.

(Passions) What are the things that drive you, or that you feel strongly about? Your work? Travel? Music? (Do you play an instrument regularly? Live to go to concerts?) Are you passionate about your religion? Anything that motivates you, defines you, thrills you, fulfills you, or that you couldn't imagine doing without…. describe.

(Dislikes) If you don't like sports, books, dogs, kids etc. make sure to let people know. It's only fair, and it will keep you from getting involved with someone with a dogsled team if you're allergic.

(Etc.) What else is interesting about you? What else should someone know? "I recently moved from …" or "I travel frequently for work" are important. As is something like, "I'm in a wheelchair, but I don't let that stop me."

(Your ideal match) What are you looking for? What are some deal-breakers in categories that haven't yet been discussed?

(Your "tell") You can use my "Three things about me" trick, or come up with your own. Either way, include something that he'll respond to that lets you know if he's read your whole profile or not.

Use this list to guide you in writing your profile. After you've written it, get a friend to proofread it. Make any necessary changes and the post your profile on your favorite sites. Don't be afraid! If you change your mind and want to add something or take something out, you always can.

I suggest using at least one of the two large sites that require profiles, such as Match.com and eHarmony, because they have the largest number of members. (I used both.) Then choose one or two other sites, depending on how much time you have to monitor your replies.

CHAPTER NINE

Marco? ... Polo!

Online dating is a two-way street. You don't just post your profile online and wait to be picked up like a box of cookies off a grocery store shelf.

Cyber-dating allows you to be an active participant—you get to look for him, too. But, to find him, you need to have the right skills. Otherwise, it's like looking for a starfish in an endless sea of possibilities.

Let's talk about how to harness the power of the dating services' computers to work for you.

The Formulas for Love

Algorithms are the new "matchmakers" in the world of online dating. Each site creates it's own algorithm or formula that is performed by its computer in a prescribed sequence to find your matches. OkCupid will use a different algorithm than Match.com because each has a different philosophy about what makes a good match.

So each site uses its proprietary mathematical formula to sift, sort, and pair up potential couples.

eHarmony talks about its trademarked "29 Dimensions of Compatibility", derived from a cross-matching of the responses to its extensive initial survey.

OKCupid offers a lengthy description of its algorithm on its website, explaining how it weights and compares the answers you give, the ones you tell it you want your ideal mate to give, the ones a potential match gives, and how important each of you said the answer is to you.

Most online dating sites don't give the specifics about their algorithm. But generally, you tell the site about yourself and what you're looking for (search variables) and the service's algorithm selects people who match your criteria.

A lot depends on you. Don't just rely on the matches that they send you. Be proactive. You can create your own search algorithm, too!

For example, on Match.com you can narrow the field of prospects by using the search function to find exactly the person you want.

If you want someone who has a graduate level college degree, earns over $150,000, lives within ten miles of your home, and is a non-smoker, you can find him! Just go into the search area and choose each of the variables. If you want to narrow the search down further by choosing his religion, height, body type, and smoking status, just keep adding variables to the search. Remember to save your search criteria so that next time you look, you don't have to start over again.

You can let the site find matches for you using its own algorithm, and you can additionally find matches using your own. The accuracy and effectiveness of a site's algorithm has a direct correlation to your efforts and honesty. The more information you give, the more information the algorithm has to work with. The more you tell it about what you're looking for, the better it can narrow the field to offer you the most likely candidates.

You have to know yourself and what you want in order to direct the search and answer the questions. So refer to all of the insights and lists you made as you went through the previous chapters of *It's a Match*. Ideally, these can be collected, or contained in a single notebook.

The algorithms begin the sifting process the instant you answer any of the questions—usually in your profile.

Age range? Tell Match.com you want a man between 35 and 49 and that cuts the list by more than 60 %.

Type in that you want someone within 50 miles of your zip code and bingo! Depending on where you live, that can bring the number of potential matches down to anywhere from several thousand to the hundreds—or less, if you live in a more remote area.

The more questions you answer, the narrower the focus becomes.

You want someone over six feet tall? Or under five feet? Snip, snip. Body type "athletic" or "a few extra pounds"? Fewer still.

Depending on the dating site, you can narrow down the possibilities even further with answers about religion, political views, favorite activities, and more.

The point is, the more specific and honest you are with your answers, the more you can fine-tune your results. The more time that you invest in the beginning, the more the efficient the process.

The Power of the Process

Both the search process and the culling process require a daily time commitment. Plus, each time you join a new site, you must invest the time and effort required to answer all their questions, complete your profile for their service, and upload your pictures. Don't join a new service if you're not willing to do this. But, once you do put in this initial effort, know that the system will be set to bring you a better selection of potential matches.

Before you start the process of online dating, you have to decide that this is going to be a priority in your life. After all, you're trying to find your lifetime partner. You have to treat the search and culling process as though it was "work" or any other priority in your life. If you want to find Mr. Right for You, you have to make the space and the time.

I've had clients tell me that finding "The One" is a top priority, but they have too little time. I ask them to list their daily activities and to list, next to the activity, the percentage of their day that this activity uses. (Your activities have to add up to 100%.)

If you say that finding lasting love is your priority, but your days are filled with so many other activities that it's difficult for you to find one hour per day to devote to finding lasting love, this indicates several things.

First, your activities do not reflect your priorities, so you need to see which activities you can cut out or reduce. Does the percentage of time you spend on each activity reflect your priorities?

Second, if you're unwilling to make room in your life to find your life partner, then it's time to examine if you have any limiting beliefs about dating or finding love. If this is the case, I suggest you revisit the chapter on limiting beliefs.

Your actions should be congruent with your priorities and your words. If there is dissonance or incongruity, you need to become a neutral observer of your own psyche in order to figure out what is interfering with your achieving your goals.

Refining Your Search

You can increase the accuracy of a site's algorithm by evaluating the matches that they send to you. If you find yourself wondering how on earth the site matched you up with "that man," it's time to go back to your profile and review your answers. Perhaps you have to refine the parameters about what you really want.

Additionally, Match.com, Zoosk, and others will send you matches every day. You have the opportunity to evaluate each one by saying "yes" or "no" or "maybe." Take the time to look at each one and answer because this helps their internal algorithms to get better at finding the right match for you.

If you invest your time, the process works. According to a recent survey by the prestigious Pew Research Center, "The proportion of Americans who say that they met their current partner online has doubled in the last eight years."

They add that, "Fully 34% of Americans who are in a committed relationship and have used online dating sites or dating apps in the past, say that they met their spouse or partner online." That's one in every three couples! Becoming one of them, though, takes both skill and work.

Know What You Want

The key to success lies in knowing what you're looking for. It's like a road trip. If you don't know where you're going, you can end up anywhere. That's why you made all those lists in the earlier chapters. They can serve as your roadmap. You're aiming for a Level III or Level IV match, your Mr. Right for You. By now you should have a pretty good idea of what he looks like.

His pictures and his profile are your guideposts. They're full of signs and clues. Some are intentional: the things he wants you to know. Other signs and clues may reveal things he does *not* want you to know, such as deal breakers.

Almost every dating site includes some additional information beyond the photos. This might be his age, height, weight, or hobbies. It might be all of the above. Or more. How he answers each question will give you valuable insights, which will serve to weed out the matches that don't meet your criteria.

The dating service's algorithms have hopefully already culled the through the possibilities to deliver some of the better candidates to you. Most sites, though, either by design or by defect, offer a wider range of candidates who might be slightly outside of your stated parameters. It's up to you to do the rest of the culling by comparing each "match" with the list of qualities that are important to you in a mate.

If you are a recovering alcoholic, you might want someone who answers the question about how much they drink with "Never." But the service might offer someone who says "Rarely" because the rest of his answers line up so well with yours.

If you're six feet tall, dating a guy who's five-foot-three might be a deal breaker for you. You might tell the service you don't want anyone under five-foot-eleven. But, again, a guy whose answers align magnificently with yours in every other way might turn up in your inbox even if he's only five-foot-nine. If height really is a deal breaker, just ignore this guy and move on.

Only you know your final answer.

Please note that there are additional things to watch for—beyond the deal breakers. You don't have to be a detective to spot them, but you do have to be alert.

According to Pew, "Half (54%) of online daters have felt that *someone else seriously misrepresented themselves in their profile.*" And, more seriously, some 42% of female online daters ... "have been *contacted by someone through an online dating site or app in a way that made them feel harassed or uncomfortable.*"

It's worth highlighting that the survey doesn't say half the online daters "misrepresented" themselves. It says, "*seriously* misrepresented." So these weren't the simple fibs of shaving off a few pounds or adding an inch to their height. These were cases of substantial fraud. These were fabrications from whole cloth, aimed at deliberate deceit.

It's a cyber jungle out there. It's up to you to *not* fall prey. At the same time, you shouldn't always stay out of the woods because you might encounter a bear on your walk. You should remain alert and take reasonable precautions.

His Screen Name

His screen name may give you indications about his personality. The same rules that helped you choose yours, also apply to him. Intentionally or not, the names "BoyToy," "PrinceCharming," or "Sarge" tell you more than a little something about him.

Actually, his screen name can tell you a lot more than he—or you—realize. It's the equivalent of a Rorschach test that reveals his personality. He may have agonized over picking the right screen name for hours or days, hoping to come up with a result that is clever, memorable, and unique. Just like you did.

If that's the case, he is intentionally trying to give you insight into how he sees himself.

If he didn't come up with a great screen name, and just put down whatever popped into his mind—that tells you just as much. Analyzing someone's screen name is similar in some ways to the free-association or word-association personality tests that psychologists use to determine how patients think about themselves or others.

If he uses "D1UWant," "AGoodThing," or "DrmComTrue," that says—or screams!—that he thinks more about himself than he's ever likely to think of you. "SayYes," "FunForYou," or "IMDPrince" are signs of a potential serial dater looking for a fling.

Your screen name is your "brand." His is his. If he wants to be known as "FastandFurious" let him. It doesn't mean you want him to think of you as "NotTooBright."

It's All "About Me"

The other items—his tagline, "About Me" and his "Idea of a Perfect Date"— each deserve scrutiny, as well. Just like yours, what he didn't answer can say just as much about him as what he did.

Beyond the obvious things like height or age, many sites include questions that are designed to reveal his personality and his purpose.

What Kind of Relationship Is He Looking For?

Some sites have a category called "I'm Looking For..." or something similar. The options range from "casual dating" to a "long-term relationship."

Guess what? Most men will tell you exactly what they want. If he says "casual relationship," he means it. If you're looking for a long-term relationship and he's looking for sex, don't blame him if it doesn't work out.

You're not looking to take on a project, or a challenge to try to convince a perpetual bachelor to change his mind. You want someone who is looking for his mate, not a date. Your Level III or Level IV match will be looking for the same thing you are: a committed, lasting relationship.

Don't think he's confused when he's actually just being honest with you. Unless he says he's looking for a long-term relationship, he's not looking for a long-term relationship. He didn't miss the question or skip over it. By not checking the box next to "committed relationship" he's already told you up front that this never will be.

Now he might say that he's looking for friendship, casual dating, a short-term relationship, *and* a long-term relationship. Chances are he's still trying to be honest. If that's the case, he might be listing everything as a way of saying he's not in a hurry, and he believes that if things don't work out you can still be friends.

On the other hand, listing all the possibilities might be a serial dater's way of casting a wider net. Serial daters are men who always need to have dates. Maybe they don't want to be alone, but are afraid of commitment. Who knows? Perhaps they have unhealed wounds from past experiences, and are unwilling to commit to marriage.

Many men are not willing to commit to marriage until they feel established in their careers, and their finances are at a level where they feel comfortable being partially responsible for another person. In Western culture, men often equate their masculinity with their job, and their financial ability to take care of someone. Of course our job is to take care of ourselves, so we're not looking for a caretaker. But many men still have this unconscious drive and need.

His reason for being a serial dater doesn't matter. He's looking for a date, not a mate. And you're not going to change that.

(If this is you, perhaps it's time to deal with any limiting beliefs, or heal emotional traumas from prior relationships. At the very least, you will be happier because you can make decisions from an empowered, healthy place instead of from a place of need or fear.)

A serial dater might check off all the relationship boxes so he can cover all the bases. He figures that if you're looking for casual sex, he won't scare you away by making you think he'll be clingy. And if you're looking for a lifetime commitment, he wants you to think that that's a possibility. Trust me, if he's looking for a mate, he won't waste his time looking for friends.

The bottom line is, you have to read all his answers carefully, and take whatever you read with a grain of salt. Compare how he answers the questions with whatever he says in his profile. As we'll cover in the next chapter, the words he uses there will help you determine what he means.

If you choose to move this man onto your list of potential candidates to get to know further, you might want to ask for clarification during the initial email or call. You might say something along the lines of, "I see that you're looking for anyone, from a friend to a committed relationship. Tell me about that." If he gives you an answer along the lines of, "Someday if I meet the right person..." he's telling you that he's not ready now.

When you talk to a man, try to find out his relationship pattern. Does he date a woman for a few years before moving on to the next one? Then he's a serial monogamist, and not for you.

His Relationship Status

Another category that tells you a lot about a man is his "Relationship Status."

Currently Separated

I made the choice not to date men who are "currently separated" because they're technically still in a relationship. He may not think of it that way, and it may not sound like he is, but he is.

Psychologists have found that there is an actual emotional shift that occurs when a man gets that divorce paper. You can be separated 35 years; it doesn't matter. The moment he gets that paper, he will experience an emotional shift which will affect the way he thinks and acts.

Even if he's been "currently separated" for three years and is involved in a protracted negotiation, he's still not 100 % emotionally available. He's still tied to that negotiation. And if he's going through a nasty divorce, he will associate you with those emotions because you were with him during the process.

Besides, why would you want to be involved in the worst part of his life, where he has to be feeling terrible about relationships because he's still negotiating with his spouse and feeling the weight of his marital failure?

If you choose to date someone who is close to finalizing his divorce, don't fall into the trap of discussing the negotiations or the process with him. Let your time with him be about romance and fun.

Divorced

Frankly, my general rule of thumb is that if you're looking for a committed relationship you should not date anybody who has not been legally divorced for at least one year.

Many men and women who are recently divorced go through what I call the "candy store" phase. They want to see and sample what's out there. They want to check out what they've been missing. So they go sampling. The world is a candy store and they want to try *all* the candy.

There are other recent divorcees, particularly the ones whose spouses left them, who will try to jump into another relationship out of need. These are not in a good place to begin another relationship, either. You can spot these because they will usually become clingy and will try to move the relationship too quickly. They will act with the new partner as they acted with their spouse. This will feel like a false intimacy to you. They will try to move from their marital home to yours. They are looking for a replacement.

Widower

If he's a widower, it's important to find out how long ago he lost his spouse. It takes time to go through the grieving process. The longer he was married, the longer it may take him to grieve his loss. Everybody is different, but you want to feel that enough time has elapsed and he's really ready for a new relationship and not just a replacement.

If his house is still full of her pictures and he has not changed anything in order to preserve things the way they were, he's not ready to move on. However if he has children, it would be natural that he would want pictures of their mother in their bedrooms.

Until a person is done with their grieving process, they're not emotionally available for a new relationship. A widower still going through the grieving process would probably be better served by seeking the help of a grief counselor so that he can move through the process of healing before he starts dating.

Never married

Be wary of this status, unless he's someone in his twenties or thirties. If a man (or a woman) is over forty and lists their status as "never married," I see a red flag. I start to think that they may have commitment issues, because in our culture, most people have been married by the time that they are forty.

Let me remind you: you're not looking for another Mr. I Should Have Known Better. You're looking for a long-term relationship. You're likely going to be wasting your time with this one. He may say he wants a lasting relationship, but his track record says otherwise.

Another variation of someone with commitment issues is what I call a "serial monogamist." I have a friend like that. He's been divorced since his late twenties and he's in his late fifties now. He's told me, "I'm never getting married again." But he never tells his dates that.

He goes from long-term relationship to long-term relationship, luring women by leading them to believe that maybe *she* will be the one who will become his last lifetime relationship. The difference between him and a serial dater is that serial daters go for one-night stands, two-night stands, or maybe a couple of weeks in a relationship. My friend has a history of many five-year relationships.

In the end, these five-year relationships fail because he refuses to commit to marriage. Meanwhile, another woman has wasted five years of her life. In between relationships, he finds dates using several sites. He doesn't like to eat alone, so he always has a dinner date.

That's great for him, but if you're not willing to spend another four or five years of your life in a doomed relationship, then that might not work for you. Again, look at what a man does, not what he says. Get his relationship history.

By the way, I know a number of women who are serial monogamists as well, and who have a fear of commitment. The "never married by age forty" rule also applies for men who are looking at women who have never been married.

Salary

Some sites ask you to list your salary. They also ask you to select for his salary range. It's important for you to be honest. If you are making $25,000 per year and you state that you earn $100,000, he or she will soon figure out the truth by observing your lifestyle. All relationships are based on trust. Your potential Mr. Right will become Mr. So Long, if he finds out you're lying.

If you really earn $25,000, isn't it better that your potential partner knows this up front, so that he or she can tailor their expectations of the activities that you can share together?

It might seem to you like this question is prying or inappropriate. It's not. Salary is a powerful socioeconomic factor, which can have a strong impact on a relationship. As I mentioned before, if he makes $150,000-plus and you make $25,000 or less, or vice versa, there's not only a major difference in income, there's a major difference in lifestyle. And the bigger the difference in your lifestyles, the less likely you are to have a significant number of shared interests, values, or educational background.

You might have a lot in common, but the odds are you won't.

Drinks

"Never" is often a code word. It could mean, "I don't drink because I don't like it." But it could also be a way of saying, "I don't drink because it's against my religion" or "I am a recovering alcoholic."

If someone is a recovering alcoholic, that's a wonderful thing for him, especially if he's doing his work and moving forward positively. But it might not be so wonderful for you. One issue, as I mentioned before, is that if you're somebody who grew up in a family of alcoholics, this man might not be the match for you because any hint of an impending relapse might trigger powerful, painful memories.

A recovering alcoholic is always, first and foremost, an alcoholic. For him (or, her) being around alcohol is always challenge at some level or other. If you're not willing to give up your nightly glass of wine or nights out at the club, this person might not be a good match for you. In order for an alcoholic to remain sober, he needs to avoid people, places, and things where alcohol is served or that he associates with alcohol. As a supportive partner, you need to be willing to understand this and comply.

If you're a recovering alcoholic you can use this search variable to find other recovering alcoholics, or people who don't like to drink, and who would be a good match for you. This gives you a great way to meet potential mates outside of the AA and NA meeting rooms. It expands your universe of potential mates.

Religion

Some sites call this category "Faith." Other sites might use other wording. But the point, and its importance, is always the same.

Faith is a core value for some. But not everyone feels similarly about the role of faith or religion. The answer "Christian/Protestant" can mean a lot of different things. By itself, it tells you little about the intensity of a potential mate's religious feelings.

There are affinity-dating sites designed specifically for Christians, Jews, Muslims, and LDS just to name some options. But deeply religious people use all kinds of dating sites.

So someone who answers "Jewish" to this question might be strongly observant or merely casual in his practice. Those who are strongly observant should mention it in their profile, as you should in yours. This advice works for every religion.

"Spiritual but not religious" usually indicates just that. This category covers those who hold a belief in a higher power, but who don't attend religious services regularly, or may not be a member of any particular faith. These people are generally open to other people's religious practices, as long as you don't impose your beliefs on them.

Ideally, someone who feels strongly about their religion will sprinkle a few clues about this in theirs profile. That doesn't always happen, but you might very well find hints in other areas. He or she might list the New Testament or *Heaven is for Real* under "Last Book Read." Or *Left Behind or Son of God* under "Favorite Movies."

If you don't see any of those clues, this might mean that you are reading the profile of someone who is not extremely passionate about their religion or faith. If *you* feel strongly about your religious practice, and he seems like someone you want to know better, then you probably want to make a note to follow up on this in conversation.

Books, Movies, Music, and More

Some dating services ask for other information that doesn't serve as a filter for the matching algorithm, but which will give you valuable clues regarding compatibility. These might be as obvious as a shared interest in a book genre or author, a shared favorite movie or actor, or a song or band. Or perhaps you learn important info from how many times a week the person exercises, or that you both like concerts or cooking.

Use this information as a peek into his personality.

Exercise: Analyze His Profile

The "About Me" Scorecard

After you've decided that you like one of the potential matches offered by a dating service, you'll want to really examine the "About Me" information to see if he's worth getting to know better.

First, look closely for any deal breakers. Is his relationship status "currently separated" or "never married" even though you marked that you wanted those men filtered out? Does he "smoke socially" and you're allergic? Did he mark every possible option under "I'm Looking For..." including "casual dating"?

If you see true deal breakers, there's no need to go further. Forget this profile and move on.

Second, if there are no true deal breakers, then look for "red flags." These are things like "has children who sometimes live at home"— info that clues you into the reality that there are potential pitfalls you need to check for and clarify before you make your final decision. You want to note everything that stands out, so you can remember to ask the right questions during your first or second phone call, or on your first date.

Third, look for shared interests. Note any of the obvious shared interests, like that you both love the same celebrity chef's TV show. Then look for the less obvious shared interests. Maybe you didn't list the same book as your favorite, but you both love reading the same author or genre.

Find as many shared interests as possible. These will give you things to talk about during your initial conversations, if you decide that there's enough to interest you.

If this candidate seems really interesting, add him to your "potential mate" file so that you have information about him when you are in that first call. I actually printed out people's profile pages to put in my files, and I added my handwritten notes directly onto this page. Add to your notes after every interaction with him.

If you disqualify him or her at any point in the process, put the notes in a file labeled "No Go." This trick can save you time, especially if you run across this person in the future and have forgotten why you passed this one by.

The Adventurer: If most of his pictures are of him enjoying base-jumping and bullfighting, ask yourself if that's what you want. An adrenaline junkie may be fun for a date, but a steady diet of danger might reveal that he's the kind of man who constantly wants new thrills—and new women. Even if he's a monogamous adventurer, he's going to want someone who can keep up and join him in the fun.

Other clues to his habits and personality might be if he's always holding a drink, or if he's always shirtless, or if he has several photos of himself astride his Harley.

I know a woman whose Facebook pictures always show her in bars or at the beach with a drink. These are true reflections of what she likes to do. The same thing holds true with the pictures that he chooses to post on his profile.

Since a person's profile and their pictures are basically an ad, what is he trying to sell?

The Little (Or Not So Little) Things

You can spot a lot in the details. Look at whom he's with, and what you see in the background. Garbage on the bedroom floor says one thing, but an immaculate background can be just as significant.

Is every "fun" shot taken in a casino? It doesn't matter whether he has his hand on the slot machine handle or not. The setting tells you what he likes. Mr. Always at the Casino loves gambling. The golfer loves golf. Beware! He may have already found the love of his life. It's going to be hard for you to compete. Maybe he's looking for a mate who can play with him. Or, he may not know it, but he may *not* really be looking for a mate; maybe he just wants a playmate who enjoys doing the same thing.

Also, do his pictures match what the profile says? Are there inconsistencies? Does he say that he values neatness, yet his selfie shows that his room has stacks of dirty clothes?

Look for Discrepancies

If his photos show him riding a motorcycle, wearing his favorite team's jersey at a sports bar with friends, paddle-boarding and fishing, that's great. This will make perfect sense if he also talks about being active and enjoying the outdoors in his profile.

If, however, he has those same pictures and his profile talks about loving opera, cooking gourmet meals, and quiet evenings at home with the "right" woman, and he makes no mention of loving sports, there's a discrepancy.

Why? The words should match the actions (or the pictures.)

The guy in the photographs is active, outdoorsy, and physical. The guy in the profile is reserved, cultured, and tranquil. He might be both, but it's doubtful. If he never mentions the active guy in his profile, then he's either trying to be someone he's not, or he's hoping that you'll think he is.

Too Much of a Good Thing

Another thing that I look for is if someone is trying too hard to portray a certain image. If a person looks too good to be true, well... you know.

An emotional predator trolling for a sex partner wants to appeal to the kind of woman who is looking for a prince to come and rescue her. He might have twenty pictures of his palatial country home (implying that he also has a city home), his many prize-winning horses, and his sailboat anchored serenely on an azure sea. He also includes pictures of his grandchildren and adult children (at the very least he shows bad judgment in putting these pictures on his site). He wants you to see that he's a family man. (Someone actually did this. You can't make this stuff up!)

A lot of emotional predators want a woman who will give herself quickly. To get this, the emotional predators will build a profile that plays to her needs and desires. Even a woman who isn't searching for her Prince Charming, or looking to be rescued, may be attracted to the fairy tale fantasy of a wealthy, cultured man who will whisk her off to his mansion.

Wealthy and not-so-wealthy predators know this. Their profiles may include photos of sunsets by their lakeside or beachside mansions, in order show you the dream setting for the fairy tale they're promising. Plus you'll get to see how wealthy they are. Remember, fairy tales only exist in books.

There is absolutely no reason for a man to post a parade of pictures straight out of "Lifestyles of the Rich and Famous" unless he's deliberately trying to impress you with how much he has—or supposedly has. Wealthy men or women who are looking for a mate tend play down their possessions, because they want someone to choose them for the person they are, not for the possessions they have. If they are flaunting riches online, it's usually meant as bait.

Women who are trying to lure in wealthy or semi-wealthy men may project a different type of fairytale. They usually play up how sexually adventurous they are, or how they'll be submissive or act like a geisha to treat their man "right"—or some variation of this. They might include a line such as, "princess looking for her prince."

Another type of profile meant to lure in older wealthy men is of a young woman who's looking for someone to take care of all of her needs. She promises to take care of all of his needs. She's telling you exactly what she wants. Remember, if it's too good to be true...

A Picture is Worth a Thousand Words

A picture really is worth a thousand words if it gives you important info about the value, or deal breaker aspects, of a potential romantic partner. His pictures are your windows into the parts of his life that he wants you to see. But they can reveal much more, including the things that he might *not* want you to suspect.

Presumably he put the same care into picking his pictures and writing his profile as you did. Then, again, maybe not.

Either way, his photos and profile offer insights into what he's *really* like. You can learn a lot about a person by carefully evaluating each picture, noting what he's doing and what you can see in each of them. Don't just focus on looking at *him*. Look at every inch of every frame. Analyze everything you see.

Me Me Me

It's great that he has enough pictures to show you that he's multifaceted. You know—one of him playing tennis, another of him laughing with friends, at work, playing guitar or singing karaoke, or in front of the Washington Square arch.

That shows he's a man of varied interests, has friends, and likes to have fun.

The same if it's pictures of him on the dock holding a prize winning marlin, putting another log on a campfire, skiing, or cooking in an apron with the words "Hot Stuff" written across his chest. Varied interests, he's fun, and he can catch it and cook it, too.

But if he's posted 25 or 50 pictures of himself smiling into a mirror, trying on different hats, driving his Porsche, or just clearly posing for the camera, beware. Take this as a clue that he's more into himself than he'll ever be into you. Ten pictures should be enough for someone to show you who they are. Make the same interpretation of the woman who has twenty pictures of herself—many in sex kitten poses.

CHAPTER 9: EXERCISE

Exercise: Analyze His Photos

A picture really is worth a thousand words. And many of them are in code. Here's a checklist to help you decipher what he's really telling you.

How many pictures are there? If there's just one, what's he hiding? Five to ten pictures is in the good range. Twenty-five is too many—is he too self-absorbed?

What's in the background?

If he's washing his car, what do you see behind him? Is the lawn trimmed or full of weeds and dirt? Are there rusty cars parked on the grass? Is the house nice or falling down?

If he's showing his bedroom, is the room clean or strewn with piles of dirty laundry? Is the bed made? Are there stuffed animals? Whips and chains?

Who's in the photo with him?

Dogs? Cats? Anacondas? Celebrities? Toothless buddies? (In every one?!)

Kids? (And does his profile say he has kids or not?)

What is he wearing?

Is he wearing the same outfit in every photo? Is he always shirtless? Or always in a suit? What do his clothes tell you? Is he fashionable (maybe too much so?) Stuck in the '80s? Are his clothes clean and well kept, or is his idea of getting dressed up to be wearing a clean T-shirt?

What's the setting? How many different settings are there? If he's always in a bar, you can guess that he expects you to be in a bar, too. The same with a baseball stadium, a golf course, or any place else that shows up repeatedly.

What is he doing in his pictures? Look for themes and range.

Is he spearfishing, bow hunting, or duck hunting? Are you ready to go to the bathroom in the woods? Or to spend every weekend alone?

Is he rock climbing in one picture, feeding the homeless in another, and playing bass in a band in the next? That's a pretty full, well-rounded life. Are you interested in that?

How many of his activities/interests do you share? How many do you like? How many do you dislike? Are any of them deal breakers? If he's working on an oil painting or playing violin and you love the arts, that's a good thing. Again, look for themes.

If he's wrestling alligators in one photo, sky diving in another, rappelling into an active volcano in yet another, he's an Adventurer or an adrenaline junkie.

If he's posing coyly in picture after picture after picture... he's probably a narcissist.

If every picture is taken in a bar, he's a partier (and, possibly, a drunk).

Is every picture from the inside of a casino? Think gambler.

And so on. If the overall vibe in the photos is what you like, good. If it's not, don't think he's ever going to give up those activities, interests, or things for you. He might, for a while, but he won't be happy about it. And this is unlikely to be a Level III or Level IV match.

The purpose of this exercise is to make sure that you *really* study his or her pictures, and look at them for more than how cute his eyes crinkle when he smiles. You know you liked how he looked; that's why you're taking your time to look more closely.

So do.

Very closely.

CHAPTER TEN

Reading Between His Lines

Your profile is important. So is his. His photos give you a look at his personality. His profile gives you an x-ray. It's a chance to see what's behind his eyes, if you know how to really read it.

What he says in it tells you a lot. So does what he doesn't.

You have to analyze his profile in context with his pictures and your conversations. You have to observe everything. Do the words in his profile match with what the pictures show? Are there inconsistencies? What is the tone of his profile? Is he upbeat and outgoing? Or is he bitter and plays the victim? Does he express himself cohesively?

Since the profile is basically an ad, what is he trying to sell? And, naturally, if it sounds too good to be true...

So, what do you look for?

The Three C's: Clues. Copycats. And Code words.

Size Matters

One of the first things I notice is how much thought he put into writing his profile. Men are not like women. He probably won't put as much time and thought into his profile as we put into ours. But a man who is serious about finding a woman will put some effort into it.

So that's a clue: If he has a five-line profile, he's probably just looking for a date, not a relationship. That may not always be the case. It may be that he's just not very good at expressing himself. But even a guy who's shy or embarrassed to talk about himself, will probably still have plenty to say about the woman he's looking for.

That's why the length of his profile matters. A short profile signals that he's casting a net and hoping to haul in whatever he can—and probably as many as he can.

Example: "Life is better when we're together. I'm looking for a special someone. Is it you?"

This tells me he is either a desperately lonely man, career serial dater, or someone still going through the candy store phase and hoping to sample everything sweet that he can.

Honestly, he may as well have written, "If you have a pulse, please reply."

Even if he's none of the above, at the very least his words should make you wonder: *If that's all the effort he's willing to put into his search, how important is the search for him?*

So, men, please put some thought and effort into your profile. At the very least, we women will know that you're really looking for Ms. Right for You, not Ms. Right Now. Also, the more clues you give a woman, the more likely she'll be to view you as a person, instead of just "Another One."

Warning: Under Repair

Sometimes, men will talk about their past relationships.

"I just broke up with the most wonderful woman and am now looking for someone else." (Please, don't. Your profile and the site is not the place for group therapy.)

That to me says, "I'm not over her yet."

There are other ways he might put these facts: "Currently separated after thirteen great years..." Or "Can you fill the hole in my heart?"

Remember, you're not Florence Nightingale. He's not ready. That's all there is to it. Taking on a project requires a lot of work, and it rarely turns into a Level III or IV Match.

Your Mr. Right won't show up in need of major repairs.

I knew a man whose wife left him. His Facebook page had about 100 pictures of his life with her—a timeline of their relationship. That was all I needed to see. (Once you know his first and last name, it's a good idea to look up his Facebook page, where he's likely to be less censored.) Men and women—does your Facebook page reflect the image you want to portray?)

God, Golf, and Good Time Charlies!

Most men will tell you exactly what they're looking for—sometimes without realizing it.

A Good Time Charlie will say things like, "Wanted: Dance partner. Dinner included." Or, "I hate eating dinner alone. Join me?" He might say, "I'm new in town and looking for someone to show me around."

He's not hiding anything. He didn't say he's looking for someone with whom to share his future. He didn't say he wants a long-term commitment. He said he wants to have dinner with you. And maybe dessert.

He's looking for a date, not a mate.

That may be great, if that's what you're looking for. But if you want commitment, and you see these clues, recognize that he's probably not the one you're looking for.

Big-time sports fans and golfers are not going to hide their passion, either.

Golfers love golf. They love doing it. They love talking about it. And they love having someone to golf with. They'll say: "Let's book our tee time together."

If he plays golf one morning every weekend, that might be a good thing. You can golf with him, or enjoy your own activities while he's out golfing. But, if he golfs every day, he's probably going to want you to be as fervent about golf as he is. If you're not a golfer, you can't fake it. And you're not going to take him away from it— you shouldn't want to. You're not looking for someone to change. You're looking for someone whose interests match yours. On the other hand, if you like a lot of free time to do your own activities, he might be the one for you.

The same holds true with a real sports fan. It doesn't matter if he's into NASCAR, football, hockey, cricket or something else. A diehard fan is fan-atical. A sports fan will often say, flat out, "I'm a Dolphins fan. If you are, too, let's tailgate.", I've seen some say, "Yankees fans need not reply. This is Red Sox territory."

If that's what you like (and you like the same teams), great! But if you don't like wearing a team jersey and being surrounded by screaming people, keep searching. At the very least, expect him to be glued to the television when his team plays.

We covered the issue of religion in the previous chapter, but it's worth mentioning again. When a man mentions his beliefs or practices in his actual profile, it's important to him.

If a man says, "My faith is important to me," or "Things I couldn't live without: God," or "I like to start my day by reading the Bible," he's serious about it. If you are, too, that can be wonderful. If a man mentions religion in his profile, he's undoubtedly looking for someone who shares the same beliefs and, usually, with the same intensity.

You'll want to keep that in mind if you decide to reach out to him. And you'll definitely want to make it one of the topics to inquire about early on. Strong religious differences can affect any relationship.

Young at Heart

Ah, to be young again—or, rather, to have someone think I am.

It seems like a lot of men (and, women) think that way. So they trim—or chop—anywhere from a couple of years to a decade or more off of their age. I've had several men lie to me about their ages, by as much as 15 years.

If they lie straight to your face, you know you have a problem. If they tell you something like, "I take a couple of years off my age so that I fall into a slightly younger search range, but I'm really... " or if he tells you before you even ask, then you're okay. He was upfront about it, so I don't consider it a lie. If I have a problem with his actual age, I can decide not to pursue the relationship any further.

Thankfully, the Internet won't just help you find potential matches; it will also help you find out about them. Google search every prospect. Always. Don't wait until you're suspicious. A Google search, as I'll remind you when we talk about the interview process, should be standard operating procedure—before you go on your first date. Also look him up on Facebook and every other social media site you've got.

You never know what you might learn.

Children

Generally, if men have younger kids, they'll have at least some time-sharing with them. As we mentioned previously, you'll probably know that from their brief biographical info, and whether they "sometimes live at home."

What a man says about his children in his profile says a lot about him. He might say, "Doing things with my children is very important to me."

No uncertainty there. You know that if you're going to be in a relationship with this guy, a lot of your activities will be with his children, at some point in your life. If that works for you, that is fabulous. If it doesn't, you've been warned. He's already told you his children are a big part of his life, and that he likes being with them. That's not going to change because he met you.

If you have children of your own this might be a good sign for you. He cares about kids. He likes them. People who like kids tend to like most kids, not just their own. If he likes doing things with his, he'll probably like doing things with yours.

If the kids are similar in age, that's even better. Somebody with children whose ages are similar to yours would probably be a good match.

He might tell you how old they are in his profile, but more often than not he'll say something like "I love coaching my daughter's soccer team." Well, she could be six or sixteen. If you're really interested in him, you'll want to make sure that you ask him the ages of his children in an email or when you first talk on the phone.

Copycats

After you've looked at a few profiles, you'll start to notice that some of them sound similar.

And some sound exactly the same.

Trust me, it's more than a coincidence. It's plagiarism. Copycats literally cut and paste things they think are good in other men's profiles. (Women do this, too. Please, don't!)

At best, copycats lack originality. At worst, they're using other people's profiles as a mask, to hide who they really are. The question then is, why? Perhaps, he's just lazy. Or maybe he's something worse.

The answer is rarely good.

That's why you should hear alarm bells ringing anytime you notice words that sound familiar. If he can't invest the time to be original, he's not seriously looking for a committed relationship. Move on!

Code Words

When a man uses code words, he does it on purpose. They're very different from the clues you can glean from the things he says about his kids, sports, or the movies he likes.

Code words are intended to be subliminal. They're meant to play on your childhood triggers, limiting beliefs, fears, and fantasies.

He might be a serial dater, or just looking to rack up as many sexual encounters as possible. He might be married and looking for a fling. Or he might be much worse.

When a man writes things like "looking for my princess," or "someone to take care of"—beware! That could be a sign of a predator, looking for women to take advantage of, or a serial dater trying to appeal to your fantasies. Most men do not want to take care of someone they have never met. At worst, he's telling you that he does not want an equal relationship. He wants to be a parent.

He could also use code sentences such as, "I like a woman who is adventurous in all areas of her life... I will let you figure that one out.

Prince Dis-Arming

I am most leery of the man who says things like, "I am a very successful, wealthy man, looking for my princess to spoil" or "I am looking for a wonderful woman to share my villa."

He might even show photographs of a lovely country cottage or a chalet overlooking a lake. We discussed him in the previous chapter.

It's a trap.

This is usually a sign of an emotional predator, or somebody looking for a quick weekend jaunt or a one or two-night stand. Truly wealthy men don't advertise their wealth. They're like everyone else—if they're looking for love, they want to be loved for who they are, not for what they have. If a wealthy man or woman is really looking for "the one," he's not going to go dangling his or her assets out there like some kind of lure.

No. Someone who tells you his yacht needs a mate is really just looking to soak you—emotionally or financially.

He's playing to the insecurities and "happily ever after" dreams that many women have. When he writes, "I'm looking for a woman I can spoil," he's trying to attract somebody who wants to be rescued. He's playing to "the princess looking for her prince." Happily ever after only exists in fairy tales—real life is messy.

He wants somebody who's vulnerable and needy.

If he says, "looking to take care of you," he's probably not. Most men aren't looking to take care of someone they don't know. They might eventually want to take care of you, after they fall in love with you. But they're not advertising for all the needy cases out there to "Come to me! I'm a sucker!"

The Not So Fine Print

Be on the lookout for the following phrases:

"Wondering where she is." "When will I meet her?" Or "Am I far too selective?"

(Often as a caption under the first photo of himself.) He presents himself as a romantic, a dreamer, who is looking for "the One." Most men don't write like this. A woman could've written this. This was written to appeal to a certain type of woman. He is also setting you up for the letdown when he doesn't select you. Some women will respond to this as a challenge to become "the One." (Check your limiting beliefs at the door before you proceed.)

> *Here's another one: "I thrive in a lifestyle that has a pace that never bores me."*

Translation: Fasten your seatbelt! He has a high need for adventure. He might be an adrenaline junkie. You'd better be ready for a roller-coaster relationship—literally.

> *"Not out to change anyone and non-controlling."*

Women who seek Prince Charming are used to being controlled by that very prince. Here he tells you he won't do that. But this might just be reverse psychology, and a way to make you let down your guard.

If you discovered you were attracted to rescuer-types when you were cleaning out your closet, you'll want to stay far away from this one. The rescuer usually rescues as a way of controlling. He is usually a co-dependent personality who gives in order to get.

He's probably using this phrase because he's been accused of doing the very same thing.

> *"I enjoy whatever we can do together—watching the Paris lights flicker on the river Seine; cuddling in bed on a rainy day; long walks on the beach. And, oh, did I mention... I have a master's degree in kissing."*

Remember what I said about "too good to be true?" Well, this sure sounds like it. It sounds like he walked out of a Danielle Steel romance novel—but, wait, that's fiction! Why is he trying so hard to lure you in? For what?

"Reality" Checking

Here are some examples of "real" men's profiles. Ok, not real, for legal reasons—but they're variations of the kinds of profiles that are often online.

> *"Hi... It's difficult to talk about myself this way..."*

You're going to see this a lot. Too much. This usually means one of two things, depending on the volume of words that follow. If he's really only written a few sentences, it's quite possibly true that he's shy. If, on the other hand, what comes after that opening could fill a couple shelves at the local library, it's a humble-brag. That's a possible warning sign that he's self-centered and just wants you to believe that he's a nice, shy guy.

> "I like all kinds of music, from Rachmaninoff (Piano Concer-
> to No. 2 in C minor, Op. 18) to the Black Keys (I Got Mine), art
> (Kandinsky), books (Plutarch, Camus, Allende, Voltaire, Bul-
> gakov, Joyce, and Chopra), travel (I did the Iditarod last year
> and spent a month in a yurt in the rain forest canopy the year
> before that), and..."

The fact that he mentions all this lets you know that he has
a wide—and refined—range of taste in music, literature, and
travel destinations. If you want to be with this guy you better
be able to keep up (and, please, look up all his references before you talk to him.) He's trying to weed out the non-
intellectuals and those who lack culture. Or he's just showing
off.

> "I believe the mind is the most sexual organ, and intelligence is
> the greatest aphrodisiac, and that there should be no limits in
> the joining of two bodies, no inhibitions in the joining of two
> souls. I want a passionate playmate, a cerebral confidant, a lov-
> er and a friend."

It's telling when a person relates his sexual preferences in a
profile. Anyone who writes specifically about sex does it because it's very important to him. This man is telling you he is a
very sexual being and he likes creative sex.

When he says, "there should be no limits in the joining of
two bodies," he's telling you that he probably has very exotic
tastes in sex.

And, with the words, "a passionate playmate" he tells you
that he is not looking for a committed long-term relationship.
He's looking for exactly what he says, "a playmate." He wants
someone to explore sex with. It's possible that this man is al-

ready married, or maybe he's a single guy who wants great sex and someone to explore with further... without any commitment. To find out more, let's look for clues in this man's description of the match he's looking for:

Height:
3' 1" (93 cm) to 8' 11" (271 cm)
Body Type:
Slender, About average, Curvy, Athletic or Toned
Ethnicity:
No Preference
Religion:
No Preference
Smoke:
No Preference
Drink:
No Preference
Relationships:
No Preference
Have Kids:
No or Yes and they live away from home

He has no preference in the relationship area. This means he doesn't care if his partner is married, single, divorced, or anything else. But he does state a preference that she not have any children living at home. She must also have a decent body. He doesn't care how much she drinks or anything else about her that would lead us to believe that he cares about who she is as a person.

This is a major red flag profile. I'd say it's pretty obvious that this guy is only looking for a sexual partner.

Here's a totally different kind of profile.

> *"Hi there,*
>
> *"I'm a nice man, looking for a good, smart and down-to-earth lady with family values... who likes to laugh. Life is short. Let's enjoy the moments.*
>
> *I'm looking for someone I can bond with, not only physically but mentally and spiritually as well."*

This is the profile of a man who's actually looking for a relationship. The word "nice" stands out—most men talk about how smart, wealthy, or accomplished they are, or how fit they are. "Nice" shows he's sensitive and considers himself a good person. (So, far, so good.)

So do the clues in the words he uses to describe what he wants in his mate: "family values," "smart and down-to-earth." And "good." The word "good" says a lot. That's an inner quality, a moral quality. And this word says as much about him as it does about the person he's looking for.

> *"I love the water... snorkeling, boating, just being at the beach are things I could never do without. I also like getting dressed up for someplace nice."*

It's pretty clear that you better like water activities, but he also lets you know that you need to also have some range, and you must be able to go from the beach to getting dressed up.

> *"I love kids. I have two I love being with (although they're at that age— their friends get to see them more than I do...) Yours are invited, too!"*

Here the man makes it very clear that his children are very important in his life. He's also letting you know his kids are older, and probably don't live at home most of the time. Also, he's willing to include your children in his life. He's clearly a family man with family values. It's pretty obvious he's looking for a relationship, and probably a serious one, since he's inviting your children into the mix.

> *"If you're looking for an honest, hard-working—and fun (I think)— man, send me a note. Who knows? It just might be right."*

This sounds like the kind of man who's refreshingly straightforward and sincere. The tone of his profile suggests that he's an upbeat person who has worked through his issues.

The "what he likes to do" section provides even more clues about his personality. And, significantly, they jibe perfectly with his profile: "Boating, any time! Walking on the beach, holding hands, kissing, gym, and great movies."

The mention of the beach and boating emphasizes its importance for him, and, if you want to be with him, for you. He also suggests he's a romantic sort with the "holding hands, kissing" reference. Then he lets you know he likes to stay in shape, and he probably also expects this of you.

He supports that even more in his description of what he's looking for in a match:

Height:
5' 0" (91 cm) to 5' 10" (241 cm)
Body Type:
Slender, Athletic and toned
Smoke:

No Way
Drink:
Social Drinker

From my criteria, he gets two thumbs up, with points for sincerity and simplicity. You may be looking for something totally different, but the point is, his profile reveals vast amounts of information about a man—whether he wants it to or not.

Red Flags

There are certain types of men and woman that everyone should avoid. I call them the Red Flags. Here are some descriptions.

The Empty Hole

This person is so needy that he or she is like a bottomless pit. No matter how much you give, it's never enough. This person will give you a lot of attention, at least initially, but they'll demand that you meet all their needs, all the time. They have a victim mentality. They'll become jealous of everyone in your life who takes up your time and attention, including friends and children. This type of man or woman sucks the life out of you. They will hide their neediness initially, and might even seem very giving, until they relax and shows their true colors.

Looking for a Surrogate Mother

He expects you to take over all the tasks his parents did. He expects you to do all the chores, pay all the bills, and make all decisions.

Emotionally Unavailable

This man could be recovering from a bad relationship, married, separated, dating someone else, just recently divorced, or so wounded from his past relationship(s) that he's unwilling to ever get close to someone else again. Or he might be a narcissist. He could tell you something like he is unhappy in his current relationship and trying to get out of it in order to convince you to be his other love interest. This man always has a reason why he can't commit to you and usually will try to string you along with something like, "I will divorce my wife when the kids get out of high school. I promise!" I will spend more time with you after...

Workaholics and Other Addicts

These men are also emotionally unavailable because their first relationship is with their addiction. These are often difficult to detect because they just seem like hard workers, or fun-loving guys, or partiers. Addictions can include gambling, pornography, sex, food, and work. In our society workaholism is socially approved, but the workaholic uses work to avoid intimacy.

The Abusive Person

He or she is usually very attentive and giving in the beginning, but you might get glimpses of a bad temper underneath. As the relationship ensues, this person will start trying to control you, they will blame you for their own bad behavior, shame you, verbally abuse you, demean you, and try to isolate you from your friends and family.

This person's reality will become your reality. They will blame you for all the problems in the relationship. They are never at fault. In fact, they will try to make you feel that you're not good enough, and that you're lucky that they even want you. An abusive person creates this insecurity in you in order to control you. Abusive behavior gets worse over time, and can escalate into hitting and other physical abuse. It's important to recognize that verbal abuse is just as bad as physical abuse.

The Liar

The liar usually gets caught because he or she can't remember what he told you last, they can't recall their own lies. So the important thing is to watch for inconsistencies in the stories they tell. Usually the stories are very elaborate, almost like he or she is trying to defend himself.

When people lie, they often cannot maintain eye contact, they fidget, and they might have defensive postures such as arms crossed over their chest. Remember that every relationship must begin with trust. If your instincts are telling you that there is something wrong with this person, then there probably is.

The Commitment-Phobic Person

One of the biggest signs that you're with a commitment-phobic man is that he is only available when it's convenient for him. This person might cancel the date at the last moment or disappear for long periods of time. In many cases you're not his top priority and he doesn't really care about how you feel.

A surefire sign of the commitment-phobic man is that he has a history of serial dating. He loves the initial rush of a relationship, but once he feels he has conquered the woman, he moves on to his next catch. His cousin, the serial-monogamist, is also commitment-phobic.

The Emotional Predator

He knows women and knows how to spot their weaknesses and target their vulnerabilities. (Likewise, she knows men and knows how to spot their weaknesses and vulnerabilities in order to target him by appealing to these.)

He uses his finely honed skills to target women for sex. He has a sixth sense to detect women who are sexually needy, hurt, lonely, or who have recently broken up with a man. Part of his skill-set is to become whatever the woman needs him to be. He is highly attuned to reading a woman's body language and subtle messages, and uses these to give her exactly what he thinks she needs. He becomes the caretaker of her needs and wounds. But beware—nothing in life is free. He usually extracts his price.

You can safe guard yourself by getting to know a person slowly. Don't allow yourself to be rushed into a relationship. As he earns your trust, tell him more about yourself.

The Financial Predator

These people are a variation on the emotional predator theme. Financial predators use the same techniques as other predators—playing on vulnerabilities and neediness. But they don't care about the sex. They want money. If he starts asking questions or probing about your wealth, your home, or even what type of car you drive—be on the alert. Don't show your wealth or talk about it until you get to know the person. Don't wear ostentatious jewelry on your first several dates.

All these men and women are to be avoided. Unfortunately, many are a combination package. The emotional predator might also be an abuser.

You are particularly at risk if your mother has been in a relationship with these types of men, or if your father has been with these types of women. If anyone in your family has been with this kind of person, you are at heightened risk. If you come from a family in which you were emotionally or physically abused, you are also at heightened risk. I suggest you work with a therapist to heal these wounds.

If you find yourself making excuses for his behavior such as, "All the good ones are taken," or "He's just like all the men in my family," or (believe it or not, I've heard this one, too), "I'm just staying until someone better comes along," then you need to take a step back and ask yourself what is it about you that makes you think that you deserve this.

It's important for you to see these problematic behaviors for what they are, and not try to minimize them. Do not believe a man when he says he'll do better, or he will try harder, or he will stop drinking so much. Words are cheap.

Watch his actions, not his words! If what he says and does do not match, run!

And don't be foolish enough to think that you're powerful enough or special enough to change him. Do not let your fear of being alone cause you to accept the unacceptable. Run! Cut your losses. No matter how long you've been with him. Move on!

Toxic Types

Toxic Types are just as bad. Those are the ones that set off our childhood triggers. The rule here is simple: Avoid them.

When I was cleaning out my closet and examining my past relationships, I discovered that I had a thing for narcissists. So, I knew that I needed to be constantly vigilant in order to avoid my past mistakes. Narcissistic men are always going to be my weakness.

The only difference now is that I can recognize them and can choose to change my reaction. I just move on when I see them.

You might be drawn to needy types, because you always wanted to be the rescuer. Or you might be drawn to "projects" or the "fixer-upper" types I told you about previously—the ones who will be better off after you improve them.

If you find yourself with any of the red flag or toxic types, ask yourself why you think you deserve them. If you feel bad about yourself, emotionally drained, or anxious when you're with someone, there's a red flag waving and they're toxic in some way, shape, or form. Listen to your body and your instincts. And then—move on!

Exercise: Profile Reading Checklist

Okay, now it's your turn. Go online. Take a look at a couple of profiles from men who seem interesting. And *really* read them.

1. Look for the things they say they want in a date.
2. And for the things they don't.
3. How do they describe themselves? What is their tone?
4. Ask yourself: What words or phrases did he use that caught my attention? Why did they? Are there any inconsistencies between things he says? How about between the things he says and the other information? (For example, in the profile he says, "My faith is important to me." Then, answering questions about what he's looking for in a match it says, "Religion: No preference.")
5. Do you sense any inconsistencies between what he says and his photographs? (For example, he says in his profile, "I work out five times a week and would love for you to be there with me." Yet, in his photographs, he's got a beer belly.)

As you practice reading profiles, you'll get better at efficiently separating your potential matches from the rest. You'll be able to zero in on the ones who match the list of qualities and characteristics you're looking for. Just as importantly, you'll be able to spot the ones you want to avoid.

Exercise: Use Your Body Consciousness as you Analyze Profiles

Once you've found two, three, or more men you think are possible matches, take a good look at their profiles. Read them. Think about them. Use the body consciousness skills I showed you. Pay attention to your gut reaction.

As you read each profile, or after any date do you feel any tightening or tensing in your body? Where? Note the word or phrase or photograph that caused the reaction.

Does your breathing become shallower at any point? Do you feel any anxiety while reading his profile or looking at his pictures? Note the word or phrase or photograph that caused the reaction.

If you had no negative reaction to the profile, and you liked what you saw, this may be a candidate worthy of exploring.

If you had some reaction, examine the words or images that made you uncomfortable. Your body is telling you something. You need to listen. Our instinct or Higher Guidance often communicates to us through our body.

It could be that he sounds like your ex-husband, or your father (this should tell you that you might still need healing but, don't discard someone just because they look like someone else).

It could be that your subconscious noticed a code word or a clue in something he wrote that you didn't consciously register as you read it. Perhaps you hadn't noticed, or were trying to ignore, one of your deal breakers. Warning signs are worth watching out for, of course, but his profile is also the first place to assess whether he fits your list of "Mr. Right's qualities." Watch for deal makers and deal breakers.

Take a good look at the complete picture he presents—in his photos, the details he provides—and, objectively, ask yourself if you're falling into old patterns. If he seems a lot like someone you used to like, and would have happily stayed with, if only... Stop! Don't rewrite the same old love story. There are plenty of other possibilities online, and you don't want to waste your time with yet another "if only...

CHAPTER ELEVEN

A Man's Perspective

What does a man look for when he looks at your profile? And what does he see?

Men sift for clues in your pictures and profile the same way that you study theirs.

You may have had the best intentions when you wrote that you're looking for a "generous, financially stable" man. But, depending on his triggers, he might see a gold-digger. Or if you write, "financially stable and responsible woman seeks same," he might interpret it to mean that you want exactly what you are: a financially stable person.

You think that picture of you with your brother's dog is cute. He might see a pit bull and fleas. Please don't even think of posting pictures of a dog licking your mouth. He will definitely think, *I don't want to kiss that mouth. Not after where that dog's tongue has been!*

No, not all men are the same. But their comments provide valuable insight, even if none of them is a Mr. Right For You. If nothing else, other men's comments might make you think about the subliminal messages you're sending, whether you mean to or not.

Picture—Wow or Oh, No

Yes, we all know how visual men are, and the importance of the photos we attach to our profiles. But let's hear it from them:

"If I had a dollar for every woman who actually looked like her photographs—I'd have a dollar," one friend said. He's kidding, of course, but he continued, "It's so bad sometimes, I don't even recognize them when we meet. They're either a lot heavier, older, or both. I know men use inaccurate photos, too, but this just ruins it for me. Even if the women still look good, I feel like they've lied. After that, everything else they say becomes suspect."

Another regular complaint is about the copycat—extremely clichéd—photos.

"I wish I could tell all those women who post that picture of their toes at the beach or by the pool to stop! This kind of photo is so overused I'm beginning to wonder if they're all using the same shot. Also, your toes say a lot about you—and it's rarely good."

"The other picture that I constantly see is the woman sitting at the beach or at the pool. The shot is taken with camera angled from above, making her breasts look huge." Most women have this as one of their photos. It looks like they're advertising for a men's club or sex."

Steve is a stockbroker, in his forties, divorced three years, online for two. But he's not the only one I've heard this from. He's one of so many.

Other no-no's men gripe about are the ones I call the "travelogue" pictures, the ones that have pictures of a beach, waterfall, forest of trees with turning leaves, Empire State Building, or the Eifel Tower—and only one of themselves.

Trust me, Ladies... you're on a dating site, not *National Geographic.* He wants to see you, not where you've been. If traveling is important to you, mention it in your profile essay.

Men say similar things about the pictures of dogs, birds, or the occasional aquarium.

They want to see you. Just you.

Which is why so many men also have such a strong reaction to the incessant strings of group shots: you at Disneyland with your sisters, you out on the town with co-workers, "Girls night out!" and all the rest.

As a writer I know told me: "What is it with all the group shots? I'm glad they've got friends, but half the time it's like a guessing game. They have shots of three or four women together, and none of them look like the one whose profile it's supposed to be. A lot of times I just give up and go to the next profile that caught my eye."

First of all, Ladies, do your friends know that their pictures are on a dating site? My advice to you is to crop your friends out of the picture if you think that you look so good in that particular shot that you need to post it. If you don't have enough photos of "just you," go get some pictures taken.

Screen Name, or "Scream" Name

You think your screen name is not that important? Guess again.

What do men say?

"'Lonely?' 'FedUp?' 'SickOfLies?' Are they kidding? It's like the Angry Ex-Wives' Club. When I see those I read, 'Run! I Have Issues!' In some ways I feel like I should thank them, though, for giving me such a clear warning."

That's the writer again. He's always got a lot to say, but several men I know echoed his sentiments.

If you are angry at men or at the world, this isn't the time to be dating. It's the time to deal with your underlying issues. Go back to the chapter on cleaning out your closet. Men are looking for inner beauty as well as outer beauty.

"I don't know if women realize what a turnoff the wrong screen name can be," a man I went out with told me. "I'll look at a picture and think, 'Hmm, she looks nice.' Then, wham! Just when I'm about to click to read her profile I see, 'CantHandleThis,' or 'Time4MeNow.' Why would anyone do that to herself? If you're emotionally damaged and not ready to date, then don't. But don't put yourself out there under a giant sign that screams 'Trouble!'"

Between Your Lines

There's a consensus among the men I have interviewed about disliking when you include any of the following in your profile essay:

"It's so hard to talk about me..." False modesty won't get you anywhere. In fact, men tell me, it works against you. Men say what they mean, and they want you to be upfront, too. "I had to talk about me," was a common statement, "why can't you talk about you? That's what this is all about. Sometimes I just won't read past that. I don't know why, but it makes me feel like she's being manipulative, or less than honest. Maybe that's a weird reaction, but I feel like she's saying one thing and doing another. If she's that way here, what will she be like later, with other things?"

"No pictures, no reply." Are you kidding? Generally, men tell me this is an automatic goodbye. "Feel that way if you want to," a man we'll call Jerry told me. "Most of us do. But, you don't have to say it. It's off-putting. It sounds bossy. 'Do this! Don't do that!'" He's not looking for a mother; he's looking for a mate.

If a man, who hasn't posted a picture, writes to you, you don't have to answer. On the off chance that he writes something really interesting, you can write back and ask him to show you his picture. That's not so hard.

I usually say something like, "You have an unfair advantage, you know how I look, but I have no clue about you." It's a nice way to ask for his picture and it gives him a clue about my personality.

I also heard: "One woman wrote her whole profile in rhyme. It was the most bizarre thing I've seen. It might have been cute for a little bit, but it just went on and on in this simple 'Roses are red, violets are blue' rhyme pattern. I don't want to date Dr. Seuss."

Another man said, "Oh, my God! There are a lot of scary ones out there. Some are so bitter and angry. It's sad they can't even tell how much anger they're pouring into their profile. They say things like, 'I don't have time for any more lies.' Or

'You better not be married. If you are I will cut off your b---s and send them to your wife.' In all caps!" If you're tempted to write anything like this, don't. Maybe it's time to take a break from dating, and heal or improve upon your skills in discernment.

If you have gone out with men whom you later discovered were married, become the neutral observer of yourself and examine why you keep choosing married men. Go back and re-read the profiles and look at the pictures of the married men you have chosen. Now that you've learned some skills and code words, ask yourself if you could have avoided them with everything you now know. Look them up on Google. Would this have helped you?

Now, back to the men's comments.

"The mixed messages are the ones that get me," yet another man said, repeating something I've heard frequently. "They say things like, 'I run my own business and I don't have much free time, but I'm looking for a man to share my life with.' Really? When? It's the same thing when I see ones that gush about how sexy, passionate, hot, and sensuous they are; and then they say, 'Not looking for a hook-up.'"

Men consistently agree that they like profiles that present the real you. As I said in the chapter about writing your profile, they're not looking for Superwoman, Wonder Woman, or Perfect Woman. The ideal match for you is looking for you. He reads your profile with the hope of being able to see the real you.

"The ones that catch me—after the pictures, of course—are the ones that sound honest and upfront," another man said. "They sound like they know themselves and they sound whole: 'I'm

> silly, sweet, and sometimes serious. I like funny movies and quiet times together.' That kind of thing. Or 'I'm an honest, hard-working, and romantic mother of two grown children; looking for a man who challenges me intellectually, likes to laugh, and is ready to be friends first and see where it goes.'"
>
> "When I read something like that, it's like I can hear her talking—and I like it! I am already connecting with her."

There is a trick to writing the way you sound when you speak. You can sound like the real you by dictating and recording your profile, then typing it out.

Remember, he's just looking for the same thing that you are, lasting love. Let him see that you are the one for him—by being   you.

CHAPTER TWELVE

3,2,1 -Contact!

Ok, you found him. Or, at least you found someone who's passed the photo and profile tests, a possible "the One." Now what?

There are certain rules to online courtship. They are, in many ways, similar to real world and offline flirting. But if you don't know what you're doing, what you think is innocent flirting may be construed as online stalking. Or what you think is being coy could be interpreted as, "I'm not interested."

The different sites may call them different things, but they all have some way of letting the other party know that you're interested. Most have variations that are, pretty much, similar to Facebook.

Some have a "wink" instead of the old Facebook poke. Some let you "favorite" him, the way you might follow or "like" a Facebook page. "Liking" his photo on a dating service is pretty much the same as "liking" a post on Facebook.

Each shows a different level of interest, and each sends a different signal. Before you send any of them, it's time to do a final internal check.

Think Before You Wink

Are you really ready for this?

It's not the end of the world if you contact someone online and then regret it. You can always stop communicating or choose to answer him at a later date. But that's a waste of his time and yours.

It's better to make sure that you're ready to swim before you take the plunge.

If you really want to bring a man into your life, you have to make room for him. I don't necessarily mean physical space. That comes later. But you have to make a time allocation for him.

If you're extremely busy and you work 80-hour weeks, you might have room for a weekend romance. But you might not have time to do the culling process of the search: to go through all the potential matches that land in your inbox, sort through the winks, exchange all the emails and phone calls, and then go on all the dates it takes to find your Level III or Level IV match.

If that's your situation, you should consider paying a matchmaking service to weed out the so-so's and offer you only the most likely pre-selected dates. There are services out there like "It's Just Lunch" or "Selective Search" that will do this for you —if you're willing to pay the price. Unfortunately, they usually only match you with their clients.

Even then, you have to make time. If you don't have time to go out and spend a few hours with a potential partner, then even a matchmaking service isn't realistic either.

Both the search process and the culling process take a lot of work and a lot of time. You won't know if he's your Level III or Level IV match until you go out with him for a while. If finding lasting love is what you really want, then you have to make this a priority in your life, and you need to give this priority all the resources you'd give a work priority or any other priority.

If you're getting ready to embark on a huge work project, you may not want to start dating now. You have to make the space and the time for love.

So if you want to start dating, you start by making room. You have to be available Friday and Saturday nights—and, probably, at least one night during the week.

You decide. You need to make a realistic assessment about all of the factors in your life—the internal as well as the external demands—and ask yourself if you have the time and space to seek out romance.

For example, if you have several children, and you are busy carpooling and doing homework, all week long—do you really have time for a relationship? How do you carve out the time? Can you hire babysitters or ask your ex to share weekends with you? Perhaps you can find people who can share your carpooling duties, so you are not exhausted on date nights.

You're also going to have to find someone to take care of the kids so you can go out. And—if things go really well—so you can stay out for the night or a weekend. Please don't let him spend the night while your children are home until he becomes an integral part of your life. You don't want to present a revolving door of men in your childrens' lives.

These are things that you have to assess realistically. And you have to plan for them.

You also have to be emotionally, psychologically, and physically ready to make finding lasting love a priority. You need to know if finding lasting love is your most important goal, of if the promotion you're seeking is your top priority at this moment.

Of course, you can sometimes have shared priorities, but you have to be a master at juggling your time.

Ready?

Then, let's go.

View, Wink, Fave, Like

Sometimes it's a "wink." Sometimes it's just a "view."

If you really like him, but don't want to seem too aggressive, you can "like" him or one of his photographs.

And, yes, you can do it first—it's electronic flirting. It's like casting that first glance across the room. Just as there's a difference between that—and catching and holding his gaze—there's a difference here.

Zoosk and Match.com let you know if anybody's looked at your profile, and vice versa. Just check the list of "Who Viewed You." If you're interested in anyone, send them a wink, you already know that they were interested enough to look. This is the online equivalent of returning a glance a man may have sent to you across a crowded room.

Other sites have other variations, but the intent, and the effect, is the same. Do either response, and you're letting him know he caught your eye. If you're interested, let him know.

Keep in mind though that traditionally men are hunters, women are gatherers. Men like to hunt. Many studies in male and female behavior support this. Our mothers knew this intuitively so they told us not to call men; let them call you. In the dating world, a man wants to feel like he's done the chasing and the catching, even if you're really the one who's reeling him in.

You want to let him feel like he's chasing you throughout the search process.

The obvious way is to let him do all the searching and let him contact you first. But in this modern age, I think that women can also search for their own man and still make him feel like he's chasing her.

That's where the power of the view, wink, fave, and like come in.

Views

Most of the dating sites send you at least one email a day announcing your "Daily Matches," or "27 Singles We Think You'll Like." It might be five. It might be 30. Doesn't matter. All of them, at least theoretically, are people selected for you based on the criteria you gave the dating service.

What you see, generally, are a single photo and a screen name. If you like what you see, you can click on it to learn more.

With Zoosk, that's all it takes. An email is on its way to the person you looked at, letting him know that you've read his profile. OKCupid lets you opt to "browse invisibly." Match calls it going "undercover." Choose either of those and no one knows you are looking (unless you want them to know). Otherwise, people can check and see who's checked them out, and decide if they want to take things further.

You can use your views the way you'd use the flutter of your eyelids or a quick, interested glance—ways to make sure he notices you. View every profile that interests you. Use your views to get a man to glance back. If he's interested, he'll come strolling across the cyber-room to say hello.

Winks

The "wink" is a step up in intensity. It says unmistakably and undeniably, "I'm interested."

Face it, someone may have viewed you and decided that they didn't really want to get to know you better. He went on his way.

Let's compare this to the non-virtual world. You see someone you think looks nice. Then he steps out from behind that group of people and you think, "No way! My mistake."

Or you see someone who fits the bill for what you like physically: nice smile, attractive hair, good physique. Then your girlfriend tells you that he has seven children from five ex-wives and he's in the middle of divorce number six. You might consider this a deal breaker.

Then again, you might see this guy's twin, the neurosurgeon, who was married for 17 years, got divorced five years ago, spent a year working with Doctors Without Borders and working on himself, then started dating again about a year ago because he thinks it would be nice to have someone to share his life with.

Sigh!

In the online dating world, the only thing these men know is that you looked. They have no idea if you liked, or didn't. Yet.

They might follow up, even if you don't want them to. Or they might not, when you do want them to.

That's where the "wink" or the "like" comes in.

These are the electronic equivalent of not just looking, but making sure that he saw you looking. Now he knows that you liked him.

It's letting him know you want to get to know him better. Honestly, you and the doctor may not hit it off (although it's hard to imagine, isn't it?). But you won't know until you talk to each other first, via email.

The wink is another way to say, "Hello! Would you like to chat?"

Likes

"Likes" come in a couple of different varieties. Some are equal to a wink. They're just a way of saying, "Hi!" He can take it from there, or not.

Other sites let you "like" a photo, or several photos, although I wouldn't do more than two. More than that seems sort of like digital drooling.

The effect is the same. "Liking" his picture or just clicking a button to let him know you really did "like" what you saw is just a variation of a wink. They're slightly more suggestive than a "view," and deliberately intended to let him know you're interested.

A like says: "This was no mistake. I saw. I like. Take a look at me and see if you feel the same."

If he does, he will. If he doesn't … ah, well, then he wasn't Mr. Right For You after all. Good thing you didn't waste any more time learning that.

Favorites

The other form, which is very subtle, is the "Favorite." Use this when you find somebody who is really interesting. Several sites have different ways of doing a "favorite," but the idea is the same.

You make him one of your favorites as a way of letting him know that you think he's special. He definitely stood out in the crowd.

The equivalent in the physical world might be locking eyes with someone or the even bolder, subtle yet unmistakable, light touch of your hand on his arm.

There's no chance he's not going to know you did it.

With Match, for example, when you make someone your favorite, the service automatically sends him a message telling him so.

Even so, it's still up to him to take it from there. Let him feel like he's doing the chasing. All you did was let him know you were there and you were curious, but he has to take charge.

When he gets notified that you "favorite" him, he'll see your picture and your screen name. If he likes what he sees, he can check your profile. If he likes that, he can reach out to you. He's chasing at this point—get it?

Continuing is all—or almost all—up to him. You just rustled the branches so that the hunter could see you there.

Special Note: No online stalking, okay? If he doesn't respond to your wink or your favorite, don't send more. Don't like a different one of his pictures every day for a week. Don't send an email. If he doesn't respond, it's the online way of saying, "I'm not interested." Don't worry, he saw you wink, your like, or your favorite.

You're looking for a Level III match or better. If he doesn't answer, he's not that person. Don't waste your time. Keep searching.

If he doesn't respond to your first email, please don't send him a second one. He received them. And when he didn't answer, that was his response. He's saying he's not interested. It's not personal. He doesn't know you. Move on. There are plenty of other fish in the cyber-sea.

Online dating is concrete. If he has to send an email that says, "Look, I'm not interested. Got it?" that's practically a cease-and-desist order.

If you keep sending messages, he's going to wonder why you don't get that he's not interested. He's likely to put a block on your profile preventing any further communication. You don't want to be that woman.

Another possibility is that he's traveling, out of the country on business or vacation, and he isn't checking his email. Or maybe he's fallen in love with someone else. Most of the services keep your messages to him online for at least 30 days. They'll be there when he gets a chance to read them. If he's interested when he sees them, he'll respond.

Blasting more winks, likes or emails his way isn't going to get you noticed any faster. It's only going to make you seem desperate. Or crazy.

So don't.

When He Winks First

Many times, it happens the other way around. He might view, wink, fave, like, or any combination of the above.

Read the level of interest the same way you would want him to read yours—if you were the one doing it.

The wink says, "Hey! I saw your photo. You look great." It might mean he's read your profile, or maybe not. He might be letting you know that he's interested, but he doesn't have the time to write right now. Still, he wants to know if you feel the same.

He might be feeling you out because he noticed that your profile said you were looking for men from 40 to 45 years old and he's 48. He still might be acceptable to you because your age range is more or less theoretical, but he's not sure. So he's winking to see if you're interested, or if the 45-year-old upper limit on your preferred age range makes his age a deal breaker.

The like, of course, says almost the same thing.

I find there are three ways to respond.

1) If you don't like him and are not interested, just don't answer. What would you do in the physical world? If some guy looked at you and smiled, but you didn't like him, you wouldn't feel compelled to go over and explain why you don't like him. You'd simply look away, turn back to your friends, return to your conversation, or maybe let him see that you're

scanning the room for someone else. You're not being rude. You're simply saying, "Not interested."

2) If you're interested but don't have time to write, just wink back. That puts the ball back in his court. It lets him know you appreciate the attention, you might be interested, but it's up to him to move things along (This is my favorite approach. I want him to pursue me; I want him be the first to write.). If he's truly interested, he'll follow up with an email or a short message. If he proceeds with the email and you like him, then you can answer the email—and the conversation has begun.

3) If he winks, you check his profile, he intrigues you, and you want to find out more, you can email him back. Write something like, "Hey! Thanks for winking at me. You sound like a really intriguing guy. I liked __(fill this in yourself)___ about your profile. I think we might have some things in common." Just send a quick email that lets him know you are interested; you took the time to look over his profile—not just his pictures—and you're ready to explore further. He winked first, so he made the first move. You're not being overly aggressive, just receptive.

If he favorites you, that's really a strong statement. He thinks you're special. He'll probably follow that up with a wink or with an email because he wants to initiate contact.

If he doesn't, and you're interested in him, you can wink, like one of his photographs, or send him an email that says, "Hi! I noticed you put me on your favorites. Thanks. I'm intrigued by your profile and I'd like to know more about you."

You can respond, just keep it short and sweet.

He might just be shy. He likes you enough to keep watch on you, but he's not ready to put himself out there by sending you an email.

Maybe he's like the shy guy at the bar. He's feels safe giving you a glance or sending you a wink, but he doesn't want to be rejected. He wants to find out if there's interest. He wants to see if you'll look back and smile. If you give him a friendly glance, he'll know it's okay to proceed.

He-mail, She-mail

I firmly believe you should wait for him to email you. If you wouldn't walk up to a guy in a bar and say, "Hi, I think you're attractive and would like to get to know you" don't email him first.

No, really—wait!

You winked. You faved. You liked. You winked again…. Guess what! He doesn't think you're his type. Move on!

If he does email, great! You're in business. He's also providing all kinds of new clues about himself, and an opportunity for you to go to the next level of the culling process.

Of course there's another possibility, which is that he's sending you an email out of the blue. You turned up in his daily matches, or he did a search and the service directed him to you. He's letting you know he likes you, and he realizes a simple wink or like isn't enough. He wants you to know he wants to talk.

First things first.

Click on his profile and see if he's someone you're interested in. If you're not interested, it ends here. You don't need to respond to him, any more than he has to respond to you. It's a foregone conclusion that if you do not respond, you're not interested. You don't have to apologize. You don't have to tell him you're not interested.

If you do like what you see and you like what you read in his profile, it's time to really study his email.

As a smart online dater, you want to use every clue you can get. Take a good look: Did he really read your profile? Remember that thing we planted in there? Now is when this pays off. Does he address your "tell"?

If what he says in his email is something along the lines of, "You have a beautiful photo" or "I like your photo," that tells me that he likes my looks, but he probably didn't read my profile.

If his email only talks about how beautiful you are, but you like his profile enough, you can send him an email thanking him—and more. Address some points in his profile. See how he responds the second time.

The reason I say to go back and answer is because not everybody has the same level of social skills. A man who's been married for a long time and recently divorced might be a little rusty in his dating skills. Give him a second chance. See if he can come back with something that's a bit better.

If he keeps it very superficial, he's probably not that interested in a relationship. He's probably just looking for a date or a sexual encounter.

If his email does address what you planted in your profile and you like what he said, it's your turn.

Generally, when a guy emails, he will say something about your profile. That means he read it. At least a good email will. Yours should, too.

Say something about his interests or something that you read in his profile you might have in common. Ask him questions about himself.

Give him something to respond to, and end the email with something like, "I really look forward to getting to know more about you."

You're inviting him to come back and chase. Keep it short. The purpose of these emails is to maintain a light and flirty attitude. You're starting a conversation; you're not delivering a monologue.

At the same time, the email is part of the interview process, just the as your initial conversation at a party or dinner function would be. It's a tool. Use it. Pay attention to the clues you see. And don't ignore your gut feelings and intuition. So before you email, prepare yourself. Study his profile. If there are points that might be deal breakers, but you want to be sure about the situation, slip in a question about them.

Here's an example: "Is that your motorcycle in the picture?" This shows him you looked at his profile and you're curious. It doesn't tell him whether you like motorcycles or not, so he's much more likely to answer honestly, rather than try to play to your cues.

You want to be able to get more information—without it seeming like you've prepared a list of questions. A good way to start a question without making him feel defensive, or like you're interrogating him, is to start with, "I'm curious about..."

If his profile says, "I have children and sometimes they live at home" you can ask the age of his children and how often he sees them. If young children are a deal breaker for you, make sure to ask. Regardless, it tells you about his lifestyle.

Try to get the deal breakers out of the way. You want to know about things you would normally notice during an in-person conversation, so you can figure out if he's got deal breakers or not.

Remember, you're trying to be efficient. It's all about optimizing the search. Your goal is to find the best candidate, deciding quickly whether to continue pursuing him and getting to the first date... or not. You're not trying to make someone fit your requirements, and you're not compromising about what you want upfront. Remember that there are plenty of other possibilities. There's someone just for you. Could this be him? Or not?

The phone call is the next step.

Get to the Phone Call

Everyone sends text messages nowadays. That's okay, but don't use texting as your primary form of communication. Texting is not going to tell you a lot more than an email or two.

Misunderstandings can occur with texting. Once you lose the voice inflection of a telephone call or a face-to-face conversation, it's easy to misconstrue what's texted.

I don't suggest that you engage in more than one or two texting conversations or email exchanges. There's only so much you can glean from an email, so definitely don't get into weeks and weeks of online exchanges.

A lot of people want to keep things online because they fear intimacy. Texting and emailing are ways to make them feel safer. If he can't deal with you one-on-one, if he has to keep you in the digital realm, that should tell you something. There are people who fall in love with a fantasy person through emailing and texting. There are people who just want an online pen pal. Those people don't ever want to talk on the phone because they're so in love with the fantasy they've created.

That's one of the dangers of online dating. You can create a fantasy relationship in your head because you're only seeing the best of this guy and you fill in the blanks to make him your Mr. Right. So move to your off-line encounters quickly. Remember that your goal is to use your time wisely and efficiently and to ultimately find him.

Do you really want to spend three or four weeks emailing back and forth with him, only to meet him and discover that there's no chemistry? Then you both have wasted a month—and who knows how many hours a day at the computer.

So don't go back and forth more than two times without saying something like, "I'm not very good at online conversations. Why don't we switch to a phone conversation?"

The primary reason for the phone conversation is that you'll get more clues about him from his tone and by how he expresses himself, than you'll ever get from his profile and emails.

He might have had help writing his profile and his emails. But on the phone he'll have to answer quickly. You'll notice things in his speech patterns and inflections that you'd never know about from texts and emails.

So text and email if you must, but get to the phone call as quickly as possible. Say, "Here's my number. Please feel free to give me a call."

That's the first step out of the virtual zone and into the real world. And that's where you want to be.

CHAPTER THIRTEEN

Into the Real World

The phone call is the interview, part two. You've shared some emails and maybe a text or two, and you've decided he's worth pursuing. It's time to move the relationship to the next step—that first phone call.

You don't want to agree to a first date without first talking to him on the phone. Believe it or not, some men will ask you on a date via email without first talking to you on the phone.

You don't want to agree to this. Someone may sound great when you are writing back and forth, but you want to see how he interacts when he has to think on-the-fly. Again, we are looking not only for dating efficiency, but also to keep you safe. Anyone can fake being nice when he's writing. It's harder for him to fake who he is once you're interacting on the phone.

Further, going on a date is time consuming. You want to make sure you're investing your time in someone who has the potential to be your mate. Going on a date takes a lot of preparation. I'm not talking about just about the time you're there on the actual date: there's also time spent getting ready, and traveling there and back. If the date's a disappointment, you've wasted three hours or more that could have been spent online continuing your search. Or having dinner with a girlfriend.

Thus, the phone call is the most effective next step in the culling process. This will give you a chance to determine if there's going to be a first date, or not.

Hear, Loud and Clear

No matter how many emails you send back and forth, you'll never hear his voice until you talk to him. His tone, his intonation, his inflections, the way he expresses himself in the course of a conversation will tell you more about him than a book's worth of written exchanges.

Done right, you can learn a lot in a short time. But you have to keep your goal in mind and guide the conversation.

It's not an interrogation; it's a conversation—a targeted conversation.

You want to gather as much information as you can, address any questions his profile or his email raised, and—if you like what you hear—get to the face-to-face encounter.

You don't want him to feel like he's answering a questionnaire, or being grilled on the witness stand by a hostile prosecutor. You want to get to know him; you want him to be relaxed and to be himself.

Conversations tend to have a natural flow. Pay attention to this flow. Do you and he have an easy rapport? Is his thinking logical? Does he project his personality while he's speaking… or is he too measured?

He may have a lot of time to compose an answer in an email. But when you're talking on the phone, he has to think on his feet. He doesn't have a lot of time to edit his words, or to make up a story that he thinks is what you want to hear. What he says spontaneously is going to tell you a lot about him.

His choice of words and how he expresses himself will tell you a lot, too. You'll see if he's nice or rude, sarcastic or sweet, funny or dry, smart or not.

His tone, too, will reveal a lot about his personality and character. His tone can tell you if he's sensitive or abrasive, angry or calm, passionate or passive.

You have to be an active listener during the call. You're listening for nuances, as well as for answers. You're also listening to what is going on in the background while he's talking to you. If little kids are running around and screaming, how does he handle this?

This means that you shouldn't be thinking about what you want to say next while he's talking. You want to listen to his answers carefully, and then compose your next question or comment.

Frankly, this is how we should listen to everybody, but most of us are too busy thinking about what we want to say next, and we don't really listen to what people are telling us. We give someone a gift when we actually listen to what they have to say, and we thoughtfully respond. So this is your chance to practice this wonderful skill. A nice plus is that he'll like you *more* because you're interested in what he has to say.

T Minus 30

Your phone call should last 30 minutes or less. At that point you can decide, by following your gut reactions and instincts, if he's someone that you'd like to meet in person.

Why spend more than that? If it's working, you want to move him to ask you out. If it's not, why keep talking?

This is an efficiency game. If you had all the time in the world, you could spend days or weeks talking to each potential match. But if your goal is to find a Level III or Level IV match, why do you want to waste your time with anything less?

As Billy Crystal says to Meg Ryan at the climax of *When Harry Met Sally*, "When you realize you want to spend the rest of your life with somebody, you want the rest of your life to start as soon as possible."

If you're looking for Mr. Right For You, don't you want to hurry up and meet him? When you think about it that way, even a half-hour seems like a lot of time to invest with a Mr. Wrong.

A friend of mine told me about a man she met online who kept calling her for hour-long conversations several times a week during a two-week period. When they finally met for a drink, it was a no-go. They had absolutely no chemistry.

She had talked with him for approximately ten hours on the phone, and in the span of a few minutes face to face, they knew they were wrong for each other. That's a pretty big investment of time for a no-go: ten hours, two weeks, and nothing to show for it.

If she had limited the calls to one or two 30-minute talks, she could have had conversations with another four to nine matches.

So when you reach 30 minutes, it's time to make a decision and wrap things up. You either move towards a meeting or, if you decide you don't like him, say goodbye.

If you don't like what you hear on the phone call, you can end things gracefully. After all, neither he nor you want to waste your time. You don't have to make a big deal of this. Just say something like, "Well, thank you so much. It was very nice talking to you. I hope you have a wonderful evening."

That's it. He doesn't need a performance review from you. This is not an employee evaluation. Just say, "Thanks" and "Goodbye" in the nicest way you can.

If it's going well, ideally you want to be the one to end the call first. You want to end the conversation while it's flowing and upbeat. You should end it at a point where he'll have wanted to say something else. That way, you're nudging him toward the next logical position.

I usually do this by saying something like, "Well, it seems like we have a lot in common and that you're an interesting man, perhaps we should meet in person." If he agrees to this, ask him first what he has in mind and when. If he suggests that you meet for dinner, kindly decline and suggest an alternative.

Tell him that your schedule is tight during this week, but that you'd like to meet him as soon as possible. So would it be okay for you to meet for coffee or a drink after work? In other words, you want the meeting to last somewhere between 30 minutes to an hour.

After all, you'll know during the first 30 minutes if you have chemistry with him, and whether he's someone you'd like to date. If you decide that you like him after meeting him, your drink can easily turn into dinner. If you don't, you have only invested 30 minutes to an hour.

A Word of Warning

There are things you don't want to reveal during the phone call.

He doesn't need to know what company you work for or where it's located; and there's absolutely no reason to tell him where you live. You can mention that you live in a certain part of town, but not the address. Breaking these rules without knowing him is risky and possibly dangerous. You do want to know his last name before you agreed to meet him. Remember to do a Google search on him *before* you go to that first meeting.

Q & A

The point of the phone call is for you to get to know him. To do that quickly, you need to know what questions to ask.

Begin by taking another look at his profile, and going over your checklists and scorecards to remind yourself of the things that stood out when you were first assessing him.

I find these conversations work best when I have a list of questions that I want to ask a particular person. As I mentioned before, I always have a printed copy of his profile with me when I expect his phone call. I highlight things in the profile or actually write down questions that I might have about him.

You might also want to ask him how long he's been single and about his experiences navigating life after his divorce.

You'll want to ask about his relationship with his ex-wife if he has children, because this can impact your long-term relationship with him. A man with unresolved issues with his ex is probably not ready to move forward with a new relationship. Plus, if they have a contentious relationship, then you may want to ask yourself, "Do I really want to get in the middle of that?"

If you had a question about the ages of his children, or about how much time they spend living with him, now is the time to get answers.

If he never answered that question about whose motorcycle he was riding in his picture, pursue this now—if it's important to you. You might not want to ask this as a direct question, you might want to phrase it as an observation such as, "It seems like you really enjoy riding motorcycles." After all, this is not an interrogation.

You want to know these things up front so that you can consider whether this is going to work for you or not before you get emotionally involved. You definitely want to address any possible deal breakers that you noticed, to find out if they really are.

One of the questions that I always like to ask is, "How long have you been divorced?" A man who just recently got divorced is in a different place from a man who's been divorced for three or four years.

If he says he flies around a lot for business, you might want to ask how often he's gone, and for how long. If he's gone three weeks out of four, then you have to recognize that your relationship might be limited to only going out one week per month.

I also like to find out how he feels about his work. If someone says, for example, "I'm an architect," I try to find out how passionate he is about that. I might ask something like, "How did you get into architecture?" or "What do you like most about your work?"

Someone who's passionate about what he does, tends to be more confident and happier than those who are just punching a clock, hate their boss, and only go to "that miserable workplace" in order to cover their bills. If that's the way he feels, he's probably not at a great point in his life.

This initial phone call also gives you the opportunity to ask him about his passions. If he included a photograph of himself rock-climbing, I might ask, "What do you like most about rock climbing?" I would then disclose that I don't like heights or physical danger. If this is a deal breaker for him, I want to find out now, not three months from now when he asks me out on a rock climb!

Maybe he says, "Oh, the thrill of being up there" or "I enjoy that it requires total focus. I feel very present." How he expresses himself and how he relates to his passion, gives me an insight into his personality, his intellect, and his drives.

If he says, "I like the danger" versus "I love the beautiful panoramic view at the summit" I know whether he's a risk-taker or someone who relishes what the world has to offer.

That's important. Risk-takers tend to prefer the rush of a new romance over the stability of a comfortable relationship. So my personal rule is, if you're an adrenaline junkie, "Thank you very much. It was nice talking to you." I'll date someone who does not shy away from adventure, but not someone who goes seeking danger just for the thrill of it.

I always find it interesting to ask men about their experiences on the dating site. Not only do I get to hear funny stories, but I also get to hear about how he perceives people and events that happened to him. A lot of the anecdotes that I have peppered throughout this book have come from those conversations.

It's important to listen to the consistency of his answers, too. If he said one thing in his profile, and another while you're talking to him, pay attention. If at one point in your conversation he says he's been divorced three or four years, and then later says his divorce just finalized in March, that's worth noting.

It doesn't matter if the discrepancy is in an area that's not significant to you. Even if it's not an outright lie, a discrepancy says something about his overall outlook on bending the truth and, perhaps, trustworthiness. Someone who's less than forthright about one thing, is likely to be less than honest about others.

Keeping Track

Obviously you're going to be seeing more than one person. This is, after all, a culling process. You're sizing up potential matches from the universe of possibilities that the dating service provided you with.

If you don't keep track of those you have considered, and why you rejected them, you can wind up writing and calling some of the same people more than once. It's not only awkward when you realize your mistake; it's a waste of your time and his.

I'm friendly with a serial dater who uses her phone's contact list to keep track of who calls. The moment a phone number shows on her ringing phone, she takes a picture of the person's profile picture and links it to the number. That's all she needs. Whenever that person calls, she immediately sees his picture and she knows who he is. There are, after all, many men named John.

I wanted a better system, so I took things a step further. When someone called me the first time, I would add his picture from his online profile, just like my friend did. Then I would add his name and, in one of the other fields, the dating service I met him on. After our initial conversation, I would add a comment. I might say, "No-go/anger issues." Or, "No-go/risk-taker." Or if things went well, I would note, "Possible/Funny/Vet." Or, "Possible/Witty/Architect."

This was a filing system I could easily keep updating. If the phone call led to a first date, I'd add a comment about that. The "Possible/Funny/Vet" might become "Poss./Funny/Vet/++." The plus symbols are a rating system I used for our chemistry together. One + means nice; two means very nice; three means wow!

Anyone who received a minus sign went from being a "possible" to a "No-go."

This tracking system was very useful in avoiding awkward situations. If a man I had eliminated for some reason, called again, I would immediately see his picture and remember. It's very important to do this because you don't want to be caught off guard. If a "No-go's" number comes up on your caller I.D., you don't have to answer. And you don't have to return the phone call. That is an implicit, and well understood, message. That's the online dating protocol. He might call twice, but when he doesn't hear back from you, he'll understand.

I had a different approach. If I met with someone for a drink or coffee and I thought they were nice, but I knew it wasn't going to work out, I would send him a text message afterwards. The message would say something like," Thank you for an interesting evening. Unfortunately, I don't feel that there is enough chemistry between us to make a relationship work out long-term. Good luck on your search." It's a different approach, but more straightforward and respectful of his time and attention. He was a nice man, just not the one for me.

Face to Face

If the phone call goes well, it's time for the next step. Your profile has done its job. You've got your first date! It's not considered rushing to push for that first date quickly—it's considered (you know!) dating efficiency.

Read all the profiles you want, talk on the phone forever—this won't be the same as that first meeting in person. That's when you'll really be able to read him in real-time, and find out if there's chemistry between you.

More than 80% of our communication with people is non-verbal. Basically, how we move, our facial expressions, and our body language account for more than 80% of what's *really* being said. So it's good to pay attention to whether someone's words match their body language. Is he leaning away from you while telling you that he wants to get closer?

The written word is good and a phone call is better. But meeting face-to-face is best, because that's the only way to find out if the combination of you + him = romance. The difference between a potential friendship and a love relationship is the frisson we call chemistry. It's not logical. It just is.

To evaluate whether or not there's chemistry between you, you need to meet. You can't tell if it exists by looking at a picture. You need a face-to-face first date.

Back to dating rule No. 1: This is about efficiency. You're searching for your ideal match. If you determine that he's not "the One," then you need to get back to searching as quickly as possible. Find out by having your date.

The Clock is Ticking

The first date is a meet & greet—and the interview, part three. So keep it short. As we said, thirty minutes should be enough. Don't meet for dinner because dinner can take up to two hours to finish. What if you don't like him and are stuck for two hours? Meet for coffee, tea, or a drink. A drink may take up to one hour, max.

Secondly, tell him there's a time limit up front. Let him know that you're meeting a friend after your drink, but you wanted to meet him as soon as possible so you arranged to come 30 or 60 minutes before your dinner date. Then, if you want to escape, you can. If things aren't going well, you can look at your watch and say, "Oh, my gosh! It's been 35 minutes. I'm late. I have to go."

Or you can have a friend call you. There are even Smartphone apps that will call you at a specified time.

If, on the other hand, your date is going well, you can always stay longer. You can tell your friend, so that your date can hear, "I'm so sorry that you can't make it. We'll have to get together soon." Never pretend to cancel a date with a friend at the last minute so that you can spend time with him. He needs to know that you value your friends and your friendships, and are not going to cancel at the last minute just because you met someone. He should value your showing this courtesy, which will be a mark of your character.

The point is that your meeting should be scheduled for only 30 minutes to an hour in case you get there and you don't like him. Or in case he doesn't like you. Maybe you're both great people and you make each other laugh, but there's no chemistry. You want to be able to leave gracefully.

If things went well during the phone call, he might suggest having dinner together before you meet. Don't. We want to maintain the efficiency of the culling process and avoid awkward situations. If he asks you to dinner, you could give him an alternative, "Well, how about if we meet for coffee or a glass of wine after work?"

How Do You Know if Your Date Was Good?

You already have the list of qualities you want in your mate. If you're going on a date, he's already passed most of the test. But now that you're at the actual interaction, what's important to you?

You might want to feel like a person understands you, gets you, or sees you for who you are. Do you feel like he's interested in getting to know you, not just your breasts?

Does he ask about you, or does he only speak about himself? Personally, I want someone who can listen as well as talk. Only you can determine how you feel after the exchange. How did he make you feel?

Chemistry is sexual. But that doesn't have to mean sex—it can also refer to attraction. You won't know if the two of you have chemistry until you meet.

You need to evaluate how your potential match interacts with you as a person. It's a dynamic, a dance between two beings. The dynamics of every interaction are always different. Listen to your instincts. Become the neutral observer of your interaction by looking at the facts. Listen actively, just like you did on the phone.

Look at how his hands move when he talks. Look at how his eyes make contact with yours. Or don't. Look at how he engages you. Or doesn't. Does he spend his time looking at everyone around him or at you? The bottom line is—how do you feel when you're with him?

Your gut instinct is never wrong.

What To Wear

My advice is to dress to impress, but not like you're ready to undress. Dress appropriately for the place you're going. You don't have to be revealing. Leave a lot to his imagination. If there's chemistry, his imagination will be working just fine. Make sure that your clothes are clean and pressed.

You want to be as self-confident as possible when you meet him. The better you feel about yourself the more confident you will be.

Take a good look in the mirror. Not just before you go out; the instant you agree to go on that date.

Check everything. Make sure that your hair is clean and looks nice. (No roots showing, please!) Check your nails and hands. (No chipped nail polish or bitten nails.) Pay attention to your wardrobe, smile, hairstyle, and everything else. Make sure you look your best on your big night. You only get one chance to make a first impression.

I once met a handsome man for coffee, but when I looked at his hands I saw that his nails were long and jagged. It said something to me, that he couldn't bother making sure that his nails had been clipped before going on a first date.

Presumably, you've worked on the big things before you started posting pictures on the dating site where you met him. You want to show up for your date looking like the person in the photos. You definitely don't want to change completely from the way you looked there.

Your photo worked. He liked what he saw. Don't change it.

Bottom line—make sure you look your best. Be stylish, but age-appropriate. Present the best you that is possible, within your budget. Neat and clean with well-manicured nails and feet are a given.

You might want to have certain outfits ready for certain types of first dates. For example, if you meet someone for coffee on the weekend, you might want to wear a pair of nice blue jeans with a well fitting top and strappy sandals. Choose a stylish bag and make sure that you've had a fresh pedicure.

Choose other outfits that you can wear for a drink after work or a lunch out. If you have predetermined outfits, you have one less thing to be nervous about before the big day. Try on these outfits for one of your friends and get their opinions.

Look, Listen, Learn

The first date is more than just a chemistry test. Yes, you want to see if the sparks fly. But the first date also gives you an important chance to see how he acts and reacts.

If he's nice to you, but mean to the waitress, he's mean. If he fidgets and looks around a lot, or constantly plays with the ring finger on his left hand, there's a chance he's married. If he doesn't bring his cell phone with him, or keeps it off every time he sees you, he could be married. Who is he avoiding?

If he's evasive, rude, gets drunk, or stares at your chest the whole time, or does anything else that makes you feel uncomfortable, run! And don't forget to continue to evaluate for your deal breakers.

Don't expect him to get better. In theory, he's on his best behavior during the first few dates and during the courtship. If he's misbehaving then, he will only get worse. Move on!

Your ideal match is respectful and appropriate from the start. His words match his actions. He's consistent and congruent. There's no need to settle for less. There are plenty of fish in the sea.

This first date is also your big chance to ask questions and actually watch his eyes as he answers. But remember that this is not an interrogation and it shouldn't seem like one. It should seem like what it is, a conversation. But you still have a purpose, and a very important one—to get to know him well.

And you want him to get to know you. You want him to feel like he's telling you about himself, not being picked apart—that he's opening up, not being dissected.

So you want to keep the conversation light and airy, a little flirty. This is a skills game. All it takes is a little practice! For example, if you say something like, "So, you're a doctor—what kind? Where'd you go to med school? When?" Then you might like his answers, but he won't necessarily like *you*.

Instead, you might say, "You're a doctor? Wow! That takes such dedication. School must have been really tough. And your residency! Is it true that young doctors sometimes have to crawl off into closets to catch a few minutes of sleep?"

You sound interested, rather than probing, and you're giving him a chance to tell you stories that will answer your questions.

"Oh, it's true," he might say. "There was this one time... I mean, you have to realize this was Chicago. In the winter. Cook County General is always the busiest hospital, and we were stuck—in a blizzard—with no way to get home..."

He's revealing. You don't even have to ask specific questions. The answers just come out. And you get to see what he gets animated about, how he expresses himself, and so much more. And you get to have fun!

A good rule of thumb is to let him talk about two thirds of the time to your one third. You already know everything about yourself, and isn't it more interesting to learn about somebody new?

Goodbye for Now, or Forever

When your 30 minutes are up and it's time for the date to end, you have options. If you're not having a good time, you will be saved by the bell. You told him from the start that you only had 30 minutes, and now you have to go.

That's it. Thank him and say goodbye. It doesn't have to be fancy.

If he suggests getting together again, it's best to be honest and polite. Don't think you're doing him a favor by stringing him along. If you don't want to see him again, he needs to get on with his search, too.

Say something like, "Oh, gosh, I don't think so. You're very nice, but I think we're both looking for someone else in our lives." Be clear, direct, and non-judgmental. Then say goodbye, and get on with your search.

The other option, of course, is that you're really enjoying yourself, and he is, too. You can choose to prolong your evening. After your friend calls, just glance at your watch and say, "You know what? I'm not going to meet my friend after all. She had to postpone." If he suggests dinner, you can choose to stay. Do not get into his car with him to go to a new place. You don't know him well enough, yet. You can, instead, use your own car to follow him to the new restaurant; or, if you don't have your own car, just have dinner where you are.

If you really can't stay, say so. But add something like, "I'd really like to see you again." This sends a clear, direct, and unmistakable message—and it puts him in charge again. He gets to chase you, and to ask you out for date number two.

Exercise: The Phone Interview Questions

One of the great things about a phone call is that he can't see you looking at the list of questions you have in front of you. He won't see you making notes, or checking things off.

So do all that.

Make a list of your four or five most important questions for him. You're not trying to get his full life story, yet. If this goes well, there will be plenty of time for that later. The goal of this call is to find out if there *will* be a later.

What kind of things should you cover?

Deal breakers— first and foremost. These are the subjects you MUST cover. Now.

Find out how long he's been divorced or widowed; or if he's never been married, then why? Try to ask in a gentle and flirty way, like, "How is it that a guy like you has never been married?" You want to find out if he's been in previous long-term relationships, and when they ended. Treat a long-term relationship like a divorce. Is he ready to move on?

You need to find out what his relationship with his ex is like *now*.

If he has kids, how often does he see them, and for how long? A man who doesn't see his kids is a red flag for me, too.

What does he do for a living? Our work makes up a major part of our life. It's only natural for people to be curious about what people do. But talking about this also gives you a chance to hear how he *feels* about what he does. Ask him how he chose his career.

His passions—What does he do for fun? What does he do with his spare time?

Refer back to this chapter for additional questions to add to your list. Above you'll just find questions for some key areas. You may have other areas you are curious about, and that can include your particular deal breakers. Include your most important questions in order of importance to you.

Exercise: First Date Conversation Checklist

There are specific things you want to cover in the first-date conversation.

First, go back to the list of the questions you had before the phone call. Are there any questions you didn't get a chance to ask? Anything you need clarified? For example, when you asked how long he'd been divorced, did he say something like, "Oh, that's ancient history" and launch into something else? Now's the time to follow up, so you can determine if he's being deliberately evasive.

Naturally, it's most important to cover any deal breakers, but I also like to ask questions about his family in general. Does he get along with his mom? Usually, the way a man relates to his mother is how he relates to the women in his life.

I definitely need to get a man's full name before the end of the first date. Ideally, I will have gotten it even earlier, during the phone call, so I can look him up online to see if his story checks out. Is it snooping? Maybe. But I might discover he once won an Olympic gold medal and was too modest to mention it, or that he recently saved a drowning kid at the lake.

If he's immediately defensive, that's a clue that he has something to hide. It's expected that someone who's interested in you is going to Google your name. And you should Google your own every once in a while to see what turns up.

For this exercise, make a list of questions that still need to be answered:

Find out about deal breakers.

Ask questions you didn't get to ask during the phone call, or that still need clarification.

Ask about his family and friends. His relationships with others tells a lot about him. How many of his friends are long-time? Listen to how he describes his friends and colleagues. Get him to tell stories, and you tell him some.

What are his passions—work, hobbies, volunteering, etc. Find out what excites him. This gives you a sense of who he is and whether he'll have time for you.

Find out about his past—self-made man or silver spoon? His stories about where he's been, what he's done, and the people he was with will tell you a lot about his character.

Find out about his present—his relationship with his ex, children, work-mates, and what he likes to do for fun.

Find out about his future—What are his dreams and desires? Where does he see himself in five years? Ten?

CHAPTER FOURTEEN

Date Two, and Three and ...

It happened! Your first date was great! It actually seems like he might be The One. You start to imagine wedding bells.

Slow down! You're only at "Phase 1" of the dating process. Before you go rushing to the altar or imagining moving in together, you want to make sure he's the Level III or Level IV match you're really looking for.

Remember, he was on his best behavior on the first date. And he'll be doing his best for a while.

So now its time to enjoy being together and doing all the things you want to explore, while you're continuing to be the neutral observer of yourself and your relationship, and reading the signs.

The more you do with him, the better. The more situations you're in together, the more opportunities you have to see how you both react in different circumstances and to each other. In the beginning of the dating process, let him be the one who asks you on dates and calls you. Remember the chase?

Look and Listen

You want to be the neutral observer to his interactions with you.

What are you looking for? Clues, red flags, consistency, and changing stories. You also want to gauge how at ease you feel with each other. Does time fly by or does being together seem like a lot of work? How do you feel about him, and about yourself when you're with him?

A man is what a man does. If he pulls out your chair as you go to sit down on your first date, that's nice. If he does it every time, he is.

So watch. Listen. And ask questions.

You want to pay attention to how he talks about his past relationships: his girlfriends, ex, and mom. Were his former lovers "bitches," "liars," or "crazy"? Is he "glad she's gone"? Does he take responsibility for his part in the failures of his past relationships? Or are those failures always someone else's fault (red flag!)

If he's divorced, you want to observe his relationship with his ex-wife and his children. Sometimes a man may say that he and his ex-wife get along, but in reality they have a contentious relationship. This matters if he has to interact with her on a regular basis—such as if they have children together.

Does he pay his child support on time? Does he pick up his children when he says? If he doesn't treat his children well, he's not going to treat you any better in the long run. If he's always trying to figure out how to cheat his ex-wife out of money, he'll do the same to you.

Observe his character: watch how he treats others, not just how he treats you. Remember, he's on his best behavior when he's with you in order to win you.

I had a client who divorced his wife of many years; their children were in their thirties. But she still manipulated him in all sorts of ways via the children. This was interfering with his new relationship. He had to learn to set good boundaries between himself and his ex-wife, and between himself and his grown children. He had to tell them all that he was not going to tolerate interference, and he had to mean it!

We all have pasts. We've all had relationships. They end for a variety of reasons, few of which are pleasant. How we handle our endings, and how we move on, is what counts. In this man's case, his new relationship provided an avenue of personal growth. In order to make it work, he had to learn about personal boundaries. As I mentioned before, one of the main spiritual goals of relationships is personal growth.

Just as we all have some negative memories from our past, we also enjoyed many happy times. After all, we did fall in love with that person. He may have been wrong for us; or we may have been wrong for each other. We may have been repeating a pattern we needed to break. Or we may have realized that as much as we enjoyed being together, our future goals were too far apart.

Maybe he wanted the white picket fence, and you wanted to live with gorillas in the wild. Maybe his career consumed him, or yours did. Maybe, because you didn't know any better, you married a Level II match, and over time realized that you each wanted more out of life.

Speaking ill of your past partners, speaks ill of you. The same rule applies to him.

If he speaks poorly of the women in his past, you have to wonder why he was with them. And what will he say about you someday?

Take notice if he speaks about his ex relationships charitably, kindly, or fondly. This means that he has probably taken responsibility for his part in the failure of those relationships. He has learned from his past mistakes.

Listen and watch.

If he's a widower, make sure that he's finished with his grieving process and that she really has been laid to rest in his mind. Many carry the ghost of their loved one with them for years, or forever. Rather than being a fond and sad memory, she continues to be a presence haunting him. She becomes larger than life, perfect. If that's the case, she'll be haunting your relationship with him, too. You cannot compete with a ghost—especially a perfect one.

If he hasn't gotten over her, you should move on. You're not looking for a project or someone to heal; you're looking for a relationship. You need to find someone who is ready for one.

You'll also want to explore your vision of your future together. If you're going to be in a lasting relationship with someone, the "future" you talk about now... may someday be your "present."

If you don't want to be in the same place as he does, then you're better off recognizing that now. A friend of mine was dating a successful lawyer. In one of their conversations, he shared with her that his goal was to retire in ten years and go to Africa to do photography and volunteer work. That definitely was not her idea of a fun future. She decided to find somebody who shared a similar vision of their future together.

You discover these things through conversations, not interrogation. If every time you get together, he thinks you're putting him under a bright light and hammering him with questions, that's going to get old, fast. Bring things up naturally, in the flow of conversation.

You can find out about his future plans, goals, and dreams by telling him about yours. "I've always wanted to learn how to paint. I have this dream of someday spending a summer in the mountains or by the sea, with my easel and my canvas, painting what I see." It's hard for him not to share his dreams, or comment on yours, after a set-up like that.

Being Present is a Present

When you're on a date, or with anyone, the biggest gift you can give them is to be fully present. Listening to him. Focusing on what he's saying and doing. Let him know that he is all that matters to you at that moment, and that what he says matters.

Therapists find that a large part of the healing process happens when someone actively listens. This shows a person that you really care about what he is feeling and thinking. And that he is valued and understood. (This is a skill that requires practice because we can easily be distracted.) Not surprisingly, he will want to talk to you *more* because he will feel that you care. (You can't fake this. You really have to care.)

In order to create greater intimacy with your partner, you may want to touch his forearm very lightly, and look into his eyes every so often. Touching his arm or his hand while he's talking encourages him to go on with what he's saying, and lets him know that you're interested in him and fully present.

Giving him your full attention is a gift he will treasure, even if he doesn't realize why. Being present and asking questions about his life, dreams, and thoughts makes him feel like he is the most important person in the world. It puts him where we all want to be—at the center of the universe, even if only for a short while. Plus, you'll really get to know him well.

Make sure that he does the same for you.

When you're on a date, is he giving you his undivided attention? Or is he looking around the room—maybe at other women who are walking by?

Is he listening to what you say? Really listening? Or is he thinking about the next story he wants to tell you, and waiting for a pause in order to shift the attention back to him?

If he's really the right one, he wants to get to know you—really know you. He'll be listening to every word, just like you do.

Red Flags

The frogs are out there. Someone who seems like a prince may very well not be.

Devil is in the Details: As you listen to what he says, look for consistency in his details. Watch to see if his story changes over time.

Was he with his buddy on that trip to the shore, or was it a girlfriend? Was he still married when he met that last girlfriend, or not? Is he 46 or 51? Was he married once? Twice? Three times?

A liar is a liar. If he chooses to lie about one thing, he'll lie about others. If he lies about his age, or his job, or his ex, or about how many exes he has, that's just the beginning. There are more lies on the way.

And if he's lying to you now, you don't want to stick around to see what else he'll lie about.

The Marrying Type

If you haven't covered this in any of your previous conversations, you should—and soon. If he says he's never been married, or he was married briefly when he was young and remained a bachelor ever since, ask him why, and listen carefully.

Then ask him if he's been in any other long-term relationships. If not, why? And don't settle for, "I never met the right woman." Or worse, "I never met the right woman—until now."

I'm not saying that he has to have been married. But by the time he's out of his 30s, it's probable—even preferable—for him to have lived with someone for at least a year or more. And I don't mean as a roommate!

That means that he has to have been in a committed relationship, even if they weren't wearing rings. This is very different from going on a date once a week, or spending a weekend together here and there. This gives people a chance to see how they function together as a committed couple. It teaches them things about each other, and about themselves.

And it tells you that he knows how to commit to someone.

You can view living together almost the same as you would a marriage. However, if he is over forty and has never been married. even though he has lived with other women, I would question his ability to make a full commitment. We discussed this when we talked about the serial monogamist.

Or if he lived with a woman while he was in college, but never again in the past twenty years, consider that a red flag. Take this as a clue that he's not looking for a long-term commitment. Not with you or anyone else. No matter what he says! Evaluate his actions and his history, not his words.

Beware if every one of his past relationships lasted only a few months. He's really not willing to commit. He might be a serial monogamist—committed and exclusive until he gets bored; or until something "better" comes along. He might also be an adrenaline junkie who moves onto a new romance after the initial rush of a current romance wears off.

As you spend more time with him, you will have a chance to find out more about what worked in his previous relationships and what went wrong. Sometimes, the women he was involved with sound very similar. Sometimes, they sound very much like you. That could mean he's still stuck in the pattern you just broke out of— he's repeating a relationship pattern that never works out for him.

You already know how that ends, even if he doesn't. Don't stick around to be the next chapter in his ongoing tragic saga. You already cleaned out your closet; he needs to clean out his.

"Friend" Me

It's only natural, as time goes on, for you to become Facebook friends with the men you are seeing. Nowadays, our digital existence is a part of our life. It's a way we stay in touch and share with our community of friends. It's a connection, with varying degrees of intimacy.

People who care about you will want to be a part of that. Sooner or later, they're going to want to be your Facebook friend and to follow you on Twitter, Instagram, and other social media. You should follow him, too.

As your relationship progresses, and if you've been going out for at least a month, ask. It's a way of becoming a part of his life, and a way of seeing what he shares with others, who he hangs out with, etc.

People are often much more revealing about their views and beliefs in their digital life than in their real life. They are often less discerning about the photos they post, as well. Most people do not clean out old photo albums on their Facebook page. Take a stroll down his memory lane.

Just Visiting

I'm always a little bit leery about men who live in faraway cities or other countries, but who want a relationship here. Maybe they're planning on moving. Or maybe they expect you to, if things work out. Maybe one of you will. But beware.

I'm not saying that you shouldn't interact. He might be the "One," after all... for that is the magic of online dating. You are exposed to people you might never have met otherwise. He might be a lot of fun. He might take you nice places. But it's easy, and sadly common, for a guy who travels regularly to try to have his cake and eat it, too.

He might have a girlfriend or a wife in his home country or state, and he wants to additionally have you here. So watch for indications that he's trying to keep you separate from his home life.

Does he friend you on Facebook so you can see his posts? Does he let you post to his timeline? Does he mind if you post photos of you and him together on his timeline? Does he ever introduce you to friends he works with, or friends from back home who come to visit? After you've been going out for a while, does he invite you to visit him in his hometown?

Another subtle clue is, when you go on a date with him, watch to see if his phone is on or off. Everybody has someone who could call with an emergency. So most people keep their phone on. Does he always leave his phone in his car, or at his place? Men never forget their phone. It's an appendage. It's in their pocket, in their hand, on the table where they can see it.

If you go out with a man on a number of dates and his phone is always off or he doesn't bring it with him, or let's say you start to get intimate with him and he doesn't have his phone on for a night or two, then you know he's hiding something. A lot of men from other countries or cities use online dating sites to have affairs or flings while they're in the United States or away from home.

I had a girlfriend this happened to. The guy was very charming, handsome, and wealthy, and he had a great apartment. But his phone was always off. Or he would go out without it. She even asked him, "Aren't you worried about missing any phone calls?" and "What if you need to make a call?" He would say, "Oh, I know you have a phone in case we need it."

Well, you know how it turned out. He was hiding his other life—and a wife—from her.

Bottom line: If you're with somebody and their phone is always off or they don't bring it with them, be careful!

On the other hand, he could turn out to be Mr. Perfect For You. I have a friend who lives in Miami and is an internationally well-known painter. She is a woman of many talents and great intellect, but she was having a hard time meeting her mate.

Her story had a fairytale ending. She met Mr. Perfect for Her on Match.com. He lived in Germany, but he met every one of her qualities. Luckily, they both had the financial wherewithal to be able to visit each other numerous times before he committed to moving to Miami. They've now been happily married for a number of years.

What About Them?

You also want to watch his interactions with others. How does he treat waiters and waitresses, store clerks, and others when you go out? The way he acts toward strangers tells you a lot about him. If he's always nice to you, but he screams at the car ahead when it doesn't race through a yellow light, be careful. His anger is not in question, only the target is. Tomorrow that anger may be turned against you, your children, or someone else you care about.

The same holds true if he belittles others.

If he barks at waiters or calls store clerks "stupid," step away. Sooner or later, he'll do the same to you.

Watch how he behaves when things don't go his way. When his food arrives cold or undercooked, does he harangue the help? Or does he politely ask for them to warm it up? It's one thing for him to berate the waitress for an honest mistake, it's another for him to say, "I'm sorry, but I wanted mine medium, not medium rare. Is it too much trouble to have them cook it a bit longer?"

The more situations you share with him, the more chances you'll have to see how he reacts to the good and the bad. After all, everyone can be nice when things are going their way.

Friends Indeed

The way a person interacts with strangers tells you a lot. The way he interacts with his friends does too.

The first question is, of course, does have any friends? If he doesn't, you should take that as a warning. Someone with no friends is either such a loner that he prefers being alone, or the kind of person no one wants for a friend. Either one is not someone you want to be with. Humans are social beings. Studies show that people who are isolated tend to get depressed because humans need social contact and support.

Assuming he's in the normal range, he'll have a few friends. Who they are, and how they act around him, can give you a sense of what he's really like. They are a reflection of him to an extent.

We all have friends we wish were a little less self-centered, and friends who always have an opinion about everything — who always think that they're right. But our friends make us laugh, are there when we cry, and we enjoy being with them for dinner, a movie, or a night on the town. We might go bowling together, to art galleries, or shopping. They are the people we choose to spend time with, and that says something about us. We do things together that we like. We discuss the things that interest us.

So look at the character and values of his friends to get a clue about him. Honest and kind people hang out with other honest and kind people. They might come from different walks of life or enjoy different things, but they share character traits and values.

There's a saying in Spanish: "Don't tell me who you are; tell me who your friends are." This was surely said first by someone who knew you could learn a lot about a man by meeting his friends. I have found this saying to be true.

This means he needs to introduce you to them. If he spends time fishing with a group of friends, but doesn't invite you over when they cook their catch, who is he hiding—you or them?

If he plays golf Saturday mornings with the same three guys, but he never suggests having dinner with them and their girlfriends or wives, why not?

If he goes to church every Sunday morning, but he never asks you along, that's odd.

It could mean he's embarrassed—about them or maybe about you. Or maybe he's worried about the stories they might tell about him.

Either way, it's not good.

It could mean he doesn't really think you're a candidate for the long term. Sure, you have fun together, but take you to the church picnic? No, thank you.

If he never introduces you to his friends and keeps you at arm's length, it's often an indication that he's just dating around. He doesn't think you're that special.

A man who likes you and thinks you may be his "One and Only" will make room for you in his life. He wants you to meet his friends. He's proud to show you off.

If he does introduce you, you want to see what they're like, yes. But you'll learn just as much or more from seeing what he's like around them. They've known him longer and he won't have any defenses or walls up when he's around them.

This is also a good chance for you to find out what his friends think of him. Surely some of them will want to tell you stories about him, including some embarrassing ones about the time they "went skiing and he..." Or that time when he was barbecuing and "his apron caught on fire!" Or they might tell you a story or two about how they were out for a walk one day in the pouring rain and he saw an old woman with no umbrella waiting for a bus, "So he gave her his and got completely soaked walking home."

Often enough, a man won't tell stories like that about himself.

You also want to observe how he behaves with them. If he seems like a completely different person with his friends than he is with you, that should give you pause. That's a sign that he's not really being genuine with you—why? He's either putting on an act for them, or for you. Most likely you.

Equally important is how he acts toward you when he's with them. Does he suddenly start asking you to get him a beer, instead of asking you if you want something the way he does when you're alone? Does he cut you off in conversation or ignore you? If he's wonderful when you're alone together, but less so when he's with you around his friends, you probably want to ask him about it or reconsider.

But, if he treats you like he wants you to be part of the gang, then he probably wants you to be part of his life.

Friends, Again (Yours)

The way he acts around *his* friends lets you witness a side of him that you might not otherwise get to experience. The way he behaves around *your* friends is equally telling.

If he doesn't want to meet them, he's probably not that into you. He knows your friends are important to you. He also knows that if he wants to be a part of your life, they should be important to him, too.... if for no other reason than that they are important to you.

If you find yourself hesitating at the thought of introducing him to your friends, you may not be as into him as you want to think you are—or you may be embarrassed—why? If you're holding back from bringing him around your close friends, the very ones whom you trust with your deepest and darkest secrets, you need to ask yourself what don't you want to hear.

Perhaps there's something you can't verbalize, and may not even recognize yet, but consider this gut reaction or instinct as a warning that there might be something wrong with him. (We'll get to this in just a bit.)

Perhaps you realize that he's not going to fit in—that should tell you something, too. What is it about him that makes you unsure about how he's going to be accepted by the people you like and trust the most? How important is this to you?

Let's say, though, that you've gone on a few dates, he's meeting all of your requirements with flying colors, and you now think that its time for the acid test - having him meet your friends. He's nice and funny; he does all the right things. You like him and you think that they will, too. So you set up the meet and greet.

How does he behave with them? And, afterwards, what did they think of him? If they're really your friends, they'll tell you the truth. If they like him, that's a good sign.

Oftentimes we are so blinded by our pheromones ("love" or excitement hormones) that we don't notice how badly someone is treating us, or that they're trying to control us.

Your friends will tell you—and you probably won't even have to ask them. If they think he's wrong for you, they'll tell you. They'll start commenting. "Oh, my God! I hate how he tells you how to behave." Or "You know, you're suddenly dressing in a totally different way because he's telling you to."

Maybe you haven't noticed him looking at other women, but your friends will. They'll tell you because no one wants to see his or her friend mistreated.

So somewhere in your dating process, (preferably, in the beginning) get him around your friends. Go out with one or two couples, and also take him to a party or to a large group setting. This will allow you to see how interacts one-on-one and in a group. See how he fits into your group of people.

Your friends will keep you honest. They know, or should, what your deal breakers are. They'll call you out on them. If they catch you settling for less, or repeating a pattern you said you wanted to break, true friends will sit you down and make you face facts.

I did this with a friend. She tended to date guys who had addictive personalities. They drank or did drugs, or whatever. She swore that she wasn't going to go through this anymore because she couldn't stand the roller coaster ride of these relationships. She was tired of trying to heal others. She made drug use or active addictions her number one deal breaker.

So she started dating a guy she swore had Level III potential. When she finally brought him around to meet our group, we discovered that he liked to smoke pot every day.

Afterwards, we called her out on it. We reminded her of her promise to herself to stop going out with guys who used drugs. She started making excuses that this guy didn't need to smoke pot every day; he just chose to do it. If you do it every day, it's a habit, and most likely an addiction. Someone who can still make a choice about smoking pot (or drinking) will do it sporadically not habitually.

When she told us how he was special, different, and all of that, we told her that she was only fooling herself. We told her she could do whatever she wanted but, as her friends, we had to tell her the truth. It's what we would expect, and want, from her. We chose to express our opinion because we loved her. We reminded her that she knew how this how relationship would turn out.

She continued to see him—until it ended, exactly like the relationships before.

Not everyone listens to his or her friends. I am advising you to pay attention to what they have to say. They often prevent us from deluding ourselves for the sake of having a relationship. Remember, you are looking for your Mr. Right not another Mr. I Should Have Known Better.

Same Old Story

OK, so you meet. The fireworks go off! You really get along and you really like him.

But …

What do you do when all that is true, but you find your-self, like my friend, accepting one of your deal breakers?

This happens. Particularly, when someone hides the deal breaker from you. In the prior example, he didn't tell her about the pot until weeks after they met. She was already fall-ing for him. What do you do?

It's time for you to love yourself enough to walk away. If you can't say goodbye to another Mr. Wrong, then you need to identify the limiting belief about yourself or relationships that keeps you there—and proceed to clean out your closet.

Those Limiting Beliefs—Again

Relationships are our mirrors. They constantly show us where we need to improve. In this case, you're able to discern another limiting belief and clear it out— forever.

Consider this as part of your journey, not as a misadven-ture. You learned; you grew. You are now ready for a better match since you have cleared yet another thing holding you back.

My advice to you is to be alert so you don't allow yourself to fall into the behaviors that caused your previous relation-ships to fail. You want to continuously check that you're not writing the same old (failed) love story with a new lead actor.

Be careful that you're not sliding past the warning signs, or accepting some of your deal breakers using the excuse that other things about him seem good. Stand up for yourself and what you deserve. You have to be your own advocate.

Never forget your list. There's no sense in delaying the in-evitable. If he's wrong for you, you'll end up breaking up with him anyhow, so the earlier you do it, the less you'll suffer. Then you can move on to finding your Mr. Right.

You should never remove something from your deal breaker list. Never. Not a real deal breaker, anyway.

If you find yourself considering dropping or excusing a deal breaker, or if you hear yourself thinking, *Well, he's really not so bad about...* or, *This time it's different...* then you need to go back and ask yourself, *Why am I willing to settle? What is it about me that makes me think I deserve to settle?*

Ask yourself, *What has changed in me that makes this suddenly acceptable?* Are you a victim of your limiting belief that, *I can't find anyone better?* Remember, you're not a victim; you're in control. So clear away. Go back to the chapter on cleaning out your closet. Re-examine your triggers and your limiting beliefs. You need to remind yourself where those come from and the damage they do.

"Mr. Almost Right" is wrong. A man who exhibits one of your deal breaker flaws is not your Level III or IV match. He might not even be a Level II.

And the time you're spending with "Mr. I Know He's Not Right For Me" takes time away from finding the person you want.

Some women go out on dates for validation. They want to feel like they're attractive and desirable, they need the external validation of a man wining and dining them, and saying pretty things so they can feel valued and attractive.

This is a limiting belief in action. Perhaps it's, *I'm not worthy,* or *I'm not attractive.* Seeking the approval of a man to feel beautiful or worthy is not healthy. Your self worth will wane with his opinion of you. Go back and figure out where your lack of self-esteem us coming from. Whose approval didn't you get? Work on this.

Going out on a mediocre date just to have a date is the same thing. Go out with a girlfriend instead. You will have more fun and feel better about yourself. Your goal is to find happiness in a lasting, loving relationship. You can have this, you just need to make room for it.

Nature abhors a vacuum. So if somebody's taking up energetic space as your partner or frequent date, even if it's the wrong person, you won't have a vacuum that needs to be filled. The universe views this as, *She already has someone, so we don't need to bring her another.*

I'm always against the idea of a "friend with benefits" because this fills the vacuum. He's filling your needs. You are sending mixed signals to the universe because you're not 100% available.

Make room for your One, and you'll find him.

Trust Your Gut

You know what's right for you. You know what's wrong. Down deep—you know.

The way a man approaches you indicates his intent. If a man is interested in having a real relationship, he doesn't rush into intimacy—emotional or physical. He approaches you with the intent of getting to know you—mind, body, and soul—and to build a friendship.

A man who over compliments you is probably trying to rush you, or may be more interested in your body than your soul. He's interested in being Mr. Right Now. He's trying to lure you in by playing to your weaknesses.

You know the difference. You can tell—if you pay attention.

You should be fully present when you're out with someone you're thinking of spending a lifetime with. This is a gift to them, as we said. But it's also a gift to you, because it will keep you safe from predators and players. Being fully present also means that you're fully present with yourself. You'll not only hear what they say, but you'll feel your own reactions.

Your body consciousness will alert you to what you need to know. Listen to that pang of apprehension that makes you stiffen, or the twinge of anxiety or fear that causes your stomach or chest to tighten.

When someone is right for you, you will know it. Your body will feel relaxed and have the feeling of expansion. This expansion can feel like joy or openness or lightness. Learn to read your own body consciousness.

Recognize the messages as they come. And make a mental note.

CHAPTER 14 EXERCISES

Exercise: Scoring the "Friends Meeting"

You will probably get a feeling or a "vibe" from his friends and the way he acts around them—and the way he acts towards you when he's with them—that will tell you a lot about him and what he thinks of you. Here's a list of things to look for, and to consider, after that first meeting with his friends.

This is all subjective, but the scores should give you a strong sense of how strong your relationship is, or isn't.

1. How did he introduce you?
   - "A friend"   -1
   - By your name   0
   - As "my girlfriend" or some other way that indicated you had a serious or exclusive romantic relationship   +1

2. How did he refer to you after that?

   - By some generic and/or sexist nickname ("Babe" or "Sweet-stuff") he has never used with you before   -1
   - Your name   0
   - By a pet name that he normally refers to you by or a positive alternative ("Honey," etc.)   +1

3. Did he mention that your relationship is serious or exclusive?
- No   0
- Yes   +1

4. Did he tell stories about experiences you shared?
- No   -1
- Yes   +1

5. Did he talk about how you met?
- No   0
- Yes   +1

6. Did he talk about how you hit it off (i.e., how he knew you were "the One" for him?)
- No   0
- Yes   +2

7. Did he treat you the same as he usually does when you're out together, or differently? If it was different, was this in a good or bad way?
- Same   0
- Differently, in a negative way   -2
- Differently, positive   +1

8. How did he act toward you when his friends were there?
- Aloof   -2
- Or worse, like you're just a fling   -5

9. How did his friends act toward you?
- Like a welcome addition to the group   +2

- Like "yet another" passing thing   -2

10. What were his friends like?
   - Nice   +1
   - Not   -1

(If they weren't nice and he let them be, it could mean that he doesn't take you or your relationship seriously.)

11. Did you like his friends?
   - Yes   +1
   - No   -3

(Remember: These are his friends. If you stay with him, you stay with them. If you try to separate them, he'll resent it.)

Now add up the points and find your score.

+5 and up = Good to great. The higher the better.

0 to 4 = So-so. Take a good look at the places in which he scored poorly and decide how important they are to you.

-1 to -7 = Uh-oh. Same as above, but this range is a warning. Maybe you missed some deal breakers or other bad signs when you were alone.

-8 and below = Bye-Bye.

Exercise: Body Consciousness

Our body tells us when something's not right. This exercise will help guide you in paying attention to your breathing, and to any tightening of your muscles in your face, your abdomen, your back, or wherever.

Find a place to sit comfortably, where you can focus.

Close your eyes

Inhale deeply and slowly through your mouth. Focus as the air comes in, and follow it as it fills your lungs. Then exhale gently through your nose. Repeat five times.

Once you're relaxed and focusing only on your breathing, let your thoughts begin to focus on him. Think about the last time you were with him. Be there with him.

How do you feel? Is your body feeling tense anywhere? Are you feeling any tightening around your chest or stomach or throat?

If you feel the corners of your mouth lifting into a smile, that's good. If you feel lighter and even more relaxed, that's great.

Pay extra attention if you feel any tension or tightening anywhere in your body. This is usually a warning.

Ask that part of your body, *What are you trying to tell me?* Continue breathing and focus on that part of your body where you feel tension. Do so without any expectation. Do any thoughts or feelings come up? Do you get any flashes of insight?

Ask yourself why that's happening. Does he remind you of something or someone negative? Are you afraid of something? Are you feeling the tightness or tension because he said or did something? Or is it because of you—are you afraid of losing him because you have an unresolved fear of abandonment or something like that?

If you're doing this exercise because something alerted you or alarmed you, think about the thing he said or did that caused it. Does it cause tension somewhere? Where? Focus on that spot. Ask yourself why you're feeling what you're feeling. Your body will tell you.

Once you know the answer, thank your body for helping you to become more aware and alert. Tell your body, and yourself, to always alert you to anything that you need to know—negative or positive.

Take five deep breaths again, just as you did in the beginning, as you return to the present.

You have to trust your gut, as they say. You have to trust your instincts. If something feels wrong, it probably is. If you're experience this feeling of "wrongness" because of a lingering limiting belief, you need to clear it. But if he's the cause, then he's probably the wrong one for you.

CHAPTER FIFTEEN

Proceed with Caution

Are We a "We"?

You met online. Your romance is developing well. That's why you're wondering whether you're ready to think of yourselves as a couple. If you're wondering whether this man could be a mate instead of just a date—wondering if this man could be The One—you're going to have to decide if you're going to be each other's "Only One." That means that, at some point, you're going to have to decide whether to date each other exclusively.

Once you progress to exclusivity, you both can really get to know each other and complete the evaluation process. After all, how can you know if he's "The One," if you're just treating him like a "Someone"?

How quickly you move to exclusivity and how quickly you take down your dating site profile depends on you. There is no hard-set rule.

Generally speaking if, after a number of weeks, a month, or two months— depending on your individual case—you find yourself basically just dating one man, it's time to at least start thinking about becoming exclusive. Since your goal here is to find your One, I'm assuming that if you are spending all your time with one person, you think he's it.

Either one of you can bring it up first, but I usually like to let the man decide when he wants to do that. That way it seems less like he's being pushed, or pulled, into a commitment. After all, men like to feel like they are doing the "catching!" If he asks, "Why is your profile still up?" you can use this as an opening.

You could just say, "Well, you know, because we've never talked about dating exclusively."

If he doesn't after two months, it's probably time for you to raise the issue. After all, you're looking for a lasting relationship. If that much time has gone by and he's not ready to commit to trying to deepen the relationship, you might want to re-evaluate whether he feels as strongly about you as you do about him.

You can take a soft lead and say something like, "You know, I still have my profile up. It seems like we are seeing each other a lot and I don't have a lot of time to pursue other relationships. How about you?"

You're telling him straight out what you're doing, but you're giving him an opening to tell you how he feels about your relationship.

He can say, "Oh well, I'm only seeing you anyhow. Why don't we date exclusively?" That's an easy, low or no pressure way to deal with it.

On the other hand, if he tells you that he's seeing other women and makes no mention of dating you exclusively, it's time to start seeing less of him and to start making time to get to know other men.

If in a few weeks he doesn't mention anything, you might say, "I really like you. But I'm not interested in just dating several men at a time, as I mentioned to you when we first met, I'm looking for an exclusive relationship with the right person. How about you?"

If he tells you that he's not ready for that commitment, you can thank him for his time and tell him that you enjoyed getting to know him, but that you seem to have different goals. Then wish him good luck on his search. Do not text, call, or email him. If he communicates with you to go out on another date, ask him if anything has changed. Again you're not looking for a date, you're looking for a mate.

You don't want to invest more time in a relationship that doesn't seem to be going anywhere.

You'll have to trust your instinct about the timing of your first soft probe. But, if he's only seeing you one day a week and it's not on Saturday night, then he's probably dating other people. Saturday night is date night. It's the night to take your favorite girl out. If you're not with him that night, then you're not it.

However, if you're seeing each other several times a week, and definitely on Friday and Saturday nights, then it's probably time to raise the question. I'm not suggesting that on the fifth date, you ask him, "Where's this relationship going?"

He's going to run for the hills.

You have to evaluate when it's the right time by how things are going and by his actions.

In therapy we say, "Don't watch what he says but what he does." If you corner a guy by asking him where things are going too soon you can push him away. It shows neediness on your part.

You don't have to be needy. Remember that you are a confident, empowered woman. You have choices. You are a catch. He should want to catch you just as much as you want to catch him.

This is not about your trapping him into a corner. A confident woman knows who she is and where she stands. If you're feeling a little insecure, then you fake it until you make it. You get past that.

When you get home, evaluate why you were feeling insecure and work on clearing that limiting belief, or see what it's telling you about his behavior and your reaction to it. Just don't show that you're insecure. Work through the neediness. If you can't do this by yourself, find a therapist. Neediness is not attractive, confidence is.

If you both come to a mutual agreement to date exclusively then it's time to take down your profile. By that I mean it's not a tacit agreement, it's actually one that you both talk about it. You clearly agree to only see each other.

Until that moment, keep your profile up, and keep interacting with other potential dates and mates. Until you both agree to try an exclusive relationship, you're still in the dating process. His delay may be a sign that he's not ready, or he's not that into you. Or he could be afraid. You need to keep looking.

To Sex or Not to Sex

Sexual compatibility is a critical part of any relationship. It can make or break a union. Sooner or later you'll want to know if his needs meet your needs—and vice versa. You will also want to make sure that the two of you have enough chemistry to make your relationship last. This is a matter of.... do you like each other's pheromones?

This can only be gleaned through experience with each other. When it comes right down to it, only you know what's right for you.

There are pros and cons to waiting a short or long time before having sex with a prospective mate. You could wait too long, or not long enough. He might seem like the perfect "One," but if you're not sexually compatible, the union will probably not work. You might want to find out how sexually compatible you are as soon as you decide that he might actually be "the One."

Some people question whether they should have sex before they agree to date exclusively. Others have the attitude that sex is just sex and should be enjoyed for its own sake. Many women have adopted the attitude that they should view sex the same way a man does.

My response to this ongoing dialogue is that everyone should make up his or her own mind after knowing the facts about how men and women bond to each other. The truth is that nature has created men and women differently, and not in the outwardly obvious way. Men and women have different sexual chemistry— which means that their bodies and brains respond differently after the sexual act.

When women have sex, their bodies release large amounts of oxytocin. After the sexual act, women begin to bond with the man—any man.

Oxytocin begins the bonding process for women by lowering their defenses and increasing their empathy towards their partner. This means that they will begin to see the man and the relationship through "rose colored glasses." They begin to physically bond with him.

Unfortunately, our body does not know or care if he is a Level I match or Level IV match.

This chemistry can trick you into believing that a Level II candidate is better than he is. It can trick you into overlooking flaws or a lack of shared values and intimacies. It can even make you forget your deal breakers, or make you delude yourself into believing that the glaring defects you see in him don't really exist. Or don't matter.

If you have sex too soon, it's easy to start overlooking his faults, even the red flags. You can become blinded because you are bonded chemically to this man. Later, even if you have a short-term relationship with the man, the break up will still hurt.

You can now understand why I am against being "friends with benefits" and other such arrangements. It's about loving yourself enough to stand for what you want—a lasting love. When you love yourself enough, you don't put yourself at risk of deluding yourself. You honor yourself.

Let us talk about a man's sexual response and his chemical response. When a man has an orgasm, his body releases a lot of dopamine. This is the "feel good" hormone. (Why do you think marijuana is nicknamed dope?) When he has sex, he *doesn't* bond—he just wants more sex in order to release more dopamine, in order to feel that rush.

Men do not bond through sex. Men bond through time, and as a result of respect, friendship, trust, and caring. So if you have sex too soon with a man, he will not be bonded with you... but you will be bonded with him. He can walk away more easily than you can. It will be harder for you to walk away, or to see the "real him." Also he might lose his thrill of the chase and move on to new hunting grounds.

This is nature at work, and was meant to be adaptive during the days of the caveman. A man wanted to make sure that he was raising his own child. Nature bonded the woman to the man so she would not want to have sex with other men. But since there were more women than men at that time, he was given the urge to continue having sex with as many women as possible, in order to propagate his genes. After all, many men died hunting for food and fighting with the dinosaurs.

The age-old question of "when to have sex" is basically a matter of intuition. You're ready when you know him well enough to know that you're interested in him as a partner, as mate material, and when he has invested enough time to show you that he is interested in you as a person, not just as a quick fling. And he has bonded with you. At the very minimum, my advice is to have sex only with someone who is willing to commit to being sexually exclusive with you.

Remember that men enjoy the chase, so the time that he waits while you build a relationship can allow him to feel the joy of the chase. As we know, men are wired to be hunters. Chemistry plays a huge part in all our functioning. If there's no chemistry, he's not your Level III or IV. It's that simple.

Leading Up To Sex

Until you're ready to have sex with him, you should avoid sending him mixed messages. I believe that you should be up front with a man and tell him that you're not ready to have sex until you get to know him better. He will respect you for this, and know that you probably tell every other man the same thing.

Being honest with him helps him to manage his expectations. He will know that you are not a "Good Time Sally" and that if he wants to go out with you, he'll have to go through the process of getting to know you. You are not a one-night stand or a three-night stand.

Your verbal message to him should be congruent with your actions. Please Ladies, this means that you definitely should not be sexting (sending sexually provocative text messages) or sending nude or otherwise provocative pictures of yourself to him via email or text before you're ready to have sex. You should also avoid having explicit conversations about sex. I mention this because many men have told me—and shown me—that far too many women do this.

If you sext him while telling him that you do not want to have sex, you're sending mixed messages. A man will get confused and, rightfully, annoyed. He'll feel like you're offering him sex; then, when you say no, he'll think you insincerely led him on.

Plus you should never send sexual or nude pictures to anyone, because you never know who will see them. I have witnessed numerous men and women showing their friends the pictures that their dates have sent them. Do you really want to be the center of his friends' attention?

If you want to wait, say so. You can tell him, "I'm really at-tracted to you, but I'm not ready to have sex." That is a very clear message. "I want to get to know you better so when we have sex it will be special." This diffuses any doubts he may have about his masculinity, or your feelings about him. This says, "I'm not waiting because of a lack of attraction. I do want to have sex with you. But right now is wrong for me."

You can still enjoy kissing him and lightly making out. But you want to avoid doing this in places such as your home or his home—where he might think it will lead to more. After all, we are adults and we've all had sex before. This is not about protecting your virginity. This is about not doing more than what you're ready to do. So don't invite him into your house, or go into his, and start making out until you're ready to have sex.

Basically, it's a delicate dance. You will have to discern when you're ready emotionally, as well as to learn to override the messages of your hormones. Part of the dance also lies in knowing how long your partner is willing to wait.

But definitely don't have sex until you are ready—even if wants to move on to greener pastures. It's your body; you get to set your own boundaries. Your Level III or Level IV match will wait for you to be ready. Just have the sensitivity to tact-fully prolong the dance by avoiding certain situations, and by continuing to reassure him that you find him attractive and interesting.

However, I don't think you should wait too long, either, because if the sex doesn't work, then the relationship doesn't work.

This is a delicate balance. You have to feel comfortable enough to have sex. And you have to feel comfortable after having sex. ⸱

I don't believe there's a one, two, or three-date rule—as some men like to say. There should be no, "Not until our second date." There definitely should not be sex on the first date (or on the second or third).

You can't set a predetermined time for what's right for you. You can't decide in advance when the time will be right. You might feel that it's right on the fourth night or on the fifteenth.

Most men want sex the first night. They will continue wanting it every night after that until they get it. You have to manage their expectations. Thus, it's important to avoid a situation in which one thing leads to the other and you end up having sex before you're ready. After that you would have to deal with the uncomfortable feeling that comes after having had sex with an almost complete stranger. You don't want that to happen with this man who could be your mate.

A man can expect whatever he wants, but if he really likes you he will wait until you're comfortable. You should *never* have sex because you feel pressured to have sex.

Even if you do think you're ready, be careful.

Sexual Compatibility

Sex is fundamentally important to a relationship. It is, after all, the very reason for having a romantic relationship. As a species, we need men and women to have sex. Otherwise, there's no species.

Sex has always been a part of what attracts men and women to each other. The courtship and the rituals were all added on later. For some other species, sex is all there is to it. They meet. They mate. They say goodbye.

Humans, though, are different. Sex is part of our connection to one another. It is part of our union. Sometimes it's the reason for the union, although I'd advise against it. A lasting, loving relationship is formed on the strength of shared values and intimacies, of common goals and dreams, not just on how well we fit together sexually. However, you might share all those other tings, but if you are not sexually compatible, the relationship might not work out.

We have to be compatible regarding how much, how often, and just plain, *how* we have sex in order to have a good and lasting relationship. If our sexual selves aren't compatible, a romantic relationship won't work. Period.

If he wants sex three times per day and you only want it once per week, you're going to have problems. I strongly advise that you find that out while you're dating.

If you want sex every day and he wants it twice a week, you might be able to compromise on three times per week. Usually, the partner who wants it more frequently will be the one to adjust his or her need. Unfortunately, it's very hard to find two people who have the exact same sexual drive. So if everything else is great, you make some compromises. Remember, there are no Mr. Perfects out there.

Now is the time to show each other what you like and what you don't. Be open about how frequently you like it, or don't. If you can't find a way to interact sexually while you're dating, don't imagine that this will get better after you're married, living together, or whatever.

We all make compromises, but we're dealing with your happiness here. Your ideal partner makes you feel satisfied, safe, and fulfilled, as you do with him.

Only you know what that means for you. Some people like tender, gentle, slow sex. Always. Some people like it rough and sweaty. Some people like all the lights off. Some like sex in public.

What you like and how you like it doesn't matter, as long as you both fully share your feelings and ideas. You both need to figure all this out, and as soon as possible. You're talking about finding a lifetime partner. Who wants a lifetime of unsatisfying sex?

So you need to be your authentic self while you're dating, and encourage him to be authentic as well. You need to show all aspects of yourself. There's nothing worse than being married and finding out that what he really likes is nothing like what you did before.

For example, someone might pretend to like oral sex and then, after they get married, disclose that they don't. That's tantamount to lying, and if oral sex had been an important part of your sexual life while dating, then he's going to feel betrayed. Good relationships are based on trust, and this is hard to regain once broken.

Don't say or do anything while dating just to "get him," because you won't be able to keep him for the long run if your relationship was based on a deception. This is about finding your lifetime partner, not about tricking someone into believing that you are his mate.

If you want to try something new in the bedroom, talk about it in a non-threatening, non-judgmental way. Often couples find that they both want to explore the same thing;

they just hadn't talked about it. Remember that sexual intimacy is developed this way—through the mutual sharing of feelings, fears, and preferences.

You have to feel safe with your partner to freely discuss these things. If you don't, you need to examine the reasons. You need to feel safe to be fully sexually expressive.

If what you'd like to experiment is a new idea for him, ask him if he'd like to try it. If he tries it and doesn't like it, then he shouldn't be forced to do it again. The same holds true for you. It's about feeling safe to express your desires and dislikes, as well as your fantasies.

If he doesn't want to try something at all, then you have to decide how important it is to you. If it's something you feel is fundamental to your sexual fulfillment, and he's unwilling to try it or doesn't like it, then you know that you're not sexually compatible.

You don't want to commit to a long-term relationship and find out that there's something that's really important to you, or to the other person, that was not disclosed when you were dating.

Thus, it's important to explore all of these areas while you're dating. Usually somebody who likes the straight and narrow doesn't suddenly become Christian Gray after he's married.

It might help you to get a good book on sex to learn some new techniques. Sit and become familiar with other things. See what might be interesting. See what might be a deal breaker for you.

STD's (Sexually Transmitted Diseases)

The reality is that the exponentially expanded pool of potential dates in the online world magnifies the need for safety precautions before having sex. You're not the only one going out with more people. The men you go out with are doing this too.

With more dates, it's more likely that they're having more sexual encounters with relative strangers. I've heard men say that they always have sex on the first and second date. Please, don't be one of those women.

No matter how long you wait, or don't, in this age of STDs and HIV, condoms are a must.

It's also good for both of you to get tested for HIV and STD's before you have sex. (Remember my advice to have sex only with someone who was willing to commit to remain sexually exclusive with you. Once your relationship has developed to that point, you care about each other and each other's health.)

Show each other your test results before things get too heated. The test results are only valid if he's not having sex with anyone else. You both should get retested after six months to make sure that you are truly free of all STDs and AIDS. Ideally, you should be having protected sex for those six months.

Venereal diseases are far too serious to be ignored. This can be a matter of life and death. It's simple: Make sure you see and understand each other's "papers."

If he is not willing to wear a condom with you—that means he has not been wearing it with anybody else. Run! Your life and health are worth more than this.

Sexting

Digital dating does not automatically include digital sexting. You have to know and set your boundaries regarding this, because someone may ask you to engage in this. Just as with physical sex, you should only do what you're comfortable with, and never— never—let yourself be pressured into doing something you don't want to do.

Sexting has become increasingly common. But you don't have to do it just because "the other women do."

Letting a man have sexually explicit videos or photographs of you is fraught with potential pitfalls. You should never give someone videos or photos you wouldn't want someone else to see.

Look at the number of times you've heard about celebrities and politicians having their intimate, supposedly private, photos racing around the Internet for everyone to see.

This sort of thing begins with trust. But it can end in disgust.

Someone you thought would never betray your confidence shows a friend— or the world. Maybe they're bragging. Maybe they're thoughtless. Or stupid. They could someday be out for revenge.

Unless you're prepared to share your intimate photos with everyone, don't share them with anyone.

The best advice I can give you is this: Beware!

Tricks and Traps Backfire

Don't ever try to trick anyone into an exclusive relationship or marriage. If someone's not ready, they may not be the right one for you. If you trap another person, you're also trapping yourself.

Over the past ten years I've witnessed two very smart men friends struggle with this. In both cases, they were at a point in their relationships where they were going to break up with their girlfriends. The women, sensing this, decided to use the oldest trap in the world—they got pregnant. Their stories did not have a good outcome in either case.

The first man never married the woman and, at age 45, he had to begin co-parenting a newborn. She had acted out of her fear of not being able to find another "good" candidate, and her attempt to manipulate the situation backfired. Raising a child as a single parent is very difficult. Having a newborn also limited her ability to find her true mate.

The second man ended up marrying the woman when she was almost due to deliver. He was resentful of her manipulation, and never let her forget it. He never trusted her again. From my point of view, they have a terrible relationship.

It's very difficult to parent children with a man who does not want them. This is unfair to all parties involved. It's particularly unfair to bring a child into this world with a father who had no intention of becoming one.

Both these men stepped up to the plate and took their responsibility as a father seriously, both financially and emotionally.

Some women are so insecure that they use certain other tricks to keep rivals away. If you feel that insecure in your relationship, you should realize that perhaps you are with the wrong person. If your man has done nothing to make you doubt him, perhaps you need to examine your limiting beliefs.

I'm the mother of two sons, and it was interesting to observe some of their dates trying to mark their territory. They would leave a bra, shoes, or a piece of clothing behind—usually hidden in a place where my sons could not easily find the item.

These women would leave evidence of their existence behind in case my sons brought another woman home. Their actions were meant to scare competitors away.

Ladies, do not do this to a man. He'll feel like you're overstepping your boundaries. I feel that it's best, if you know you're going to spend the night at a guy's house, to bring what you need—and to take everything away with you when you leave. Everything. Don't even leave a toothbrush—until he asks you to do this. A man wants to be with a woman who is confident, and who knows she is a "catch" and does not have to rely on tricks or manipulation. Remember, self-confidence is magnetic.

When you are in his house, it's *his* territory—and men are very territorial. When he asks you to leave a toothbrush, you know he really wants you there. Wait to be invited into his life. If you're inflicting yourself upon him, he'll feel resentful or pressured. Women react the same way towards a man who does this to them.

Meet the Family

It's always tricky to figure out when you should introduce a new man to your family. It's best to be cautious because men and women view this milestone in the relationship differently. If you suggest this meeting too soon with a man, he might think that you're rushing the relationship and pressuring him to commit.

You need to think about how he will interpret your suggestion, and how the meeting and its setting will make him feel. Use your intuition to guide you.

Obviously, if you're invited to a family wedding or some other major event for which you would normally have a date, there's less pressure. But if your parents are coming into town and want you to go out to dinner with them, asking a date along means a whole lot more.

Think about the situation. Then talk to him. Ask him how he feels about meeting your family, and really listen to his answer. Watch his body language. Be body conscious with yourself, as well.

As I mentioned, meeting the family has a different connotation to men and women. If you ask a guy to meet your family, he usually thinks, "Oh, she wants to get married." But this isn't always the case. If, for example, you're in the middle of the holiday season and your family is having a get-together, asking him to join you is a bit different.

You have to use your own judgment as to when you want to introduce him to your family.

If your family lives in the same town and you see them regularly, then at some point, when you feel comfortable, you might say to him, "We're just doing our usual Sunday dinner at my parents house. Do you want to come over?"

Make it a non-threatening event.

Or if you've been dating for a few months and your parents live someplace else and are coming into town, you might say, "My parents are coming to visit. Would you like to join us one night for dinner?"

Again, make the invitation nonthreatening. Let him decide whether he wants to join you or not. He can say, "No. It's okay. You go ahead and spend time with your family."

If you've been dating for a few months, your parents are coming in from out of town for a few nights, and he doesn't want to join you for one night, he's sending you a message. He's saying, "I'm not ready to get that serious with you yet."

If he does meet them, watch how he reacts to them, and vice versa. How does he act around them? You know your family. This is a chance to get to know him better and for them to get to know him.

The same thing is true when he invites you to meet his family. You get to see what they're like. And the experience will also provide an opportunity for you to learn more about him.

Watch how he interacts with his family, and how he behaves with you in front of them. Also watch how they treat you and how they behave in general. What do they "expect" of you? How important is religion, politics, race, etc., to them—especially if yours are different from theirs?

Meet the Kids

Introducing him to your children, or your children to his, deserves special consideration. You have to think about when to do it, and how.

You know your kids, so you know what situation is best for the initial meeting—over dinner, for a movie, or at a sporting event. Make the initial meeting a short one. Sometimes, everyone can meet when he comes to pick you up for a date.

Briefly introduce him as your friend. Let them interact for five or ten minutes.

Your children's ages will also help determine what you say when you introduce him, and what you tell them about him.

Just don't force him on them, or force them on him. That could lead to resentment. Your kids might need time to adjust to his being a part of their lives—maybe even their stepfather— whether they like it or not.

It's probably better—again, depending on their ages—to introduce him as a friend you think they might like. You might tell teenagers or older children that you like him and you think they will too. Tell them that you are still getting to know each other so they don't feel like they're interviewing a potential stepfather.

When you do introduce them, watch how he interacts with them. You must, of course, watch for any signs of inappropriate touching or sexually suggestive acts. Beyond that, though, you need to watch how he resolves conflicts with your children, and with his own children as well. And how does he deal with conflicts between your kids and his?

Generally speaking, if one of your children is rude to him, you need to set proper boundaries with your child by taking the child aside and saying that this behavior will not be tolerated. State the consequences of continued rudeness. Your date should do the same with his. Children will generally act out at some point because no one likes change. It's how you deal with their inappropriate behavior that matters.

Adult children can often act out also. Again, it's about setting proper boundaries with your children and not tolerating rude behavior. If he doesn't defend you when they are rude to you, then perhaps you need to take a pass on this man. His children are part of the package—and you'll be sharing him with them. If he allows them to be disrespectful while you're dating, the situation will only get worse after you're married.

Please, don't let your special someone spend the night with you when your children are home, until you're dating exclusively and you're fairly certain that he's the One. You don't want to expose your children to a revolving door of men (or women). Children can get attached easily, and you don't want them to go through all your break-ups.

Blending families brings a whole new set of complicated dynamics to a relationship. The pressure can strain any union. You need to be prepared. You also need to spend a lot of time doing things with both sets of children (especially if they're younger) before you commit, so that everyone feels comfortable together.

Remember, you also need to do things as a couple, without the children, because he's looking for a mate, not a replacement mother for his children. Same as you.

Living Together

I highly recommend living with somebody for a limited period of time before marriage. That's how you *really* get to know someone.

And I do mean "limited." If your goal is marriage, set a time limit before moving in. I suggest six months to one year. If he doesn't want to get married at the end of the period, move out. This means that he doesn't feel the same way that you do, or he has commitment issues. Either way, don't waste more time.

Never make ultimatums. He knows his time agreement with you. If he doesn't take the next step, then say, "When I moved in, we agreed to a time limit. That time is now approaching. It seems like you have changed your mind. I need to make arrangements to move out." Do not make recriminations or accusations. He is entitled to his feelings. If he doesn't feel like he's ready, then he's not. Move on. But go with class and dignity.

And, who knows, he might come back.

Here's why I believe in a trial period of living together. Even if you spend long weekends together, or go on vacation together, it's not the same as sharing space together. Somebody who wants to hide his defects can do so for short periods of time. He can't do it if you spend a lot of time together.

When you live with somebody full time they can't hide who they are. Six months to a year is a good trial period. Of course some of this depends on your age. If you're in your twenties, you could prolong the trial period for up to two years. (But if you're looking for marriage, don't agree to a longer period of time.)

Many times people aren't hiding things intentionally. For example, usually people clean their homes just before someone comes over. What if, when you live together, he finds out that when no one's coming over you leave toothpaste spattered on the sink? Or what if you leave dirty plates piled up in the kitchen—for days? What if you don't take out the garbage, even when it's overflowing?

And what about him? Maybe he leaves his dirty socks and underwear tossed on the bedroom floor. Maybe he never hangs up his wet towel after he's done with it, and instead he tosses it onto the furniture, causing mildew? Or what if one of you is a neat freak who constantly wants to vacuum? You need to know if you are comfortable with each other's domestic habits. You get the picture.

We all have little (or not so little) things we do without thinking that might bother someone else. It's also good to find out if you can compromise, and if you're able to modify any annoying habits so that you can both feel best.

Does he always have to have the TV on when he's home? Loud? Does he always watch sports, even when you want to watch your favorite cooking show or cable drama?

No matter how good a match you are as a couple, you're still two individuals coming together with your own habits, likes, and dislikes. Some differences won't matter. You'll be able to compromise on others. But some might be bigger hurdles. You won't know until you live together, and see.

Living together also gives you a chance to see him in even more situations. You are still in the evaluation process.

See what happens if you're late some day, or when he's in a stressful situation. If he has anger issues, you want to know. You will see this when he's in his own environment, over time.

If you have an argument you want to see how he argues. Does he keep the focus on the argument? Or does he start belittling and ridiculing you? Does he yell and scream? Does he twist your words around, until they no longer sound like what you just said? Does he blame you too much? Or can he discuss things rationally?

Any abuse —whether verbal or physical—is an absolute deal breaker. If anything abusive happens, leave. Don't look back. He won't change. The abuse will only get worse.

The purpose of a trial period of living together is to determine if you're with your ideal mate. If you realize you're incompatible, for whatever reason, then it's better to move on, sooner rather than later.

Even if you spend eight or ten months with him, if you find out that he's the wrong man, don't stay with him because you've invested that much time. View the situation as a learning experience, not as a failure. Every relationship plays an important role in your growth and self-knowledge. Learn your lesson and move on.

You know that if you end up marrying the wrong person, the relationship will not last for the long run. A divorce is a lot more costly—financially and in wasted time. You'll be back at the same game, only a few years older.

It's always best to cut your losses, and not make a fear-based decision to stay in a relationship that's not working for you.

CHAPTER SIXTEEN

Lasting Love

How do you know if you have found lasting love with "The One" or just "another One"? Unfortunately, love is easier to discern than its longevity.

Real love is the feeling of intense affection, safety, warmth, emotional attachment, and acceptance of the person as he is. It survives trials and tribulations. It is much more, too. It is not just a strong sexual attraction and desire for the person. That's lust.

There's an element of lust needed for romantic love, but love is much more.

Some questions to ask yourself: Do I feel really good when I'm with him? Do I feel safe? Am I happy when I'm around him and do I feel free to be myself? Am I happy when I think about him?

Do you give to him because you really just want him to be happy? Or do you give to him because you want something back?

As a couple, do you encourage each other to be the best you each can be? Do you encourage each other's goals and dreams? Are you there for each other when things are tough? Are you each other's best support?

Do you trust each other? Are you committed to each other and the relationship?

If you've answered yes to most of these questions, then congratulations! You've found love. However, that's just the beginning—a relationship for a lifetime takes a lifetime of effort.

Making It Work Takes Work

Good relationships don't just happen; they take a lot of work and maintenance. Just ask anyone who has been happily married for over thirty years!

After all, you're two independent people trying to be interdependent. You have two different life histories. It's natural that there will be points of conflict in a relationship.

Relationships are often a delicate balance of tension. As you will see later, the amount of tension or conflict can depend on the stage of your relationship. It's important to know which stage you're going through, so you don't throw away an overall great relationship.

Many relationships in the "Struggle Stage" have a push-pull pattern—like a seesaw or a dance. When she gets too close and personal, he withdraws because he feels smothered. Then she feels hurt and pulls back from him in answer to his withdrawal. This triggers his reversing his position and pulling close to her—seeking to reconnect. And the dance starts over again.

You can see that this push— pull pattern is based upon fear— of being too close or too distant.

A healthier relationship will achieve a delicate balance between giving and receiving, doing and asking, closeness and distance.

Sometimes, when you think something has gone wrong in a relationship, what actually went wrong was your interpretation of what was happening.

Let's say he starts working longer hours because his boss gave him a big job. He's facing a challenging deadline. But you interpret his long work hours as his withdrawing from you; so you withdraw your energy from him and the relationship, giving him the silent or distant treatment. This might all be due to your misinterpreting of his motives. His withdrawal might have nothing to do with you. But your reaction did. Perhaps you were acting on a fear of abandonment.

When you face a challenge in your relationship, become the neutral observer. First, examine what is actually happening—the facts. Then determine whether your reaction is based on what's really happening, or if you're responding to some fear or limiting belief about yourself or relationships. You now have the tools to clear these, so use them.

Address your fear by talking to your partner. You'll find out the truth, feel closer, and grow your level of intimacy with each other. Talking about any fears or problems in a timely manner, before resentments build, can prevent damage to your relationship.

If he loves you, you're a priority in his life. But you might not always be his first priority. His work may be demanding more of him at times. Or your children may need more attention. Our priorities temporarily shift as we face new challenges. In a great relationship, you're always one of each other's top priorities, even if you're not always the only one, or number one at that moment. As long as you're his first priority over the long term, and he's yours, you'll be fine.

Still, for a relationship to be successful for the long-term, you have to make time for each other. Sharing means caring, and showing you care shows that you love.

Keep The Romance Alive

You have to keep your romance alive to keep your relationship healthy. You have to do things for, and with, each other.

One thing I suggest is having a date night, for just the two of you. Have certain rules for this evening: you don't discuss the children, and you don't discuss work. You talk about the things that make you uniquely you. You talk about your goals, your dreams. You talk about the things that you love to do, or the things you'd like to try together. You learn more about each other.

Even though you're a level III or level IV match, don't assume that you're not changing and growing as time passes. This is the time to talk about things that you might be dreaming about exploring. Or you might be talking about ways to make your areas of commonality larger. As you grow as a person, you'll have new dreams and new aspirations.

Date night is for getting to know the real you, and for maintaining your bond with each other. It's not about discussing problems with a coworker or your children. It's about romance.

Get dressed up. Look beautiful.

Another important aspect is to keep the passion in your sex life. Send a fun little text: "I keep thinking about what you did to me last night." Or "I'm looking forward to doing something special with you tonight."

Believe me, he'll be thinking about you all day.

You want to keep things fresh. Do something interesting. Buy beautiful underwear and make sure that you always make an effort to look good—even when you're just hanging out at home. Dream up little surprises to keep the relationship and your sexual life fresh and romantic.

Also, just because you have your man, don't let your looks slip. Don't stop wearing makeup. When you wake up every morning, make an effort to look your best.

Why should you put in less effort now that you have him, than you did when you were trying to get him? This wasn't a sales job. It was a union.

Most people tend to fall into the trap of focusing on the flotsam and jetsam of life when they are in a committed relationship. Relationships can devolve into doing joint errands and mundane chores. Don't let your relationship fail.

In the middle of your errands, take time to go for a romantic lunch. Do something different. Keep the fun in the relationship. Tell him how much you love him in the middle of the hardware store. Designate a weekend for a romantic getaway.

Try new things together. Surprise him one day by suggesting, "Hey, let's try kayaking together." Try something different on a weekend date. Explore new hobbies or new museums together.

Try to avoid falling into routines unless it's a fun routine— like taking a walk together every night where you catch up with each other. Definitely don't fall into the routine of sitting in front of the TV. That works against the relationship. You're not having a relationship with each other; you're each having a relationship with the TV.

He's the most important person in your life. Show him that he is. Your relationship should be the most important focus for both of you. Every action should be viewed in terms of, "does this make the relationship better and stronger? Or worse." If it's worse, don't do it.

Keeping the romance alive after you have children is just as important. It just gets a little more complicated.

Sex may not happen exactly when you want it, but you still can—and should—make an effort. You may not be having sex seven or ten times a week, like you did when you first moved in together, but if you do it three times a week, make it romantic. Plan for the evening. Sex is about showing love and tenderness, as well as gratification, even if it's sex "on the run" in ten stolen minutes during a busy day.

By the time you reach the point in your relationship where you've been together a couple of years, sexual incompatibility shouldn't be an issue if you have kept the lines of communication open between the two of you. Presumably, you both shared a satisfying sexual relationship before you moved in together, and developed it even more during those initial months of committed cohabitation.

You should feel safe and open to discuss your desires, fears, and fantasies with each other. If one or both of you is going through a stressful period that's affecting your sex drive, talk about it. It's normal for this to happen during periods of stress, and you should feel free to bring it up. Let him know that you still desire him.

The key is that in a healthy relationship you should feel safe about voicing all your opinions and revealing what's going on with you emotionally.

Little Things

Romance is not just about steamy sex and candlelight dinners. We all have different ways of showing each other we care.

It might be so simple as his holding the door open for you, or helping you slip on your coat, or telling you that your hair looks particularly nice before you go out—and meaning it.

You can show your affection and love by doing something special for him such as sending him a text that says, "I love you" out of the blue.

Cards. Little gifts. Staying home with you when you're sick. These little things say, "I care." They say, "I love you." We all have different ways of feeling loved. I feel like I'm loved when someone does thoughtful things for me. I love waking up to find that my special man has made me breakfast. Other women love to receive little gifts… "just because."

Part of the bonding process is learning how to express your love in the way that he wants to receive love. Find out what makes him feel loved. Do it.

The point is: Don't stop after you get married, or move in together, or however you define your long-term relationship.

Lasting love lasts because we show we love, and we both are committed to the relationship. We trust each other.

It's also important for you to evaluate if he respects you. Does he treat you like a partner? Does he ask for your opinion on important things, even if it's questions about his work? If a situation comes up, does he seek your advice?

You want a relationship in which you're treated as an equal. You want somebody who respects you, and encourages you to pursue your goals. He believes in you. And you do the same for him. You want to know that no matter what... he's in your corner and has your back. And you have the same exact feelings for him. That's a sign of a healthy love.

Communication is Key

No one can read minds. If you don't tell him what bothers you, he won't know. He might keep on doing the bothersome thing over and over, forever. He might even think that you like it. Tell him what's going on.

The same is true if he does something you like. Tell him. If you want him to do it more often, tell him that, too.

Encourage him to do the same. Ask him to tell you if you do something he likes, or if you do something he doesn't. When he does, let him know that you're glad that he did.

That's all part of having good communication.

If you run into a problem, or do something that irritates your partner or hurts his feelings, apologize. Each person needs to take 100% responsibility for his or her 50% of the relationship.

There are ways to communicate without making the other person "wrong" or feel defensive. Your aim is to express how you feel—not to win an argument or make the other person wrong.

You can control your emotions and reactions to anything. Learning to control your mind and your thinking requires practice and vigilance.

You are responsible for your own emotions and well-being; this means that you need to let him know how you feel when he does a certain thing.

In a compassionate, empathic relationship the person at fault might say, "I'm really sorry you felt that way when I did this. It was not my intent to cause those feelings. It was my intent to let you know that I feel unappreciated when you don't acknowledge the little things I do."

When you communicate without blaming and shaming and are empathic, you both feel understood.

A compassionate response to his apology would be, "I'm sorry that you felt unappreciated because I did not acknowledge what you did for me. That was not my intent. I was busy, but I should have stopped to tell you that I love you."

This is an example of a win-win communication. He explained himself in a non-blaming way that communicated his feelings. He apologized for his hurtful response. She realized that he never meant to hurt her so she doesn't feel resentful. She apologizes for her slight, and they both feel better at the end of this conversation. Practice this with your partner by using your own words.

How to Argue

Still, despite good communication and sharing, every relationship hits rough spots. How you deal with them is a critical factor in how successful and enduring your relationship will be.

You have to learn how to argue or discuss points of disagreement.

First, make sure you focus the argument on the actual problem, not on how wrong your partner is. Say something like "When X happens, I feel "Y." He cannot control how you feel, but he can address the action. If he answers, "That's silly! How can you feel that way?" you can answer, "Emotions are not rational, they just are. It's the way I feel."

Never say anything like "You're inconsiderate or stupid!" This takes the focus away from the problem and makes it personal. Even though you are angry, don't let your disagreement escalate into disrespect. Words are like swords; they wound and are seldom forgotten. These wounds are not visible, but they can cause irreparable damage to a relationship.

If you follow certain protocols for arguing and communicating, you have a better chance of reaching an outcome that will be a solution that's workable. And a better chance of being happy with each other afterwards.

Protocol for Arguing

First, identify the problem.

Let's say he leaves his dirty clothes on the floor—all over the house. The problem shouldn't be expressed as, "You don't love me." Or, "You're a pig!"

The problem is that, "I really feel like you're invading my space and being disrespectful when you leave your clothes all over the floor."

Second, focus on the problem.

You don't say, "You're an insensitive slob."

You're looking for a solution, not a fight. It's about the clothes, not about him. You can explain how having dirty clothes all over the floor makes you feel. You might say, "I feel really stressed out when our room is a mess."

Third, attack the problem, not the person.

It's about the problem, not him. "Perhaps, we could put a clothes hamper at the entrance of our bedroom, so you could throw them in there. Would this be helpful?

Fourth, listen with an open mind.

Don't have your answers ready before you've heard what he has to say. Actually stop and actively listen. That means you should look at him with a relaxed face, and your arms down by your side, not crossed over your chest.

Most people are so busy thinking about their argument that they're not really listening to the other person. After listening to him, you can reflect back to him what you heard him tell you by saying, "What I'm hearing you say is that you're in too much of a hurry to…"

Fifth, treat a person's feelings with respect.

If you tell me that you feel like I've invaded your boundaries, I'm not going to tell you, "That's ridiculous" or "You're being unreasonable." These statements only serve to devalue your partner or undercut his or her feelings. Remember, feelings aren't rational.

A better answer would be to say something like, "I'm sorry you feel that way. That's not my intention."

Sixth, take responsibility for your actions.

When you're wrong, you apologize. Take ownership and responsibility for your actions and behavior. And then follow through: because it's not what you say, it's what you *do* that shows the other person the way you feel.

A good response would be, "You know what? You're right. I should've taken more care in keeping my mess contained. The hamper is a great idea. Yes, let's put the hamper by the entrance of our room. Would this work for you?"

Make sure that you thank him. Then, kiss him.

A win-win solution is when the relationship wins, which means that the solution brings back harmony. It's not about a personal win. A personal win means somebody loses. That means the relationship loses.

You should learn to argue so that the relationship wins and you both feel good about the solution.

So... No name-calling. No blaming. No shaming. And no making excuses for bad behavior.

Sometimes that's easier said than done.

Another rule for arguing is that if the argument is getting heated, or it's going nowhere, call a time out. Each person has the right to call a time out. No matter who calls it, the other one has to respect it. Immediately.

You step away, but you agree to come back in an hour, or at some other specific time, to try again. After you've had time to cool down. Then be willing to do just that. "I'm not able to discuss this right now because I'm too upset. Can we talk about it in an hour?"

No matter how hard you try, sometimes you have to realize that you just have to agree to disagree. And sometimes, if the thing you're arguing about is not as important to you as it is to the other person, it's okay just to give in. You have to pick your battles. In a healthy relationship both are willing to compromise—its not just about one partner always agreeing with the other.

Remember, the goal is for the *relationship* to win.

The Five Stages of Relationships

No matter how well we communicate and show each other we care, relationships evolve and change. Dr. Susan Campbell identified five stages through which successful relationships must evolve. When a couple gets stuck in any one of the stages, they usually break-up unless they seek help. Or they continue in a bad relationship.

Understanding these natural stages of a relationship will help you understand your feelings and experiences and not misinterpret them as... *It's time to find my next partner!* You will be able to identify where you are and what is happening. This information will empower you to make better decisions.

We need to be aware and understand, for example, that fading passion doesn't necessarily mean the relationship is ending. It's just changing and maturing. In order for a relationship to be healthy, it has to proceed through these stages.

Stage 1: The Romance or Honeymoon Stage

The first six months (or sometimes as long as two years) of a relationship are known as the honeymoon stage. You both fall in madly in love and feel the magical bliss that poets write about. You both look starry-eyed at each other. You are driven by infatuation from that initial attraction.

Remember those hormones that create bonding and minimize our differences? They are fully in charge during this stage. You see each other through rose-colored glasses, seeing each other as your idealized "Other" and minimizing any differences. You can't get enough of each other.

This is the stage in which you decide to date each other exclusively. And, when you move past lust and first fall in love. Everything seems wonderful. One partner may be more infatuated than the other, at this stage, so sometimes the other partner has to wait until the infatuation levels are about the same.

It's all systems go until the drug high wears off and you remove your rose colored glasses. This stage cannot last, because it's not based upon reality. Eventually, you have to be yourself, and allow the differences between you two to surface.

Stage 2: The Power Struggle

Then you pass into the Power Struggle Stage, in which you begin to see the real person underneath. You see his faults and annoying habits. And he has many! Your differences are magnified.

The crazy sex that you had in the beginning has settled into a more established pattern. You begin to wonder what happened. Unfortunately, when Mr. Perfect is no longer perfect, you may think that it's time to move on, that he wasn't the One.

Many couples break up at this stage of the relationship, thinking that they are no longer compatible. (Serial daters often suffer from this syndrome, only to have the same experience happen with the next person.)

Hold on! Being in this stage is normal and it's supposed to happen. Your relationship is evolving, even though it seems like it's doing the opposite.

Conflicts, anxiety, and disappointments will start to surface. This is where you must be your own neutral observer: watch your reactions and address unrealistic expectations.

This is the stage in which you can best evaluate and decide if this person shares your values, interests, and a congruence of intimacies which will allow you to have a level III or a level IV relationship.

You can also learn how to work through conflict with each other in a healthy way—or not. This is where a lot of your limiting beliefs about yourself and relationships start to really show up. Your cultural and socio-economical differences are also highlighted.

Each partner has to negotiate how to remain him or herself while being part of a "we." This is when the real relationship between two individuals actually begins, as you start to maneuver the struggle of independence and interdependence. You learn to accept your partner as he is—at his best and worst—without trying to change him. Or, not!

You have to learn to deal with the anxiety of the disillusionment of the broken fantasy, and of your different ways of relating to one another. You move from being in love with a fantasy person to discovering your perfectly imperfect partner.

This is where couples are working out their relative roles within the relationship. They struggle over personal boundaries and clearly defining unacceptable behaviors and deal breakers. Many struggle with the idea that they've wound up in a relationship that's not living up to their expectations. Some feel trapped, and their differences cause friction and resentments.

Arguments may devolve into yelling and disrespectful behavior. If a couple is stuck in this stage, they may leave the relationship instead of appreciating the growth opportunity it presents. It is here where they must learn and practice communication and conflict resolution skills.

They will pass this stage successfully if they treat their relationship as the primary goal, instead of focusing on maintaining their independent selves. They must learn to become interdependent. Relationships can be stuck for years at this stage.

This stage presents an opportunity for your greatest personal growth by allowing you to address childhood wounds and limiting beliefs in order to improve your interactions with your loved one. If you don't do this personal growth work while you're with this partner, you will end up having to address these issues with your next partner.

I believe that many Level II relationships will give up at this stage, while Level III or IV relationships will continue trying to grow. Every relationship takes work, but higher-level unions will have more shared intimacies, values, and goals that will naturally keep them interested in one another and working together. They know that it's difficult to find this type of partner, and each person will work hard to preserve the relationship.

If you progress through this stage, you will have a deeper and more fulfilling relationship, because you'll have learned to relate to each other as individuals and accept that your differences are healthy. You've both clearly chosen to be together at this stage; while during the honeymoon stage you *need* to be together.

You're in a process, a journey, which requires hard work... both individually and as a couple. Don't forget to find the joy in the journey.

Stage 3: The Stability Stage

When you both decide that you can accept and live with each other's faults and give up the illusion that a good relationship is always harmonious, you move into the next stage of learning to become partners.

You survived the Power Struggle and you're somewhat in mourning for the loss of the fantasy relationship. You are tired. Now is time to rest and enjoy. You are seeing each other clearly, and making clear choices about who you both are and want.

The danger at this stage is the couple may start to grow apart as each person does their own thing. If you have not been exploring your shared intimacies and mutual goals, you may now realize that each other's paths in life may be different.

There may be a feeling of boredom because you're no longer struggling and fighting. When you're fighting, you are negatively engaged with each other. This creates a feeling of connection, albeit negative.

Now, that you're at peace, you may have a sense of not being connected. Your future together is still undecided. Thus, you need to find ways to strengthen your connection through finding additional shared interests and goals.

Stability may feel boring to some people. They may wonder if the relationship is really over, because there is no longer that bliss of infatuation or the adrenaline rush of the struggle.

No. This is when you have to work to put the romance back into your evolved relationship. After all, you know that you have what it takes to stay together. Isn't being a "we" worth the investment of time and effort?

You also need to learn to be part of the team. Try to make decisions based upon "what's good for the relationship," while continuing to grow as a person. You learn to balance developing yourself with developing the relationship.

You look at your differences as an opportunity to grow. Some moderate levels of incompatibility are healthy and will add spice to your relationship. After all, you don't want to be with your clone.

You can also perfect your communication and conflict resolution skills, to make your relationship even stronger.

During this stage you navigate how to work through disagreements and learn to make compromises on things such as the frequency of sex. This is also the stage in which you build mutual trust, expand your intimacies, and show acceptance for each other's differences... or you go back to the Struggle Stage.

This is the second most common stage for counseling or breaking up.

Stage 4: Commitment Stage

This is the only stage in which there really is a readiness for marriage (though many couples have already married during the romance stage).

You have grown as individuals, and are also a stronger couple because you worked through your differences either through compromise or by accepting each other as you are.

This is the time when you fully commit to the relationship and the person. You now choose each other with full awareness of who you each are. You have a clear direction in your future together.

You share a balance of love, belonging, fun, personal identity, and freedom. You don't need each other; you choose to be with each other.

You now have a strong base for dealing with any future problems because you have the skill set and trust to do so.

When couples choose to live together, they are usually at Stage 3 (Stability) and not at Stage 4. Many couples, even those who have been married for years, will never reach Stage 4 of commitment. They remain ambivalent to their relationship through their own fear of intimacy.

Stage 5: The Co-Creation Stage

This is the stage in which you're a bonded team. Believe it or not, few couples make it this far. In this stage you're each *truly* committed to your shared vision of the future together; and secure in the relationship, trust, and commitment to each other—for better or for worse.

You turn your joint focus towards something bigger than the two of you. You move out as a team to create something new—through charitable work, a joint business, or a project.

The dangers at this stage are that you may become over-involved with your project or work, which can lead to your neglecting your relationship. Remember, your relationship is the key to everything, and you must continually nurture it. There needs to be time for you, for me, for us, and for them. Finding balance can be difficult sometimes and choices must be made.

These stages are not perfectly linear. You will sometimes move back and forth between the stages. Hopefully, you continue to work on yourself and your skills in order to align your relationship to where you want it to be. And to co-create lasting love.

How Fast Should You Move in a Relationship?

There is no "correct" timeline for going from dating to marriage. This depends on your culture, your relationship, and particularly your age. If you're 22, dating for five to eight years might be appropriate. If you're 65, dating for one year might be more realistic. The future seems longer or shorter at different stages of life.

You need to follow your heart and realize that you will go through each stage of the relationship. If you have the commitment to the process and to each other, plus the conflict resolution and communication skills, you and your level III or IV partner can succeed.

CHAPTER SEVENTEEN

Ready, Set, Go!

Wow! You've done a lot of work and covered a lot of ground. You are now ready to embark on the journey of your life.

Finding your true love is actually about the journey, not only about the destination. It's about the process of discovering yourself and reclaiming yourself and growing through each experience.

Let each stumbling block be a marker showing you that you are that much closer to finding your mate. You are that much wiser and knowledgeable.

Use each bump along the road, and each perceived failure, as an opportunity to learn more about yourself and to heal any limiting beliefs you still hold. This will bring you closer to finding your lasting love.

I absolutely believe that there is someone out there just for you. He or she is looking for you right now. Sooner or later you're going to find each other.

Know and *accept* that this is going to happen. Be joyful in your certainty. And take the first step of your journey, so that when you find each other, you are ready.

All you have to do is modify your mindset. When I was younger I was afraid to examine my past and my limiting beliefs, triggers, and drives. Heck, I didn't even know what those were! I was afraid to explore the dark recesses of my mind.

After two failed marriages, I became more afraid of continued failures than of looking for the bogeymen in my psyche. I knew that I had to change how I was dealing with my life. That's when I went to therapy for the first time in order to learn how to date and make better choices.

Many of us never had good role models for creating successful relationships, so we have no idea what these looks like.

Just know that with the right skills and knowledge that I have taught you in this book, and with a lot of perseverance, you too can succeed. I did. You can too!

Do not miss out on the wonderful opportunity to experience love because you're afraid of failure. Many people will convince themselves that they no longer want to be with a man or want romance, as a way of avoiding failure at all costs. Don't be like that.

Have faith in yourself. Learn from every mistake, for these are a natural part of learning. Do not measure yourself against the success of others. You have your own journey.

You are no longer a prisoner of your past. You are not a victim of past wrongs or faulty parenting. You are an empowered person with the opportunity to create the life and the love you want and deserve. So take charge now!

Perhaps, you can become the new role model of a happy marriage for your children and family, giving them a better chance to find success themselves.

I know that you are afraid to keep failing and getting hurt. This is natural. But this time is different. You have new knowledge, you are learning to become psychologically minded, and you have learned about the 4 Levels of Love. You now have the tools to find, co-create, and experience a level III or level IV match.

It might take six months or six years, but if you work through the process and remember to enjoy the journey, you will find your *One*.

As Ambrose Redmoon said, "Courage is not the absence of fear, but rather the judgment that something else is more important than fear."

A Recap

Let's talk about what you've learned so far. This can serve as your roadmap.

I guided you through my five-step process for finding him, getting him, and keeping him.

First you do an accurate self-assessment of all of your emotional and physical qualities—the good and the not so good.

Second, you inventory the things that you can realistically change, and decide which of those you are willing to change. You start the process of becoming your best version of you—both internally and externally. This is a lifelong process that requires introspection and discipline.

We talked about the importance of self-love. You can only attract what you are. You need to truly love yourself in order to attract someone who truly loves you. That means you must learn to be your own best advocate. Show more compassion towards yourself and monitor your self-talk when you make a mistake. Love yourself enough to clear away all your limiting beliefs. Clearing your limiting beliefs is really about reclaiming yourself and lifting the barriers that prevent you from being you. It's part of your becoming the best version of yourself.

Once you excavate your authentic self, you raise your energetic vibration, which allows you to attract better partners into your life. So by loving yourself more you're capable of attracting people who love you more because they reflect your self-love.

Third, it's time to focus on the search process. You begin this by analyzing what you want and don't want in a mate. After all, if you don't know where you're going, how do you know you've arrived!

Write your online profiles, have your photos taken showing the improved version of you, and chose the dating services you want to use. And the fun begins...

You get to interact with your potential candidates—online, on the phone, and on actual dates. You now know what to watch out for, what to ask, and how to assess.

Four, you choose several potential candidates and begin the culling process. You narrow down the potential list of candidates to those who can be your potential Level III and Level IV matches. You keep your 4 Levels of Love guide next to you. You choose the best one for you.

Finally, five, you've chosen to date your potential One exclusively. It's time to evolve your relationship while continuing to evaluate it. You have new skills, and you know how to address any limiting beliefs or anything else that comes up.

You've learned about the stages of romance, which will help you to address any issues by understanding exactly what is happening. You've also learned some new communication and conflict resolution skills.

Don't worry. I will be with you every step of the way. My words will follow you when you're in doubt.

I am currently working on my new book, *The 4 Levels of Love: Finding the One.* Those who have read the book you are reading, *It's a Match: The Guide to Finding Lasting Love,* have asked for more information on the 4 Levels of Love principles. And they want to know more about Divine Partnerships!

They want to know how to use the 4 Levels of Love to evolve their romantic relationships. They also want to know how to become more intimate with their special one. They wanted to know so much more. I realized I had to write a whole book on the subject instead of just one chapter. So stay tuned.

You can also follow my blogs and ask any dating or relationship questions on my website, www.NatalieMoore.net.

So long, for now... I wish you great success and I send you much love. Remember to embark on your journey of a lifetime with a feeling of anticipation and great joy.

Ready, set, go!

ABOUT THE AUTHOR

Natalie Moore is a Marriage and Family Therapist specializing in relationship coaching, dating and marriage. After her experience coping with her own divorce, Moore, a Harvard graduate who runs her own financial firm specializing in estate tax planning, went back to school to earn her Masters Degree in Marriage and Family Therapy from the University of Miami.

Through years of working with clients, Moore has developed a psycho-spiritual approach to relationships. She wanted to write a book that would give the average person the opportunity to find lasting love. This book is meant to be a guide that includes everything that the reader needs to know in order to find *the One*.

A resident of Miami, Moore is the mother of two sons, ages 23 and 26. In addition to her therapy credentials, she is a Clinical Hypnotherapist.

If you want more information on relationships, dating, and marriage, subscribe to her blog at www.NatalieMoore.net and follow her on Twitter, Instagram, and FB at NatalieMooreExpert.